KT-150-289
le Shuttle
EURO TUNNEL
RAC
Weekends across the
CHANNEL

The parts of France, Belgium and the Netherlands covered by this guide all lie within a distance of about 150 miles/240 km from Calais – that is, roughly 2½ to 3 hours' drive. The arc described by this limit encloses at its northern extent the Dutch bulbfields and Amsterdam, Brussels and northern Belgium, and includes parts of northwest France from Reims to Paris and west to the Normandy coast. The map opposite shows the major through-routes and identifies the areas into which the book is divided. At the beginning of each chapter is a map of the area covered by that chapter, showing main regional routes, minor touring roads and scenic routes, as well as some of the places of special interest to visit in the area. There are also town or city plans of a principal town in each of the areas the guide focuses on, as well as city plans of the three capital cities: Paris, Brussels, and Amsterdam.

Published by RAC Publishing, RAC House, PO Box 100, South Croydon CR2 6XW

ISBN 0 86211 263 X

A CIP catalogue record for this book is available from the British Library

Written by Helen Varley
Photography by Christina Jansen
Design by Simon Bell
Cartography by Mapworld for RAC Publishing
Area maps and town plans drawn by Nick Fryer
Cartographic Design by David Fryer
Editing and research by Gene Ferber, Barbara Fuller and Anne Mancillas
Edited, designed and typeset in Gill and New Baskerville by Book Creation Services Ltd, London
Colour reproduction by Pixel Tech Prepress Pte Ltd, Singapore
Printed in Great Britain by Varnicoat Ltd, Pershore

Acknowledgements

The Publishers would like to thank the following for their assistance in the preparation of this book:

Nissan (UK) Limited
Association Samara (photograph on page.28)
Musée Vivant du Cheval (photograph on page 49)
Barrie Smith (photograph on pages 62-3)
Belgian Tourist Office (photograph on page 102)
Glen Breeds, Talkback International Ltd

Special thanks to all the tourist offices who have been so helpful in providing information for this book

Above: Mosaics in the crypt of the Basilique de Ste-Thérèse at Lisieux.

Contents

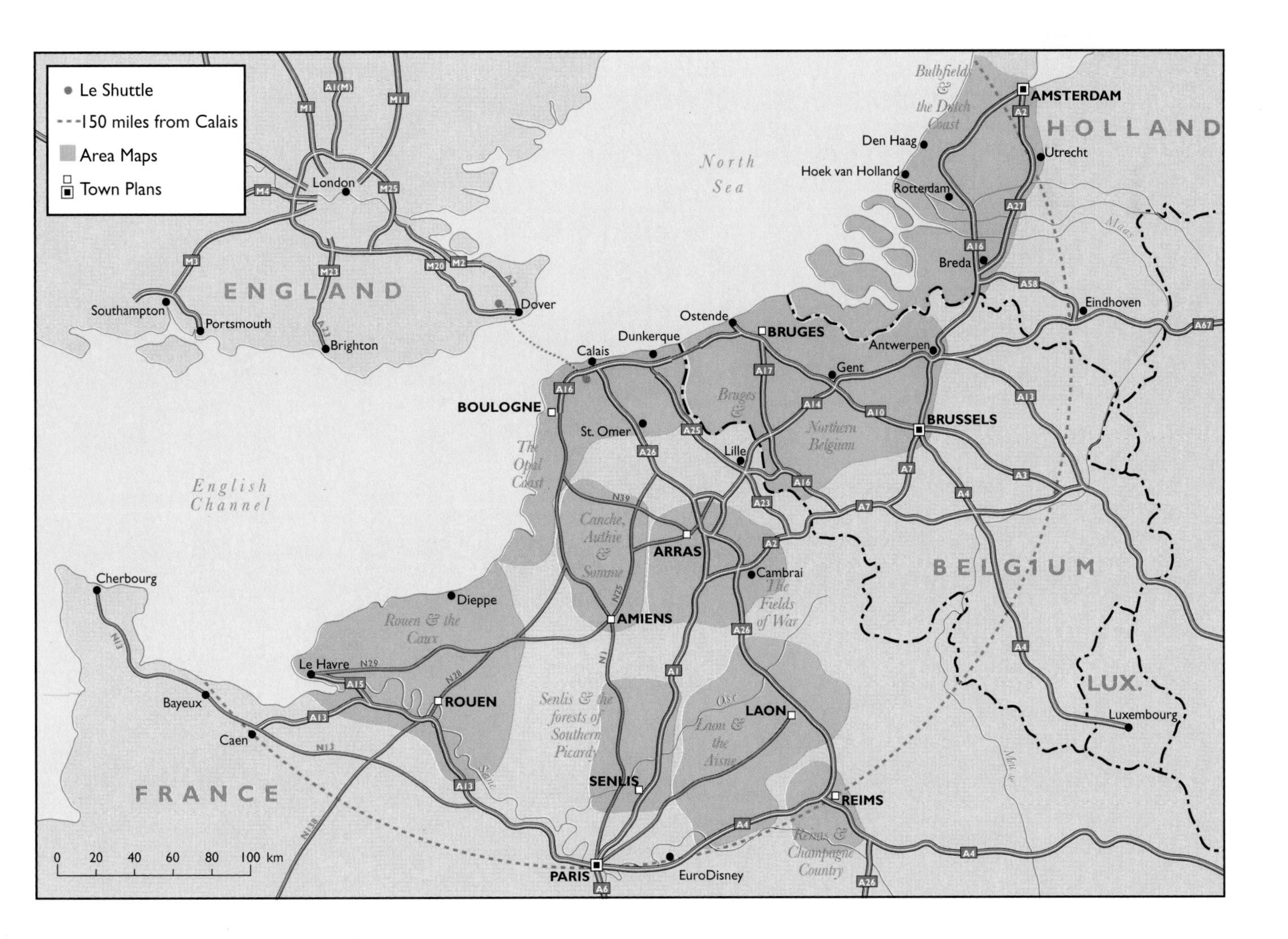

Le Shuttle
150 miles from Calais
Area Maps
Town Plans
ENGLAND
FRANCE
BELGIUM
HOLLAND
LUX.
North Sea
English Channel
London
Southampton
Portsmouth
Brighton
Dover
Calais
Dunkerque
Ostende
BRUGES
Antwerpen
Gent
BRUSSELS
BOULOGNE
St. Omer
Lille
ARRAS
Cambrai
AMIENS
Dieppe
Le Havre
ROUEN
Cherbourg
Bayeux
Caen
SENLIS
LAON
REIMS
PARIS
EuroDisney
Luxembourg
Eindhoven
Breda
Rotterdam
Hoek van Holland
Den Haag
Utrecht
AMSTERDAM
Bulbfields & the Dutch Coast
Bruges & Northern Belgium
The Opal Coast
Canche, Authie & Somme
Rouen & the Caux
Senlis & the forests of Southern Picardy
Laon & the Aisne
The Fields of War
Reims & Champagne Country
0 20 40 60 80 100 km

BANQUE

Three hours' drive from **Calais**

Le Shuttle brings the richly varied region covered by this guide within faster reach than ever before – and widens the scope for rewarding weekend breaks. Drive off Le Shuttle and out to beach resorts and wild sand dune reserves; high plateaux ringed with castles and walled towns; the wooded Seine Valley and the Dutch polders; the battlefields of Ypres; or the rolling hills of Champagne.

Within easy reach of Calais are ideal spots for short breaks – Chantilly and its surrounding forests; Le Touquet and the Opal Coast; the medieval towns of Flanders. Each chapter takes one of these areas as its theme, and explores it with a map, and suggestions for interesting destinations, illustrated with specially commissioned photographs. Each page features points of interest – the Astérix theme park near Senlis; the cheese towns of Normandy; tastings run by the wine-producers of Champagne.

Accompanying each section are selected listings, giving useful information – distance from Calais; parking; the nearest tourist office; suggestions for places to eat or drink; sights or places of interest; and many things to do.

The parts of northern France, Belgium and the Netherlands covered in this guide have remained largely undiscovered in the past by visitors, who were usually passing through, en route to Germany, Italy, Spain or the South of France. Now Le Shuttle is here, it is easier than ever to make short visits to see the beautiful cathedrals of Amiens, Reims, Tournai and Gent; the winding waterways of St-Omer and Flanders; the fortified churches of the Thiérache; the Trappist breweries of Belgium; and the many other memorable places across the Channel.

The Leopold Canal, Flanders.

The old gatehouse in Cambrai.

The Fact File Listings

Where possible, we have given the following information:

• **Place names:** Local names have been used. Where there are several of these – notably in Belgium, where French and Flemish and sometimes even English are all used from time to time – Fact Files list them all.

• **Distances and routes from Calais:** Quick reference so you can plan and time your journey.

• **Postal zip code:** So that you can write for information and brochures, or make bookings.

• **Tourist information:** It is useful to contact local tourist offices to make arrangements ahead of your visit. They will send details of forthcoming events; provide lists of hotels or campsites; make reservations; and even book courses or tuition. Addresses, telephone numbers, and opening hours are listed. Someone usually speaks English.

• **Telephone numbers:** The area code is given as part of the number. Country codes from the UK are:

France: 00 33–
Belgium: 00 32–
The Netherlands: 00 31–

• **Parking:** The most accessible parking spaces are noted. Tourist offices can often provide a town or area map showing car parks.

• **Sightseeing:** Sights of special interest and those that are hard to find are listed. Pick up a comprehensive guide from the local tourist office.

• **Camping:** Telephone numbers are given so you can book ahead during high season. The RAC's *European Camping and Caravanning Guide* lists more campsites.

• **Children:** Check opening hours and admission charges for children's theme parks and special events. The tourist offices also have details.

• **Eating and drinking:** In addition to the bars, cafés and restaurants described in each chapter, we make a few suggestions in the listings for places to eat and drink. More are recommended in Gault Millau's *The Best of France* and *The Best of Paris* (1993), published by the RAC. These guides list good-value places, as well as the best. They also list hotels. Ask at the tourist office in Brussels for *Gourmet Restaurants*, a guide by Belgium's leading restaurant critics, and at the Paris tourist offices for *Maîtres cuisiniers de France*. All the smaller tourist offices have lists of the best local bars and restaurants.

Always book restaurants in advance and check menu prices before setting off. Last orders are normally around 9pm. Listings indicate the cheapest menu prices, without wine, in pounds sterling.There is no need to leave a tip – 15% is added to your bill.

Where the proprietor is also the *chef de cuisine*, she or he may close for a well-earned evening off once a week.

• **Hotels:** Some pleasant hotels are listed on pages 125–127.

Top : Ostende Harbour.

Eating & drinking

The quality and variety of the food and drink of the area covered in this guide is justifibly renowned. It includes two cities that can claim to be the gastronomic capitals of Europe: Brussels and Paris. Within easy reach of Calais is Europe's most prestigious wine-producing region: Champagne. At the south-western limit of the guide's coverage lie the pastures of Normandy, France's gastronomic heart and soul. And in the north are the fine market gardens of Flanders and the Netherlands. Additionally, in the fishing ports and harbours along the coast, catches of the day are served fresh from the boats in harbourside stalls and restaurants.

Beer

Belgium and the Netherlands are the beer-producing giants of northern Europe, and their traditional beers are discussed on pages 104 and 122. But northern France competes with both in brewing excellent top-fermenting beers in the area between Boulogne, Lille and Valenciennes. *Les Brasseurs* in Lille is one notable brewery.

Cider and calvados

The Normandy Pays d'Auge, where the cider is so good it has an Appellation contrôlée label, is signposted with a Cider Route through pretty apple orchards to farms where you can sample the produce. Calvados is the spirit made from cider. Calvados country is on the west side of the Pays d'Auge, around Lisieux. The cheapest
-de-vie; the best is matured for five years or
a small drink of calvados in the course of a
of course.

Vegetarian food

There are vegetarian restaurants and cafés in the larger towns. Elsewhere, vegetarians who are not too worried about the content of stocks and sauces can indulge in some wonderful dishes. Normandy boasts a potato and cabbage soup with beans and leeks,

and a repertoire of baked egg dishes, omelettes and soufflées. Cabbages and potatoes are treated with respect and imagination in Champagne. The market gardens of Amiens produce crunchy-fresh vegetables, which appear in magnificent carrot soups as well as leek tarts and *flamiches* – tarts with a yeast crust.

Normandy

The most famous Normandy dishes include roast pressed duck with wine or liver sauce, tripe cooked in calvados, sausages made with pork and cream, hare with cream sauce, and Dieppe's famous fish stew (*marmite dieppoise*). It is also hard to resist the local apple pies and dumplings, buttery pastries and biscuits. You can follow a 'cheese route' by car across Normandy. It begins in Neufchâtel-en-Bray, home of strongly flavoured, heart-shaped cheeses, in north-east Normandy, then travels west to Pont-L'Evêque, and on to Livarot and Camembert farther south. Bars and cafés often serve local cheeses in inexpensive *plats de fromages*.

Champagne

Freshwater fish from the rivers and lakes of Champagne-Ardennes make classic dishes based on pike and trout, garnished with wild mushrooms, a regional speciality. Wild boar is a celebrated delicacy of this forest region, which also specialises in rabbit made into dumplings, pheasant, quail, and venison. Tangy Ardennes ham is mixed with pork, sausages, and vegetables in the *potée champenoise*. Local cheeses, like the delicate, creamy Caprice des Dieux, and chocolates complete a meal.

The Netherlands

At its most modern, Dutch cooking is nourishing, simple, and fresh; at its most traditional it can be heart-warmingly solid. Dutch restaurants have improved immeasurably over the last decade and, to date, no less than 30 had been awarded Michelin stars – De Bokkedoorns in Overveen near Haarlem and Inter Scaldes in Kruiningen, Zeeland, each have two – and many others have succeeded in modernising and lightening traditional Dutch cuisine.

Flemish cuisine

Flemish cooking is country cooking, based on very fresh ingredients, especially superlative vegetables. *Smakeluk* (rabbit cooked in beer) and *charbonnade de bœuf* (beef with prunes and beer) are often served with a salad of local ingredients – lettuce, chicory, cabbage, beetroot, onions, perhaps petits pois or haricots, and walnuts.

Sports

The year's big sporting events are the best places to glimpse the French, Dutch and Belgians at their most festive. Most famous is the Tour de France, a three-week event in July, finishing at the Arc de Triomphe in Paris. June is the season for horse racing at Deauville, Compiègne and Chantilly. Spring is the season for the 24-hour car rally at Ypres. And midwinter is the time for skiing in the Ardennes, or city-to-city skating races along frozen Dutch canals.

From archery (in the Valois, France) to golf, fishing, riding, sailing and swimming everywhere, all regions share their sports with visitors all year round.

Coast sports

Le Shuttle takes you to a watersports paradise – weather notwithstanding. From Deauville to Zeebrugge, covered and heated seawater swimming and diving pools stand by for inclement days. Strong winds combine with wide beaches and shallow seas to make perfect conditions for windsurfing and sand-yachting around Le Touquet in France, between De Panne and Oostduinkerke-Bad in Belgium, and along the coast of the South Netherlands. And there are wild and windy days when the Dutch and Belgian shores boast breakers big enough to test the skills of practised surfers.

Golf

France has a countrywide network of Tourist Golf Courses (minimum 18 holes) – and arrangements with a local golf club are among the facilities considered *de rigueur* for a good French hotel. Thus, within easy reach of Calais are two courses laid among the humpy dunes and pine woods of Hardelot; the hilly, 9-hole beginners' course in the Olhain Leisure Park, near Arras; the course at Nampont-St-Martin near Montreuil, with a clubhouse in a 16th-century fortified manor house; and an international championship course at Le Touquet. Ask at the tourist offices for detailed brochures on golf in northern France, Belgium and the South Netherlands. Golfing weekends at the Château de Raray near Senlis in France include accommodation as well as beginners' tuition or coaching for improvement by stages – or simply an opportunity for a good game in lovely surroundings.

Yachting

There are many yachting harbours along France's northern coast. In Belgium you can hire a fully equipped fishing boat (about £20), or a dinghy, in Nieuwpoort and Ostende, and it is easy to hire boats anywhere along the Dutch coast. The seafaring Dutch will teach you to sail almost any type of vessel, from a kayak to a clipper.

Sea fishing

Contact the tourist offices for details of the hundreds of ports along the coast that operate deep-sea fishing trips. Otherwise, hire a boat, set up a line from a pier or a breakwater, or just wade out into the surf. You need no licence or permit to fish in coastal waters. The North Sea yields eels (from Nieuwpoort), conger eels (from the pier at Zeebrugge), cod (from the pier at Blankenberge), ray (from the Zwin estuary), and sole (from Ostende's East Jetty), plus sea perch, dab, whiting, turbot, plaice, flounder, and sea pike.

River fishing

The French say fishing is their most popular sport and prove it by realising the full fishing potential of their many rivers, lakes, canals, ponds, and coastal waters. Prime sites in the region covered by this guide are the loops and lagoons of the Somme downriver from Péronne, the *étangs* of the river Sensée near Cambrai, and the winding *watergangs* near St-Omer. Close to Calais, there is good trout fishing along the lovely river Course.

Fishing regulations

In Belgium: these are complicated, but clearly summarised in *Fresh and Salt-Water Fishing in Belgium*, produced by the Belgian Tourist Office in London. The various licences are available from Belgian post offices. For regulations governing specific waterways, check with the local tourist office.

In the Netherlands: there are an estimated 60,000 hectares/ 150,000 acres of fresh waters, and year-round fishing. To fish in public waterways, you need a permit (from a post office: ask for a *sportvisakte*). To fish in Angling Association waters you need a licence (from the Nederlandse Vereniging van Sportvissersfederaties – NVVS; Tel 033 634924).

In France: sea-fishing is free, but you should contact the local tourist offices well in advance for information about fishing inland, and to obtain help with registration, in order not to lose time with such arrangements during a short break. Waters are categorised as 1 (for salmon and trout) and 2 (for other species) and a different type of stamp is required for each. Permission from local angling societies or private owners may also be required before you can fish. Waters are further categorised as public (*eaux libres*) and private (*eaux closes*).

Fairs & Festivals

A few key events of the year, in France, Belgium and the Netherlands, are listed below. More French events, with their dates, are listed in *Festive France*, a publication produced by the French tourist office toward the end of each year.

FRANCE

APRIL
Aire-sur-la-Lys (Flanders): carnival parade with giants.
Cassel (Flanders): Carnival with giant figures.
Les Andelys-Gisors (Normandy): Festival of theatre, dance, and music.

MAY
Amiens (Picardy): Carnival.
Arras (Artois): *Fête des Rats* (Rat Festival) – 4-5 June in 1995.
Lille (Flanders): *Montgolfiades* – hot air balloon meeting.
Marais Vernier (Normandy): Marking of the Livestock.
Rouen (Normandy): Jeanne d'Arc Festival.
Tourcoing (Flanders): Free Fair.

JUNE
Chantilly (Oise): *Nights of Fire* fireworks contest.
Chateau-Thierry (Aisne): Jean de la Fontaine Festival.
Douai (Artois): *Gayant* Festival with giant figures.
Fécamp (Normandy): Sea Festival.
Le Havre (Normandy): Sea Festival and blessing of the sea.
Paris: Waiters' Race – to and from the Hôtel de Ville.
St-Valéry-sur-Somme (Opal Coast): William the Conqueror Festival.
St-Denis (Paris): Festival.
Versailles (Ile de France): Festival.

JULY
Bastille Day celebrated countrywide, especially in **Paris**.
Forges-les-Eaux (Bray, Normandy): Horse Festival.
La-Haye-du-Routot (Normandy): St Clair's Fire.
Opal Coast: Music Festival.
Pierrefonds (Aisne): Festival of theatre, music and crafts, July-September.
Reims (Marne): Music Festival and *son et lumière.*

AUGUST
Arras (Artois): Carnival with giant figures.
Cambrai (Artois): annual parade.
Dunkerque (Flanders): Blessing of the Sea.
Wimereux (Opal Coast): Mussel Festival.
Wissant (Opal Coast): Flobert Festival (the flobert is the traditional fishing boat).

SEPTEMBER
Amiens (Picardy): Festival of the *hortillonnages.*
Champagne: grape harvest.
Paris: *Fête de l'Humanité*.
Saint-Michel de Thiérache (Aisne): *Son et lumière*.

OCTOBER
Rouen (Normandy): National Antiques Show.

BELGIUM

JANUARY TO MARCH
Carnivals celebrate the coming of spring. Most take place on the Sunday following Ash Wednesday or on the fourth Wednesday before Easter. **Ostende Carnival** is one of the grandest, with processions and dances. Every carnival has its ball, and Ostende's '*Bal du Rat Mort*' is one of the biggest and grandest carnival balls in Europe. Reservations are essential.

APRIL
Gent: Flower Show (end of April, every five years. The next is from 22 April until 1 May, 1995).
Tournai: Carnival.

MAY
Bruges: Procession of the Holy Blood (Ascension Day) – one of Europe's oldest religious festivals.
Ypres: Kattestoet (second Sunday in May): Cat Festival.

JUNE
Knokke-Heist (coast): Cartoon Festival (June-September).
Mons (Hainaut): The Golden Carriage Procession and 'Lumecon' Combat.
Ostende: Blessing of the Sea (Sunday service).
Tournai: Day of the Four Processions (two days) – a carnival parade and procession.

JULY
Festival of Wallonia: music and drama events all over Wallonia from July to Oct.
Antwerp: Steenfestival (held every two years – 1996, 1998, etc): music and events.
Blankenberge (coast): Blessing of the Sea (morning).
Brussels: *Ommegang* (first Thursday in July).
Gent: Festival (ten days) of music, theatre and events.
Knokke-Heist (coast): Summer Festival (seven days): popular music.
Schoten (Antwerp): World Folklore Festival (second Sunday in July).
Veurne (W. Flanders): Penitents Procession (end of the month).
Countrywide: National Day (21 July): fireworks, processions and entertainment all day.

AUGUST
Festival of Flanders: dance and music events are held all over Flanders in August.
Blankenberge (coast): Floral procession (day at end Aug).
Bruges: Pageant of the Golden Tree (every five years; the next is from 18 to 25 Aug, 1996).
Brussels: Planting of the Maypole.
Gent: Festival of Flanders – concerts and events.
Knokke-Heist (coast): Firework Festival (five days in Aug) – four countries compete to stage the best firework display.

SEPTEMBER
Antwerp: *Op Signoorke* (second Sunday in Sept) – a giant doll tours the streets.
Gent: Annual Flower Show (first Sunday in Sept): marks the end of the flower season.
Poperinge (West Flanders): Hop Procession and Beer Festival (afternoon).
Tournai: Procession of the Plague (afternoon) on the 2nd Sunday of September.

OCTOBER
Beer festivals take place in towns and villages all over Belgium in October. The biggest in West Flanders are held in **Ostende, Wieze** and **Diksmuide** (West Flanders). The Diksmuide *Octoberfest* (three successive Saturdays) is Belgium's biggest beer festival.

NETHERLANDS

JANUARY
Leiden: Keytown Jazz Festival – third weekend in January.

MARCH
Amsterdam: *Stille Ommegang* – procession to St. Nicolaaskerk.

APRIL
Amsterdam: Queen's Day – celebrations on 30 April.
Brielle (near Rotterdam): Festival – to celebrate the liberation from Spanish occupation in 1572.
Haarlem to **Noordwijk:** Flower parade through the bulbfields.

MAY
Den Haag: Flag Day – a fishing festival to open the herring season.

JUNE
Amsterdam: The Netherlands Festival – June-Aug.
Den Haag: International Arts Festival. International Rose Show held in Westbroek Park, June-Sept.
Hoek van Holland: Harbour celebrations.
Rotterdam: Arts Festival.

JULY
Delft: Jazz Festival, featuring trad jazz.
Den Haag: North Sea Jazz Festival. Scheveningen Kite Festival.
Leiden: Summer Festival; Cloth Festival.

AUGUST
Den Haag: Flower parade (last Saturday of month). Scheveningen Firework Festival.
Noordwijk: Flower parade from Rijnsburg.

SEPTEMBER
Amsterdam: Flower parade from Aalsmeer to Amsterdam (first Saturday of month). Jordaan Festival. Arts Festival.
Den Haag: Opening of Parliament – by the Queen, 3rd Tuesday.

OCTOBER
Delft: Art and Antiques Fair.
Leiden: Festival celebrating the Relief of Leiden.

DECEMBER
Gouda: Lighting the Christmas Tree.

Driving *in* Europe

Think ahead about passports, insurance, Green Card (International Motor Insurance Certificate, to extend insurance from minimum Third Party cover in EU to level of insurance normally held in Britain), and a Vehicle Registration Document.

Drivers in Europe should buy the ***RAC Motoring in Europe*** (updated every year), which gives all the up-to-date, detailed information you could need for a Continental journey, including a country-by-country guide. London branches of European tourist organisations also provide leaflets detailing regulations, help and information services, and current petrol prices.

B = Belgium; **F** = France; **NL** = the Netherlands.

Drive on the right (B; F; NL). At junctions, cars coming from the right have priority, unless otherwise indicated (**B**; **NL**); traffic on major roads has priority (*passage protégé*) unless a sign indicates: *priorité à droite* ('cars coming from the right have priority') (**F**); priority roads are indicated by diamond-shaped orange signs with white borders (**NL**).

CHILDREN AND TEENAGERS
The minimum age for driving is 18 for cars, 18 for motorcycles (**B**, **F**, **NL**).

Children under 12 (**B**), under 10 (**F**) are not allowed in front seats if there is room in the back of the vehicle; children under 4 must sit in safety seats if travelling in front (**NL**).

BREAKDOWN/ACCIDENT
All drivers must carry a red triangle to display in case of breakdown (**B**; **NL**); red triangle or hazard warning lights (**F**).

Dial 100 for medical help (**B**); call for assistance from orange emergency telephones located every 2 km along motorways and main roads or dial 17 for police/ambulance (**F**); refer to local telephone directories for all emergency services (**NL**).

DRINKING
DO NOT DRINK AND DRIVE ANYWHERE.

LIGHTING
Dip headlights in towns and on open roads. Do not use side lights only (**B**; **F**; **NL**). Amber headlights are not needed (**B**; **NL**); are not compulsory for foreign registered cars (**F**). Headlights must be adjusted for right-hand drive (**B**; **F**; **NL**).

MOTORWAYS
Toll-free (**B**); toll roads (**F**; **NL**).

PETROL
Unleaded petrol – *essence sans plomb* (**B**; **F**) or *loodvrije benzine* (**B**; **NL**) – is readily available.

ROUNDABOUTS
Traffic on the roundabout should give way to traffic wishing to enter (**B**; **NL**). In France, traffic on the roundabout usually has priority; this is indicated by a triangular sign with a red border showing a roundabout symbol, plus another reading *vous n'avez pas la priorité* ('you do not have priority').

SEAT BELTS
Compulsory for anyone in the front seats (**B**; **F**; **NL**); must be fitted, back and front (**B**).

SPEED LIMITS
(cars, caravans, small trailers). **In towns** 50 kph/31 mph (**B**; **F**; **NL**). **Outside built-up areas** 90 kph/55 mph (**B**; **F**; **NL**). **Dual carriageways and toll-free urban throughways** 110 kph/68 mph (**F**). **Motorways** 120 kph/74 mph maximum (**B**; **F**; **NL**); some motorways 100 kph/62 mph (look for signs) (**NL**); 70 kph/44 mph minimum (**B**; **NL**); 80 kph/49 mph in overtaking lane (**F**). Lower speed limits come into force in bad weather and when towing trailers weighing more than the car. Check in ***RAC Motoring in Europe.***

TRAMS
Trams – and anyone crossing the road to get off or onto a tram – have priority (**B**; **F**; **NL**).

Le Shuttle:
easy access to Europe

Turn up, pay, drive on, and go. This is Le Shuttle's minimum-stress, cross-Channel service for travellers. You just buy your ticket, drive on to the next available shuttle, and 35 minutes later you're in Calais.

Turn up and go. Eurotunnel's Le Shuttle services operate between terminals at Folkestone and Calais. There's no advance booking. You simply turn up, pay and go. Buy your ticket at one of the tollbooths, pass through frontier controls, and board the next available shuttle. Plain sailing! If you want to do some shopping and have a snack or a meal in the Passenger Terminal Building, take as long as you like – another shuttle will be leaving soon.

The shuttles run day and night every single day of the year, regardless of sea conditions. When the service is fully operational, there will be up to four passenger-vehicle shuttles per hour at peak times. Even during the quietest periods of the night there will be a minimum of one departure an hour.

Although advance reservations are not taken, tickets can be bought beforehand from selected travel agents or from the Le Shuttle Customer Service Centre at Cheriton Parc, Folkestone (telephone 01303 271100).

Getting to Folkestone

There are motorway connections to Le Shuttle's Folkestone Terminal from most parts of the country via the M25 and M20. Once you've reached the M20, look out for the signs to the Channel Tunnel. Exit at junction 11A, which leads straight into the terminal. (Travellers from the east Kent area can reach the terminal via local roads and the A20.)

On the M20, tune into Channel Tunnel Radio which gives up-to-date information about the weather and driving conditions on both sides of the Channel.

Using Le Shuttle

Here's a simple step-by-step guide:

1. Buy your ticket at one of the tollbooths. Credit cards, Switch, cheques, and cash (sterling and francs) are all accepted.
2. Now there's a choice. Either visit the Passenger Terminal Building or head straight for Le Shuttle.
3. Pass through British and French frontier controls. This is another innovation – both frontier controls are located at the departure terminal. On the other side of the Channel you drive directly off Le Shuttle and on to the motorway.
4. Head for the allocation area where you wait to drive on to Le Shuttle. Attendants will direct you down the loading ramp and on board. Drive through the carriages until another attendant directs you to stop.
5. Turn the engine off and put the handbrake on. Loading takes about eight minutes, and then you're off. During the journey Le Shuttle staff are available to answer any questions.
6. 35 minutes later Le Shuttle reaches Calais. Attendants will direct you to drive to the front of the shuttle and

Double-deck or single-deck?

Each shuttle normally consists of 12 double-deck and 12 single-deck carriages. Cars under 1.85 metres high (including any roof load) and motorcycles travel in the double-deck carriages. The single-deck carriages are for coaches and other vehicles more than 1.85 m high.

Freight lorries travel on their own specially built shuttles, and follow an entirely separate route through the terminal area.

Below: The Eurotunnel Terminal at Folkestone, with a passenger-vehicle shuttle leaving the platform area on its way to Calais through the tunnel.

Above left: Loading cars on to a passenger-vehicle shuttle at the Folkestone Terminal.
Above right: Inside a passenger-vehicle carriage.

then out on to the exit ramp. This leads straight to the exit road and on to the motorway network – *Voilà!* You're in France. Just remember to drive on the right.

On board Le Shuttle

During the short journey you remain with your car inside the spacious, well-lit, air-conditioned carriage. Sit back and relax, perhaps tune in to Le Shuttle Radio (95.6 and 99.8 FM). Look out for messages on the dot-matrix screen giving you information about your trip.

If you want to, get out of your car to stretch your legs. In the double-deck shuttles there are toilets in every third carriage.

Coming home

On the way home, leave the A16 *autoroute* at junction 13, which leads directly to the Calais Terminal. From here, repeat the process described above.

When you reach Folkestone you drive straight on to the M20. Both sets of frontier controls are at Calais.

Eurostar services

If you prefer travelling without your car, take one of the new high-speed Eurostar passenger trains that pass directly through the Channel Tunnel. The London–Paris journey takes just over three hours, London to Brussels three hours ten minutes. A number of Eurostar trains stop at Lille, where there are connections with other high-speed services, and some stop at Frethun, just outside Calais. Telephone the Eurostar Information Line (01233 617575) for more information.

Take a break

The Folkestone Passenger Terminal Building is a good place to take a break from driving. There are eating-places, a duty-free shop, a bureau de change, plus a range of well-known high-street shops, together with toilet and motoring and information facilities. Spend as long as you like here and head for the next shuttle when you are ready.

On the way back, the Calais Terminal has similar facilities. In addition, 1995 will see the opening of La Cité de l'Europe next to the terminal, with shops, a hypermarket and other leisure facilities.

Le Shuttle Fact File

- **Speed:** 140 kph/87 mph.
- **Journey time:** Folkestone–Calais, 35 minutes; in the tunnel, 26 minutes; motorway to motorway, just over 1 hour.
- **Frequency: up to** four shuttles per hour in each direction at peak times when fully operational; one per hour at night.
- **Cars per shuttle:** maximum 180.

Exhibition Centre

Located beside the Folkestone Terminal and close to the M20 (junction 12), Eurotunnel's Exhibition Centre brings to life the past, present and future of the Channel Tunnel through the imaginative use of interactive videos, a full-size shuttle, and the 'talking head' family. Other highlights at the bilingual (French/English) Centre include a viewing tower over the terminal, a 33-metre model railway – the longest in the UK – a French-style café and a shop.

Open: *Summer,* 10am to 6pm daily;
Winter, 10am to 5pm daily.
Admission: Adults £3.60, children/OAPs £2.20.
St Martin's Plain, Folkestone, Kent CT19 4QD (telephone 01303 270111). Access from Junction 12 of M20, and follow signs.

Centre d'Information

In France, the Centre d'Information, superbly located overlooking the Calais Terminal, uses an exciting, modernistic audio-visual and laser show to relate the Channel Tunnel story and take you on a journey through the system. Practical information is available from video screens, and a superb panoramic view of the loading platforms can be enjoyed from the observation tower. There is a cafeteria and a souvenir shop.

Open: *May-Sept,* daily 10am to 7pm;
Oct-April, daily 10am to 6pm.
Admission: Adults 32 francs, students 27 francs, children 22 francs
Centre d'Information, 62231 Coquelles, (telephone 21 00 69 00). Access from junction 12 of A16 *autoroute*, and follow signs.

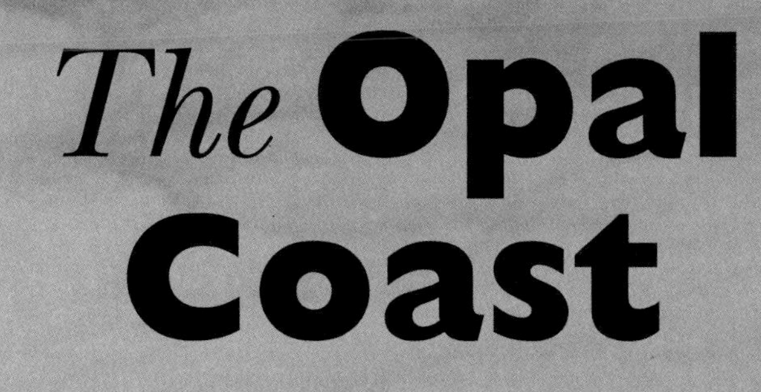
The Opal
Coast

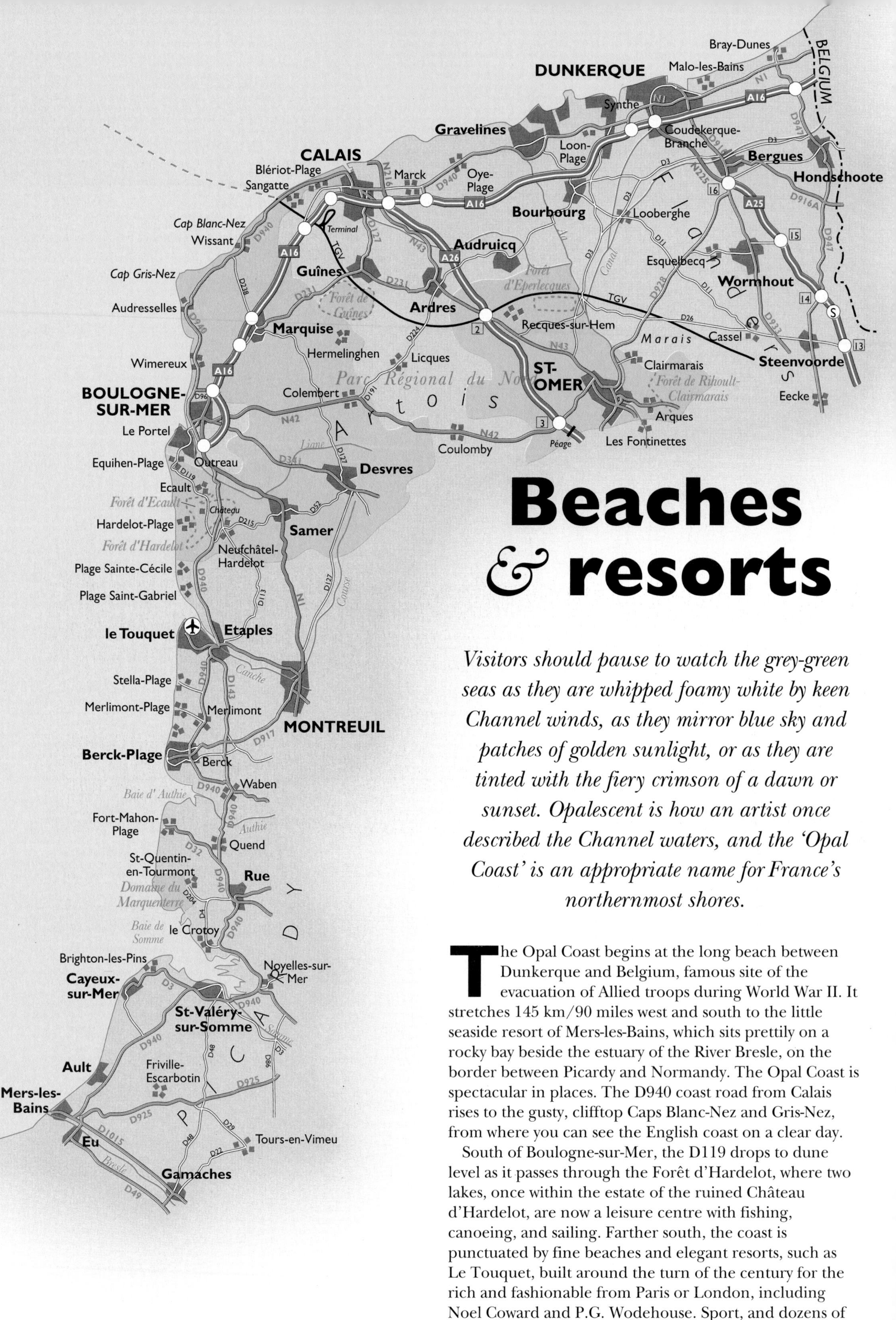

Beaches & resorts

Visitors should pause to watch the grey-green seas as they are whipped foamy white by keen Channel winds, as they mirror blue sky and patches of golden sunlight, or as they are tinted with the fiery crimson of a dawn or sunset. Opalescent is how an artist once described the Channel waters, and the 'Opal Coast' is an appropriate name for France's northernmost shores.

The Opal Coast begins at the long beach between Dunkerque and Belgium, famous site of the evacuation of Allied troops during World War II. It stretches 145 km/90 miles west and south to the little seaside resort of Mers-les-Bains, which sits prettily on a rocky bay beside the estuary of the River Bresle, on the border between Picardy and Normandy. The Opal Coast is spectacular in places. The D940 coast road from Calais rises to the gusty, clifftop Caps Blanc-Nez and Gris-Nez, from where you can see the English coast on a clear day.

South of Boulogne-sur-Mer, the D119 drops to dune level as it passes through the Forêt d'Hardelot, where two lakes, once within the estate of the ruined Château d'Hardelot, are now a leisure centre with fishing, canoeing, and sailing. Farther south, the coast is punctuated by fine beaches and elegant resorts, such as Le Touquet, built around the turn of the century for the rich and fashionable from Paris or London, including Noel Coward and P.G. Wodehouse. Sport, and dozens of things for children to do, are among the many attractions of Le Touquet. There are riding, show-jumping and horse-racing, golf on a championship course, and sand and sea sports. Le Touquet has a casino and some lively nightlife. Bagatelle is a huge summer fun park for children outside Merlimont, with a water slide, donkey rides, a ghost train, and, it claims, 87 other attractions.

People collect mussels in the flat estuary of the Canche River opposite Le Touquet. Etaples, just inland, is a charming old seaport with a famous fishermen's restaurant above the modern fish market. This part of the coast is moving gradually seawards, and its silting estuaries and creeping dunes, widening salt marshes and lagoons are a haven for coastal wildlife. There are nature reserves at the estuary of the Authie River, south of Merlimont, and, among the huge dunes and shingle beaches at the wide mouth of the river Somme, the Marquenterre bird sanctuary (Parc ornithologique du Marquenterre) is a haven for rare species. There are hides for ornithologists, and signposts for children and interested amateurs.

Coves and bays all along the coastline are overlooked by towns and fishing villages straggling around their ports and harbours, and ruined castles command sea views from once-strategic vantage points. The delightful old town of Rue began as a medieval castle on the Somme estuary. The older part of the Church of St-Vulphy, the Chapelle du Saint-Esprit, is a masterpiece of 15th-century Flamboyant Gothic architecture and sculpture, and the town has a Gothic town hall with a Flemish belfry.

At the old port of Le Crotoy on the Somme Bay, famous as the place where Jules Verne wrote *20,000 Leagues under the Sea*, are the ruins of a fortress where Jeanne d'Arc was imprisoned in 1430. On the opposite bank of the Somme, fortifications remain around the Ville Haute, the medieval centre of St-Valéry-sur-Somme. The scenic D940 gives lovely views over the Somme and across the wide sands and marshes between the Somme and Normandy.

Touring the coast

A pleasant route of about 112 km/70 miles follows the coast between Calais and the Normandy border on the most scenic roads, then returns on minor roads through the hilly countryside of the Boulogne hinterland. There are also delightful drives inland, along the D49 which follows the south bank of the Bresle River, and along the D22 and D86 between the Bresle and the Somme. Another pretty road, the D127, follows the river Course from Montreuil through the little town of Desvres, famous in the 17th century for its porcelain. It continues through the rural hinterland to Marquise, whence the D238 joins the coast at Wissant close to Cap Blanc-Nez.

Previous pages: The wide beaches and the wild sea of the Opal Coast are delightful to walk along or watch. Others may prefer to mess about in boats at a harbour such as Le Crotoy (below), or join the children as they explore the attractions of Bagatelle Park (inset).

Best beaches & resorts

Audresselles fine sand beach.
Berck-Plage 12-km/7.5-mile long, uncrowded beaches with fine sands.
Boulogne Le Portel children's beach with sand, rocks and rock pools, 4 km/2.5 miles from Boulogne.
Brighton-les-Pins 14 km/9 miles sandy beaches to **Cayeux-sur-Mer** on a windy stretch of coast.
Calais to **Blériot-Plage** and on to **Cap Blanc-Nez** 13.5 km/8 miles sand beaches.
Dunkerque (promenade and beach), and **Malo-les-Bains** to **Bray-Dunes** 4 km/2.5 miles sand beaches.
Equihen-Plage pretty dune beach.
Fort Mahon-Plage sandy beaches stretching south to the nature reserve on the Somme Estuary.
Hardelot-Plage, **Plage Ste-Cécile**, **Plage St-Gabriel** sand beaches.
Le Crotoy sheltered, enormously wide beach on a beautiful bay.
Le Touquet miles of dune beaches with fine sands, crowded in summer; huge sea-filled swimming pool on the beach.
Merlimont-Plage sandy beaches, crowded in summer.
Mers-les-Bains sandy beach in the shelter of a rocky cove.
Stella-Plage sandy beaches, crowded in summer. A pleasant new resort with lawns and trees.
Wimereux children's beach of sand, shingle and rock pools.
Wissant beautiful curved white sand beach.

Calais & around

England's gateway to France, and the French town with which Britain has the closest historical links is, ironically, a part of France we rarely get to know. The hypermarkets always exert a pull, and shoppers explore the cheerful bars and eating places. But Calais has some treasures to discover.

It is all too easy to get onto the motorway network and head off away from Calais and see nothing of the French town that was part of England for some 200 years. Follow the signs to the Vieille Ville, and you find a lively town, its northern part a fishing port and tourist resort, its southern half a hard-working industrial city. Out in the harbour is a plaque commemorating the last stand against the Nazis by the Green Jackets in 1940 and in the War Museum is the record of the devastation that was the sad reason for the soullessness of the modern port.

A German blockhouse, part of World War II coastal defences.

The Burghers of Calais stand mournfully in front of Calais town hall.

Rodin's moving statue, *Les Bourgeois de Calais* (*The Burghers of Calais*), in front of the 19th-century town hall is the most famous of Calais' treasures. The oldest is the Church of Notre-Dame, begun in the 12th century but built in English Perpendicular Gothic style. The Wednesday market in the main square, the place d'Armes, and the Thursday and Saturday markets in the place Crèvecœur are both lively events. Calais' magnificent beach extends south-west to Blériot-Plage, from where the aviator Louis Blériot took off to make the first flight across the Channel in 1909. The Musée des Beaux-Arts et de la Dentelle (Fine Arts and Lace Museum) tells the story of the Calais machine lace industry, an export from Nottingham in the early 19th century.

Around Calais

From Calais, you can set off along the coast to the golf courses of Wimereux, the varied beaches stretching south-west to Boulogne-sur-Mer (see pages 14-15), or inland to the woods and rivers of the Pas-de-Calais. You can walk in the forest outside the old town of Guînes, or fish in the lakes near Ardres – worth visiting to see the Basilique Notre-Dame of St-Omer. Audruicq, to the south-east, has a church and two châteaux, all built in the 18th century.

Beside the D231 between Ardres and Guînes is the site of the Field of the Cloth of Gold, where a meeting in 1520 between Henry VIII of England and François I of France was celebrated with extraordinary pomp and splendour.

Some of the French hypermarkets offer an extraordinarily wide choice of products, often at very attractive prices.

Shopping and markets

In season, Le Touquet, with its northern branches of Parisian boutiques, is the focus for style on the Opal Coast. Boulogne-sur-Mer's two main shopping streets have a good range of general shops, as have those of small inland towns such as St-Omer. But food is the main shopping theme along all of France's northern coastline.

Discerning visitors shop at the aromatic *boulangeries* (bakers) and the old-fashioned *pâtisseries* of coastal towns and villages, and at several outstanding cheese shops. Of these, Philippe Olivier's *fromagerie* at 45 rue Thiers in Boulogne-sur-Mer is deservedly the most famous; and in Dunkerque, a *crémerie* on rue du Président-Poincaré specialises in the cheeses of the Low Countries. Montreuil is becoming famous for its *chocolateries*, where you can watch chocolates being made by hand.

Best buys at the hypermarkets

Wines and beers are usually competitively priced in all the hypermarkets, but for other goods Prisunic and Leclerc tend to be the cheaper of the chains. British shoppers thinking only of stocking up with alcohol are likely to miss some of the other good buys in these emporia. Some bargains to look out for include: canned and bottled soups; fruits; vegetables (2 kg/4.5 lb are the customs limit, but potatoes are not allowed); mustards, vinegars and olive oils; *charcuterie* (which can be brought back if it is purchased in sealed packs); coffees; and chocolates. You can also buy good boxed cheeses (camembert is at its best before Christmas and in the spring).

Market days

Street markets bursting with street life are pricier than the supermarkets, but more fun, and great for fresh foods. Markets are usually held weekly in the villages and two or three times a week in the market towns. The range of foods is breathtaking – in addition to fruit and vegetables there may be stalls specialising in dairy produce, dried fruits, *charcuterie*, tarts and cakes... Along the coast, fish markets are irresistible. Boulogne-sur-Mer (open mornings Monday to Saturday) is one of the best – oysters are a particularly good buy. Dunkerque specialises in herrings and kippers, and in the village of Audresselles, fishermen sell fish and shellfish from their cottages. Mussels, clams and turbot feature prominently in the Etaples fish market, and in Le Crotoy, where fishermen sell fish and shellfish from their boats. Those with limited time should ignore the temptations of the fish markets and head instead for the restaurants of Boulogne-sur-Mer, Dunkerque, and other coastal resorts to try the excellent local fish dishes.

Most markets start early in the morning and finish near noon.

BOULOGNE-SUR-MER Wednesday, Saturday (main market days)
CALAIS Wednesday, Thursday, Saturday
CAYEUX-SUR-MER Tuesday, Friday, Sunday
DUNKERQUE Wednesday, Saturday
ETAPLES Tuesday, Friday, daily fish market
FORT MAHON-PLAGE Tuesday, Friday in summer
HESDIN Thursday
LE CROTOY Friday; fish market Sunday
LE PORTEL Tuesday, Friday
MERS-LES-BAINS Monday, Thursday, 3rd Wednesday every month
MONTREUIL Saturday
QUEND Monday, Thursday
RUE Saturday
ST-OMER Wednesday, Saturday
LE TOUQUET Monday (summer only), Thursday, Saturday
WIMEREUX Tuesday
WORMHOUT Wednesday

The tall belfry of Calais town hall reaches high above the surrounding buildings and is easily identified from miles around.

Local drinks

Northern France is not a wine-producing area, but there are some excellent wine dealers within easy reach of the Channel ports. One example is the proprietor of the Château de Cocove, a château hotel off the N43 near Recques-sur-Hem, who sells quality wines to a mainly English clientele. Small breweries dotted around northern France produce tasty local beers – St-Omer is a good example. If you decide to take a detour to the cultural centre of Lille, try the juniper-flavoured spirit called *genièvre* sold in the delicatessens (*traiteurs*).

Calais Fact File

CALAIS
Postal zip code 62100.
Tourist information 12 blvd Clemenceau. Tel 21 96 62 40. Fax 21 96 01 92. ***Open*** Mon-Sat 9am-7pm; Sun 10am-1pm, 3-5pm.

SIGHTSEEING
Calais
Centre d'information d' Eurotunnel See pages 10-11.
Musée des Beaux-Arts et de la Dentelle (Fine Arts and Lace Museum) 25 rue Richelieu. Tel 21 46 63 17. ***Open*** Mon, Wed-Sun 10am-noon, 2-5.30pm.
Musée de la Guerre (War Museum) Blockhaus du parc St-Pierre (opposite the town hall). Tel 21 34 21 57. ***Open*** daily 10am-5.30pm.
Dunkerque
Musée portuaire (Port Museum) 9 quai de la Citadelle. Tel 28 63 33 39. ***Open*** Mon, Wed-Sun 10am-12.15pm, 1-6pm.
Musée d'Art contemporain (Museum of Modern Art) avenue des Bains. Tel 28 59 21 65. ***Open*** Mon, Wed-Sun 10am-noon, 2-6pm. An outstanding gallery of modern and contemporary art.

FOR CHILDREN
Sportica place du Polder, Gravelines. Tel 28 65 35 00. ***Open*** Mon 2-9pm, Tue-Sat 9am-9pm, Sun 9am-8pm. A huge sports complex with cinema and shops.

CAMPING
Camping-caravaning Les Peupliers NE of town, signposted turning on the N1. Tel 21 34 03 56. ***Open*** *all year.*
Camp municipal W side of harbour. At roundabout below fort take turning 'Plage' off D940 to Blériot-Plage. Tel. 21 97 89 79. ***Open*** all year.

EATING AND DRINKING
Calais
Aux Côtes d'Argent 1 digue Gaston-Berthe. Tel 21 34 68 07.
La Buissonnière 10 rue Neuve. Tel 21 96 22 32. Menus from £12 to £17.
Le Channel 3 blvd de la Résistance. Tel 21 34 42 30. Menus from £11 to £35.
La Diligence 7 rue Edmond-Roche. Tel 21 96 92 89. Menus from £13 to £33.
Recques-sur-Hem
Château de Cocove. Tel 21 82 68 29. Menus from £14 to £42.

St-Omer *& the* Clairmarais

The deer woods, waterways and old fortified towns of French Flanders are a barely known pocket of northern France – yet the charming old town of St-Omer on the Flemish border is less than an hour's drive from Calais.

The river Aa between Gravelines, a fortified town and beach resort east of Calais, and the 18th-century inland town of St-Omer marks the border between the provinces of Artois and Flanders. Flanders is the northern half of France's Nord *département.*

French, not Flemish, is the language spoken here, but it has strong cultural links with the neighbouring Belgian province of West Flanders. French Flanders is etched with canals and their associated engineering works – for

An elegantly sculpted fountain complements the fine architecture of Mansart's Palais de Justice in St-Omer.

The Marais audomarois at sunset.

instance the 19th-century hydraulic boat lifts at Les Fontinettes near the glass-producing town of Arques. Windmills and curved gables are evident in the lines of fortified towns that punctuate the roads along the Belgian border. In restaurants and cafés, Flemish favourites – rabbit with dried fruits, endives, asparagus, eels – appear on menus in Gravelines, Dunkerque and St-Omer.

St-Omer became part of the Kingdom of France only during the 17th century, and thankfully escaped destruction during the world wars. Its large, cobbled Grand-Place is surrounded by merchants' houses, shops and cafés dating from the mid-18th century. A 16th-century astrological clock and a Baroque organ are among the many sculptures, paintings and other treasures that fill St-Omer's large Basilique Notre-Dame, begun in the 13th century.

Just east of St-Omer is the beautiful Marais audomarois, formerly marshland, now an area of woodland and forest drained by still, almost hidden, waterways called *watergangs*. Visitors can row or take guided boat trips from Clairmarais village on the peaceful waterways bordered by woodlands, fields and market gardens. The area is a sanctuary for freshwater marsh plants and wildlife. Frogs call in the evening, waterfowl rest and feed there, and deer and wild boar roam the denser forest areas.

The roads parallel to the Belgian border lead to pretty villages with paved squares – Wormhout, with a 17th-century church; the riverside Esquelbecq, with its decorative, gabled 16th-century church and picturesque château with turrets and a moat; and Eecke, with a wooden belfry. There are old windmills and pretty Flemish houses in the little town of Steenvoorde. Municipal museums in the hilltop town of Cassel and the moated, lowland town of Bergues explain the bellicose history of the region. And plentiful woodland and waterways give scope for more energetic activities – walking, canoeing, swimming, and fishing.

Around Calais Fact File

Tourist information Comité départemental du tourisme du Pas-de-Calais, 24 rue des Villes, 62200 – Boulogne-sur-Mer. Tel 21 83 32 59. Fax 21 30 04 81.

SIGHTSEEING
Tours the regional tourist office publishes a driving tour of fortified towns in the Pas-de-Calais. Bergues tourist office (Tel 28 68 60 44, ask for 'Office du tourisme') organises guided tours in the Nord *département* (1st Sun of every month at 10am and 3pm).
CASSEL
Musée d'Art, d'Histoire et de Folklore Hôtel de la Noble Cour, Grand-Place. Tel 28 40 52 85. ***Open*** Mon, Wed-Sun 2-6.30pm. (Closed from Nov 1994 until Apr 1995). A museum of Flemish life.
CLAIRMARAIS
Grange-nature ('Nature Barn'), rue du Romelaëre. ***Open*** *Apr-Jun, Sept-Oct* Sat 2.30-6.30pm; Sun 9.30am-12.30pm, 2.30-6.30pm. *Jul-Aug* daily 10.30am-12.30pm, 2.30-6.30pm; *Nov-Mar* Sat, Sun 2.30-5.30pm. Nature trails and information on the *marais*.
Guided tours through the **Parc naturel de Romelaëre** (wildlife sanctuary) Tel 21 98 62 98, **Lande de Blendecques** (heathland) and **Forêt de Rihoult-Clairmarais**.
Boat trips along the *watergangs*. Tel 21 39 15 15 or 21 95 10 19.
ST-OMER
Musée Henri-Dupuis 9 rue Henri-Dupuis. ***Open*** Wed, Sun 10am-noon, 2-6pm; Thur-Fri 10am-noon, 2-5pm. Flemish food and natural history.

EATING AND DRINKING
ST-OMER
La Belle Epoque 3 place Paul-Painlevé. Tel 21 38 22 93. A good place to try Flemish specialities. Menus from £8.50 to £22.
Les Frangins 5 rue Carnot. Tel 21 38 12 47. Fax 21 98 72 78. Menus from £6 to £17.

Boulogne

British visitors often pack Boulogne-sur-Mer's bars and restaurants and throng the steep streets of this seaside town so full of character, delighting in its easy mix of familiar welcome and distinctly French atmosphere.

Boulogne-sur-Mer and Britain go back a long way. In the 1st century BC, Boulogne-sur-Mer was Rome's northernmost fortress, the forward position from which Julius Caesar's expedition to conquer the Britons was organised and directed. In the 18th century the town harboured a colony of English writers and doubtful characters avoiding their creditors. In World War I, it was a strategic base for the supply and evacuation of British troops; and in World War II Hitler's troops were billeted there ready for the intended invasion of Britain.

In recent years, Boulogne has launched at least one successful invasion of Britain in the form of exports to the cheeseboards of British high-grade restaurants from the establishment of M. Philippe Olivier, *Maître fromagier.*

Left: Fresh fish on sale in Boulogne-sur-Mer.

Below: Gardens are planted along the 13th-century ramparts that enclose the Upper Town.

Opposite top: Nausicaà Centre is one of several museums of marine life along the coast of northern France.

What to see

Boulogne-sur-Mer is an important fishing port, built on a sheltered bay at the mouth of the Liane River; the catches brought in by the large fleet, then sold in the stalls of its quayside fish market from Monday to Saturday, are a major attraction. Its many excellent restaurants, specialising – naturally – in fish, are another.

Although most of the Lower Town (Ville basse) was destroyed by Allied bombing during World War II, Boulogne-sur-Mer is still a picturesque town, crowding the slopes of two hills. A network of small shopping streets connects the hotels, houses and harbour buildings of the Lower Town with the old hilltop town. The concentration of good food shops on these streets, plus the cheerful main street markets held twice a week, make Boulogne-sur-Mer a useful and colourful spot for general shopping.

The crowning glory of the town is its encircling 13th-century wall, with broad ramparts pierced by four fortified gateways. The walls enclose the charming Upper Town (Ville haute) which has narrow, cobbled streets lined with tall, dignified houses many embellished with ornate doors and windows. Cafés and restaurants surround a lively pedestrian area.

The Château de Boulogne was built in the 13th century and restored on an octagonal plan by the French military engineer, Vauban, in the 17th century. The dome of the 19th-century Basilique Notre-Dame dominates the whole town.

The vast, beautiful beach, first 'discovered' in the 18th century by English bathing aficionados, lost its fashionable status long ago to the resorts of Le Portel, Equihen-Plage and Hardelot-Plage, further south.

Boulogne-sur-Mer is a good starting point for excursions along the coast and through the pretty countryside to the east. Attractions include the hilly oak and beech Forest of Guînes; the attractive rural town of Ardres, its central square surrounded by old houses; the museum at Desvres, whose ceramics were famous in the 17th century; and pretty country villages, like Hermelinghen and Licques.

Boulogne Fact File

BOULOGNE-SUR-MER from **Calais** A16 35 km/21 miles. **Postal zip code** 62200. **Tourist information** BP 187, quai de la Poste (beside the Pont Marguet bridge over the Liane River). Tel 21 31 68 38. Fax 21 33 81 09. ***Open*** *Jul-8 Sep* daily 9am-7pm. *9 Sept-Jun* Mon-Sat 9am-7pm, Sun 10am-1pm, 2-5pm.

Parking There are parking spaces on the opposite side of the Liane river from the main tourist office in the Ville basse. The tourist office provides maps showing official parking places.

SIGHTSEEING

Beffroi (Belfry) and **Hôtel de Ville** (Town Hall) place de la Résistance. ***Open*** Mon-Fri 8am-noon, 2-5 pm; Sat 2.30-5pm. The belfry, partly dating from the 13th century, is the town's oldest building and is open to visitors, together with the 18th-century Hôtel de Ville.

Basilique Notre-Dame place Godefroi-de-Bouillon. ***Open*** daily. The Romanesque crypt can be visited Tue-Sun 2-5pm.

Château-Musée Château de Boulogne, rue Bernet. Tel 21 80 00 80. ***Open*** *15 May-14 Sept* Mon, Wed-Sat 9.30am-12.30pm, 1.30-8.15pm, Sun 9.30am-12.30pm, 2.30-6.15pm; *15 Sept-14 May* Mon, Wed-Sat 10am-12.30pm, 2.30-5pm, Sun 10am-12.30pm, 2.30-5.30pm. The story of Boulogne-sur-Mer from Gaulish times.

Guided tours can be arranged from the Château-Musée. Tel 21 80 56 78 for information.

Ramparts Entrance near the Porte des Degrés, on the S side, which is open to pedestrians only. Steps lead up to the walks and gardens along the walls.

DESVRES

Maison de la Faïence rue Jean-Mace. ***Open*** *Jul-Aug* daily 10am-noon, 2-6.30pm. *Sept-Jun* Tue-Sun 10am-noon, 2-6.30pm; Exhibition of Desvres pottery and porcelain.

FOR CHILDREN

Nausicaà Centre national de la Mer (Sea Museum) blvd Sainte-Beuve (beside the Liane river E of the tourist office). Tel 21 30 98 98. ***Open*** *15 May-14 Sept* daily 10am-8pm; *15 Sept-14 May* Mon-Fri 10am-6pm; Sat, Sun 10am-7pm. ***Closed*** 9-20 Jan 1995. About £6 adult, £4 child. A huge living museum of marine life, with 1,400 cubic metres/49,500 cubic feet of aquariums and 4,000 fish, plus exhibitions, activities and a cinema.

CAMPING

Airotel le Phare Signposted on S side of Le Portel. Tel 21 31 69 20. ***Open*** *Easter-30 Sept.*

SHOPPING

Main shopping streets rue Faidherbe, Grande Rue, rue Thiers, rue Victor-Hugo.

Markets Morning to early afternoon, Wed, Sat, place Dalton. Mornings daily: market at the harbour on the seafront (fish).

Le Chais Wine Cellars (wine shop) rue des Deux-Ponts. Extensive cellars of wines.

EATING AND DRINKING

Favourite restaurant areas are around the place Dalton off the Grande Rue in the Ville basse, and in the pedestrianised area of the Ville haute, near the Porte des Dunes.

Bar Hamiot opposite the fish market. ***Open*** daily 6am until after midnight. A fishermen's bar and restaurant serving snacks and meals.

La Liégeoise 10 rue Monsigny. Tel 21 31 61 15. Menus from £12 to £40.

La Matelote 80 blvd Ste-Beuve. Tel 21 30 17 97. Menus from £15 to £43.

Mimi d'Anvers 124 blvd Ste-Beuve. Tel 21 99 90 90. Menus from £11 to £18.

Le Relais de la Brocante 2 rue de Ledinghem, Wimille (5 km/3 miles N of Boulogne off D940). Tel 21 83 19 31. Fax 21 87 29 71. Menus from £16 to £35.

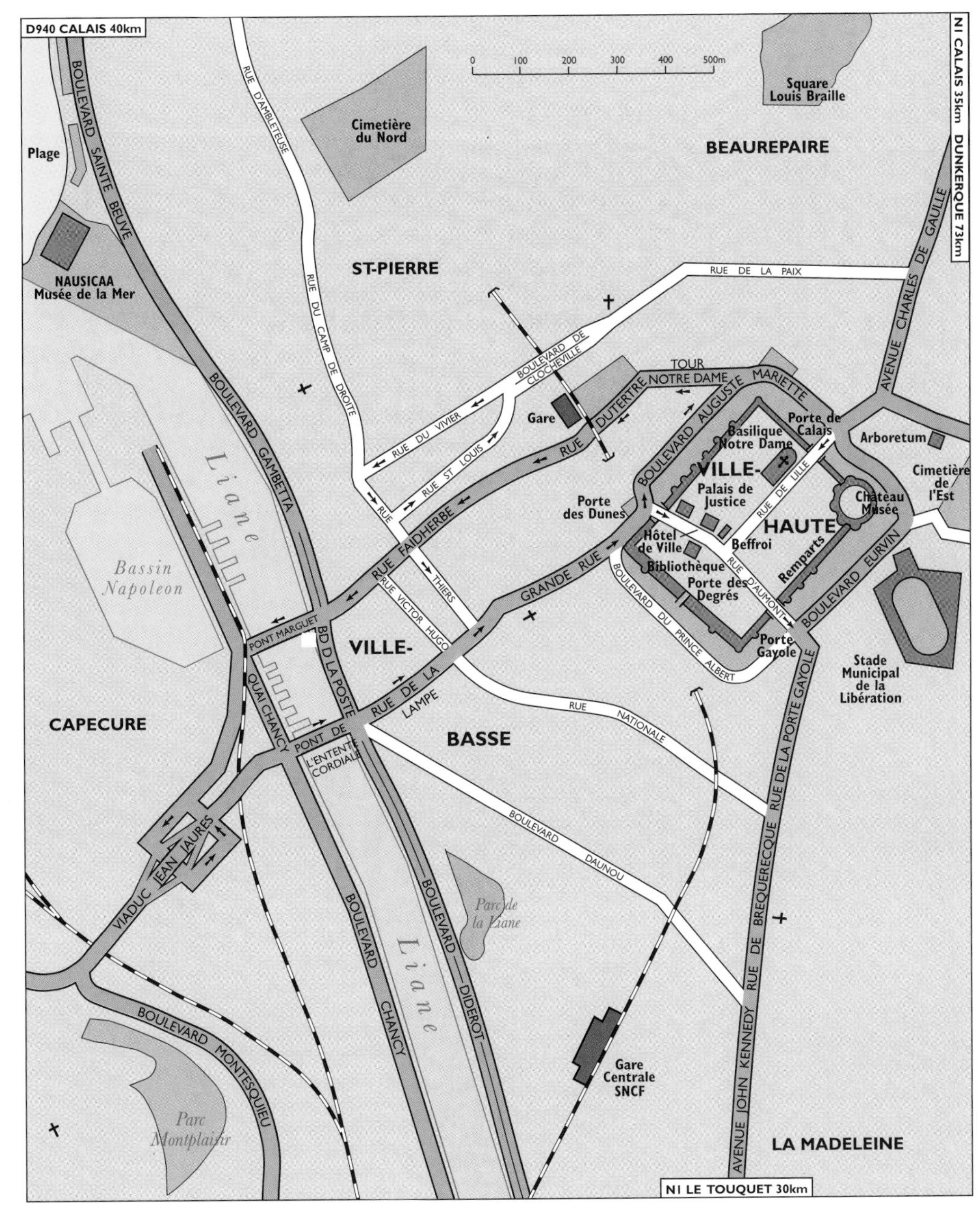

Canche, Authie & Somme

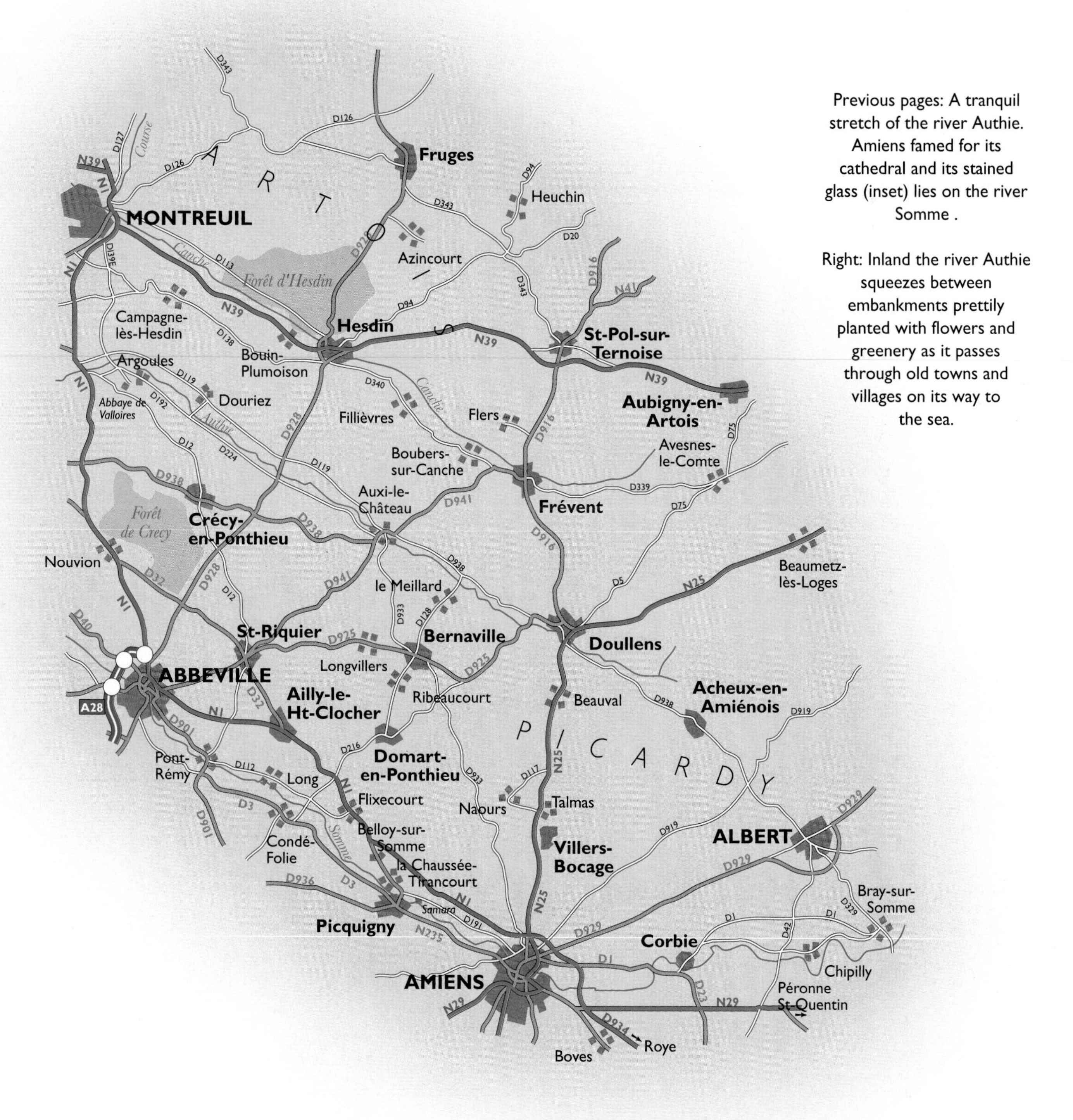

Previous pages: A tranquil stretch of the river Authie. Amiens famed for its cathedral and its stained glass (inset) lies on the river Somme .

Right: Inland the river Authie squeezes between embankments prettily planted with flowers and greenery as it passes through old towns and villages on its way to the sea.

Three rivers

The wide plains of Artois and Picardy are hatched with rivers and their attendant lakes, marshes, islands, and lagoons. The Somme is a wide, majestic river, its banks magnificently wooded in places, crossing grassy marshlands, and edged along its route by chains of 'étangs', or inland lagoons. On its circuitous route to the sea it passes through the major towns of Picardy, turning parts of Amiens into a city of canals. The pretty Authie River crosses and recrosses the Artois/Picardy border on its course to the coast at Berck-Plage. Country roads run northwards from the Authie to the Canche, which flows through the medieval towns of Montreuil and Hesdin, and on through the 'Villages fleuris', or villages in bloom, of the Artois, with their narrow footbridges, watermills, and still ponds. From source to estuary, fishing is the regional sport along these scenic waterways.

The lovely Course River, flanked by the pleasant minor road D127, joins the Canche on its circuit beneath the ramparts of Montreuil, a fortified hill town since Roman times. Some 3 km/2 miles of ramparts make a spectacular walk around the medieval Upper Town, and give panoramic views across the Picardy landscape.

The ramparts enclose the remains of the medieval citadel, steep cobbled streets with 18th-century half-timbered cottages, the abbey church of St-Saulve, founded in the early Middle Ages, but much rebuilt over the centuries, and the old hospital, or Hôtel-Dieu, built in the 18th century.

Following the Canche south-east from Montreuil, the D113 crosses Hesdin Forest to Hesdin, a little 16th-century town with a former palace (now the Town Hall and a museum) at its centre, and a church with a Renaissance doorway. On Thursdays, a lively market takes over the central square. North of Hesdin, off the D928 towards Fruges, is the site of the battlefield of Agincourt (Azincourt in French), where in 1415, England's Henry V and a small English army defeated a French army nearly twice its size by strategic deployment of its longbowmen.

The Canche Valley is very pretty to the south-east of Hesdin, where the D340 runs through award-winning villages – Fillièvres, with its water mill, and picturesque Boubers-sur-Canche. South of Montreuil, the little D139E joins the D119, which runs alongside the river Authie through some pretty villages and countryside to Auxi-le-Château, a town with a Flamboyant Gothic church. South of the river near the village of Argoules lies the 12th-century Cistercian abbey of Valloires. The countryside to the south is sprinkled with châteaux (not all open to the public). At Le Meillard on the D128 is the Château de Remaisnic, and near Bernaville are the châteaux of Ribeaucourt and Longvillers.

War can never be long out of the mind in this part of France. To the south is the majestic but battle-scarred River Somme – and to the west, near the village of Crécy-en-Ponthieu, is the site of the Battle of Crécy, where in 1346, the army of Edward III of England, en route to claim the French throne, defeated the army of the French king Philippe VI de Valois. The wooden tower built for visitors to survey the Crécy battlefield also overlooks the cool green deer forest of Crécy. A drive is signposted – 'Route des chênes' or 'oak tree route' – through the forest. At its centre is a menhir, or ancient standing stone.

Below: The belltower of the venerable abbey church of St-Saulve in Montreuil. The church was founded in the 12th century, but suffered great destruction. The belltower was added by a local architect in the 18th century.

Underground city

The cave-city of Naours (above) was a Gallo-Roman refuge where Romanised Gauls used to hide from invading barbarians, and it has been a refuge for local inhabitants through all the wars that have afflicted this region since. There is, indeed, a complete underground city in these caves. Leading off its 26 galleries, 3,000 m (nearly 2 miles) long, are 300 chambers big enough to accommodate whole families. The cave-city has squares, roadways, stables, wells, and three chapels. Today, the caves contain a museum of life in a Picardy village, showing village crafts typical of the region. The band of light in the photograph (above) reveals the path of the guide's torch.

Right: The western side of the ramparts of Montreuil, with five round towers built between the 13th and 17th centuries. From the northern side of the ramparts you can see the Carthusian monastery at Neuville on the north bank of the river Canche.

Three Rivers Fact File

MONTREUIL-SUR-MER from **Calais** N1/D940 72 km/46 miles. **Postal zip code** 62170. **Tourist information** 6 place de la Poissonnerie. Tel 21 06 04 27.

SIGHTSEEING

HESDIN

Beffroi (Belfry) and **Musée**: call the tourist office for visits (Tel 21 86 84 76). Guided visits of Hesdin can be arranged by the Sept Vallées tourist office (Tel 21 86 19 19).

Forêt d'Hesdin (off the D928 N of Hesdin): quiet zone (no driving, no radios) at the heart of the forest; marked walks; picnic areas; orientation tables.

MONTREUIL-SUR-MER

Remparts and **Citadelle** ***Open*** *Jan-Sep, Nov-Dec* Mon, Wed-Sun 9am-noon, 2-6pm.

NAOURS

Grottes-refuges (Cave-city). On the D60, about 3 km/2 miles W of Talmas (on the N25 N of Amiens). Tel 22 93 71 78. ***Open*** *Mar-Nov* daily 9am-noon, 2-6pm. *16 Nov-Feb* group visits by appointment. About £5.

RIVER AUTHIE

Centre permanent d'initiation à l'environment CPIE du Val d'Authie 25 rue Vermaelen – B.P.23. Tel 21 04 05 79. Guided walking tours of the Authie Valley; talks on the river environment; restoration and conservation of area's natural features. Also river canoeing and cycling.

RIVER CANCHE

Etaples Tourist Information Le Clos St-Victor building, blvd Bigot-Descelers, Baie de la Canche. Tel 21 09 56 94. Walks and tours of the Canche estuary with talks on its wildlife and ecology. Canoeing trips.

Centre nautique de la Canche Ask at tourist information about activities at the marina: navigable sea-canoeing route from **Montreuil-sur-Mer** to **Etaples**, fishing, windsurfing, diving, sailing, coastal boat trips and bird-watching hides.

Abbaye de Valloires Argoules (S bank of the River Authie on the D192). Tel 22 29 62 33. ***Open*** *Apr-11 Nov* daily 10am-noon, 2-5.30pm.

CAMPING

Camping du Blanc Pignon La Calotterie (on the N39 about 3 km/2 miles NW of Montreuil. Tel 21 06 03 64. Wooded campsite with swimming pool, 12 km/7 miles from sea. Tel 21 86 98 12.

Camping Les Peupliers Off the D113E nr Bouin-Plumoison, close to the Canche. Tel 21 86 98 12.

EATING AND DRINKING

Auberge La Grenouillère La Madeleine-sous-Montreuil. Tel 21 06 07 22. Fax 21 86 36 36. Menus from £19 to £45.

Château de Montreuil 4 chaussée des Capucins. Tel 21 81 53 04. Fax 21 81 36 43. Regional food is served by Roux Brothers-trained chef-proprietor, Christian Germain. Menus from £25 to £50.

Le Darnétal place Darnétal. Tel 21 06 04 87. Classic French cooking. Menus from £16 to £23.

Touring *the* Somme

Straight, fast roads, first laid some 2,000 years ago by the legions of Augustus and Julius Caesar, take you from Abbeville, Doullens and Roye, across the wooded marshlands of the Somme *département* into Amiens, its capital. En route, frequent signposts direct you to *Camps de César* – where Julius Caesar's legions rested before venturing northwards to subdue the local Celtic tribes and, eventually, Britain.

Aristocratic Amiens has been a capital for almost as long as it has been a settlement. The Romans first reported its existence as Samarobriva (meaning 'bridge over the Somme'), capital of the Ambiani tribe of Gauls. The Somme Valley between Amiens and Abbeville has been a rich focus of archaeological finds. At sites in the area, archaeologists have found traces of human habitation dating back some 400,000 years. Samara, on the D191 north of Picquigny, is an archaeological theme park on the site of a hill fort, where the life, industries and crafts of the region's prehistoric peoples are displayed and demonstrated.

Treasures of the Somme

Gems of French Flamboyant architecture dot the towns and villages of the Somme. The 15th-century abbey church of St-Vulfran in Abbeville's place de l'Hôtel-de-Ville was restored after the town was bombed and burned at the end of World War II. The sculptures of the Flamboyant West Front record the marriage in 1514 of King Louis XII to the English monarch Henry VIII's sister Mary Tudor. The town has an outstanding archaeological museum, and on the outskirts is the 18th-century Château de Bagatelle: both the house and magnificent park are open to the public.

The huge abbey church of St-Riquier is an outstanding example of Flamboyant Gothic architecture. It was built in the 15th and 16th centuries, and its West Front is crowded with carvings. The church and abbey buildings – the cloister and belfry – are very well preserved. In Amiens, the church of St-Germain is another example of Flamboyant Gothic style.

Castles and châteaux along the banks of the Somme bear witness to conflicts in this region long before the batles of this century. The Somme forms the moat of the Château Pont-Rémy; Long has a brick and stone château

Left: Samara, where the dwellings of Neolithic people who lived on the banks of the Somme some 7,000 years ago have been reconstructed.

Above: The manor house in Argoules, one of the many pretty villages in the valley of the river Authie. Stopping at the riverside cafés and *auberges* often found in converted mills and manors is one of the great pleasures of touring the Pas-de-Calais.

overlooking a chain of river lagoons; and the ruins of a stronghold still guard Picquigny, a pretty village on the left bank.

East of Amiens, the Somme meanders through a series of loops to Péronne and on to St-Quentin. There are some lovely drives around the river's loops between Corbie and Bray-sur-Somme, which is the focal point for people wanting to fish in the Somme, its lagoons, lakes and canal.

West of Abbeville, the Somme estuary (although the Somme is a canal between Abbeville and the sea) is wild in places and very peaceful. You can drive around the salt marshes on the D940 and D3, but it is well worth while driving to Noyelles-sur-Mer or St-Valéry-sur-Somme and taking the little steam railway on its scenic tour of the Somme bay around the salt marshes to the seaside resort of Cayeux-sur-Mer, and back (see map on page 14).

Somme Fact File

ABBEVILLE from **Calais** N1 116 km/72 miles. **Postal zip code** 80100. **Tourist information** 1 rue Amiral-Courbet. Tel 22 24 27 92. Fax 22 31 08 26. ***Open*** *Jan-Jun, Sept-Dec* Tue-Sat 9.30am-noon, 2-6.30pm, Sun 3-6pm; *Jul-Aug* Mon-Sat 9.30am-noon, 2-7pm, Sun 10am-noon, 3-6pm.

Boat trips on the Somme
To Corbie and Samara from La Capitainerie, 31 rue Belu, St-Leu quarter, Amiens. Tel 22 91 88 55.

Rail trips around the Somme bay on the Somme Railway. Tel 22 26 96 96. Departs *15 Apr-Jun* and *4-24 Sept* Sun, *Jul-3 Sept* Tue-Sun from St-Valéry for Noyelles and Le Crotoy at 3.30pm, 5.30pm; and *Jul-Aug* Sat-Sun Cayeux for St-Valéry and Noyelles at 3.30pm. About £7 adult, £5 child.

Around the Upper Somme from Froissy 14-km/9-mile trip to Cappy and Dompierre on a steam train, ending with a visit to a railway museum. ***Open*** *May, Jun, Sept* Sun 2.15-6pm; *15 Jul-5 Sept* Wed, Sat 3pm, 4.30pm; Sun 2.15-6pm. About 90 min and £5 adult, £3.50 child. Check with tourist office for tickets, point of departure, or tel 22 44 55 40 (mornings only). See map on page 80.

SIGHTSEEING

ABBEVILLE

Château de Bagatelle 135 route de Paris. Tel 22 24 02 69. ***Open*** *Jul-Aug* Mon, Wed-Sun, 2-6pm. Château and museum about £6.

Eglise St-Vulfran's Parvis St-Vulfran. ***Open*** 9am-7pm.

Musée Boucher-de-Perthes 24 rue Gontier-Patin. Tel 22 24 08 49. ***Open*** *May-Sept* Mon, Wed-Sun 2-6pm. *Oct-Apr* Wed, Sat-Sun 2-6pm. Prehistory rooms explaining the archaeology of the Somme region. Exhibits on the birds and other natural history of the Somme Bay.

MARQUENTERRE

Parc ornithologique du Marquenterre (bird sanctuary) Off D4 from Le Crotoy. Reception: St-Quentin-en-Tourmont on D204. Tel 22 25 03 06. ***Open*** *18 Mar-12 Nov* daily 9.30am-7pm; *13 Nov-17 Mar* tours on Sat at 2.30pm, and on Sun at 10am and 2.30pm.

SOMME

Abbaye St-Riquier On the D925 9km/5 miles NE of Abbeville. Tel 22 28 20 20. ***Open*** *10 Feb-Sept* daily 9.30am-noon, 2-6pm; *Oct-11 Nov* daily 2-6pm.

Château de Long On D218 about 15 km/9 miles SE of Abbeville. ***Open*** *20 Aug-Sept* daily 10am-noon, 2-5pm. About £4 adult, £2 child. 18th-century château in lovely grounds.

Samara On the right bank of the Somme, on the D191 just E of La Chaussée-Tirancourt, N of Picquigny. Tel 22 51 82 83. Fax 22 51 92 12. ***Open*** *5 Jan-20 Dec* daily 9.30am-6pm. About £7.50 adult, £5.50 child. Demonstrations of prehistoric crafts; reconstructed iron age houses, model of prehistoric oven; tours of fortifications; nature circuit through the marshes; boat trips on the Somme.

CAMPING

Airotel Château des Tilleuls On D40 about 1 km/⅝ mile SE of Port-le-Grand, outside Abbeville. Tel 22 24 07 75. ***Open*** *Mar-Oct.*

EATING AND DRINKING

Auberge de la Corne 32 chaussée du Bois, Abbeville. Tel 22 24 06 34. Fax 22 24 03 65. Quality but simple food from local river and forest produce. Menus from £12 to £25.

Escale en Picardie 15 rue des Teinturiers, Abbeville. Tel 22 24 21 51. Notable cooking based on coastal fish.

Hostellerie Belloy 29 route nationale, Belloy-sur-Somme (on N235 between Abbeville and Amiens). Tel 22 51 41 05. Fax 22 51 25 14. Menus from £10 to £24.

The *hortillonnages*, or marshland market gardens, of Amiens can be explored on foot or in the flat-bottomed punts that are used by gardeners to take their produce to market.

Amiens

Amiens is famed for its cathedral, but is also a pleasant city to explore for the few remaining old town houses, and the maze of waterways in the St-Leu quarter.

Modern Amiens, dominated by its medieval cathedral, is an important stop on a cathedral tour of northern France. St-Firmin brought Christianity to Roman Samarobriva from Spain. He converted the Gallo-Roman population during the 4th century and became the town's first bishop. The first cathedral was destroyed by fire in 1218, and the present Cathédrale de Notre-Dame was begun two years later.

Most Gothic cathedrals took centuries to complete, but Amiens was built within 50 years. Begun at the height of a cathedral-building fever that gripped France after its development of Gothic architecture, it is the supreme example of the early maturity of French Gothic. Conceived as a symbol of civic pride, its plan and scale are audacious – it has the largest area of any Gothic church in France, and its classic, three-stage nave is the highest: 42 m/139 ft from floor to the ridge of the vault.

There is a lot to see in Amiens Cathedral, but especially captivating are the 110 medieval oak choir stalls, carved with scenes from the Old Testament and everyday medieval life. And do walk around the ambulatory at the east end which contains the famous 17th-century 'Weeping Angel' carved by Blasset. The cathedral's sooty façade – its West Front a riot of medieval sculpture – still towers high above modern industrial Amiens. Although much of its precious medieval glass was shattered, the cathedral was not seriously damaged in 1940, whereas the entire city to its west was laid waste.

Walking around the former old town with a camera can be rewarding. The old quarter of St-Leu is cut across by waterways, with old gabled houses on their banks. The puppets in the *Maison du Théâtre* keep the disappearing Picardy language alive. There are shops, cafés, restaurants and night clubs in this old quarter.

Farther east are the *hortillonnages,* a large area of market gardens on former marshes originally reclaimed by the Romans. The island gardens are surrounded by waterways and the *hortillons* – market gardeners – manoeuvre around the area on punts. Boat trips can be taken around the *hortillonnages,* which cover an area of some 300 hectares/741 acres, with 90 km/55 miles of waterways fed by the Somme and Avre rivers.

In the streets to the east of the cathedral are restored town houses from the 16th and 17th centuries, and to the south the Jules Verne Information Centre – the house where the famous novelist lived.

Art lovers should spend time in the Musée de Picardie, which displays works by Fragonard, Delacroix, Géricault, Bonnard, and Matisse, plus finds from St-Acheul in Amiens and other archaeological sites.

Amiens Fact File

AMIENS from **Calais** D916/N25 148 km/92 miles. **Postal zip code** 80010. **Tourist information** 12 rue du Chapeau-de-Violettes. Tel 22 91 79 28. Fax 22 92 50 58. ***Open*** Mon-Sat 9am-12.30pm, 1.30-6pm. **City Information Centre** SNCF Station. ***Open*** daily 10am-7pm. A **museum card** gives admission to **Musée de Picardie, Musée d'Art local et d'Histoire régionale**: About £2.

SIGHTSEEING

Guided boat trips all year in traditional high-prowed punts from quay at 56 boulevard Beauville (Tel 22 92 12 18), through the *hortillonnages* and to L'Ile aux Fagots Nature School, 43 chemin du Halage (Tel 22 91 44 96), an ecology centre introducing the *hortillonnage* environment.

Cathédrale de Notre-Dame place Notre-Dame. Open daily.

Jules Verne Information Centre 2 rue Charles-Dubois. Tel 22 45 37 84. ***Open*** Tue-Sat 9.30am-noon, 2-6pm. Organised tours of Jules Verne's favourite haunts. About £1.50 adult, 50p child.

Musée de Picardie 48 rue de la République. ***Open*** Tue-Sun 10am-12.30pm, 2-6pm. Museum card. Free Sun.

FOR CHILDREN

Ferme d'Antan Creuse on D162, off the N29, 13 km/8 miles SW Amiens. A farm using methods, materials and breeds in use at the beginning of the century. ***Open*** all year. For times check with tourist office or tel 22 38 98 58. About £2 adult.

CAMPING

Parc St-Pierre northern Amiens. Ask tourist office for details.

SHOPPING

Flea market held second Sunday of each month on Quays at St-Leu.

Puppet shop (Mr Faquier) 67 rue du Don. Tel 22 92 49 52. Shop selling traditional Picardy puppets (*cabotans*).

Maison du Théâtre 24 rue St-Leu. Puppet shows.

Waterside market place Parmentier every Thur, Sat morning.

EATING AND DRINKING

Auberge du Pré Porus 95 rue Voyelle. Tel 22 46 25 03. Fax 22 46 75 23. Menus from £12 to £23.

La Couronne 64 rue St-Leu. Tel 22 91 88 57. A respected restaurant in the St-Leu area. Classic cooking based on fresh ingredients. Menus from £11 to £20.

La Mangeoire 3 rue des Sergents. Tel 22 91 11 28. Late-opening *crêperie* for vegetarians. £1 to £8.

Les Marissons 68 rue Marissons. Tel 22 92 96 66. Fax 22 91 50 50. Menus from £14 to £30.

Le Petit Chef 8 rue Jean-Catelas. Tel 22 92 24 23. Modern French food at very reasonable prices. Menus from £7.50 to £27.

La Soupe à Cailloux 16 rue des Bondes. Tel 22 91 92 70. A small, friendly restaurant. Menus from £8 to £11.

Le Vivier 593 route de Rouen. Tel 21 89 12 21.

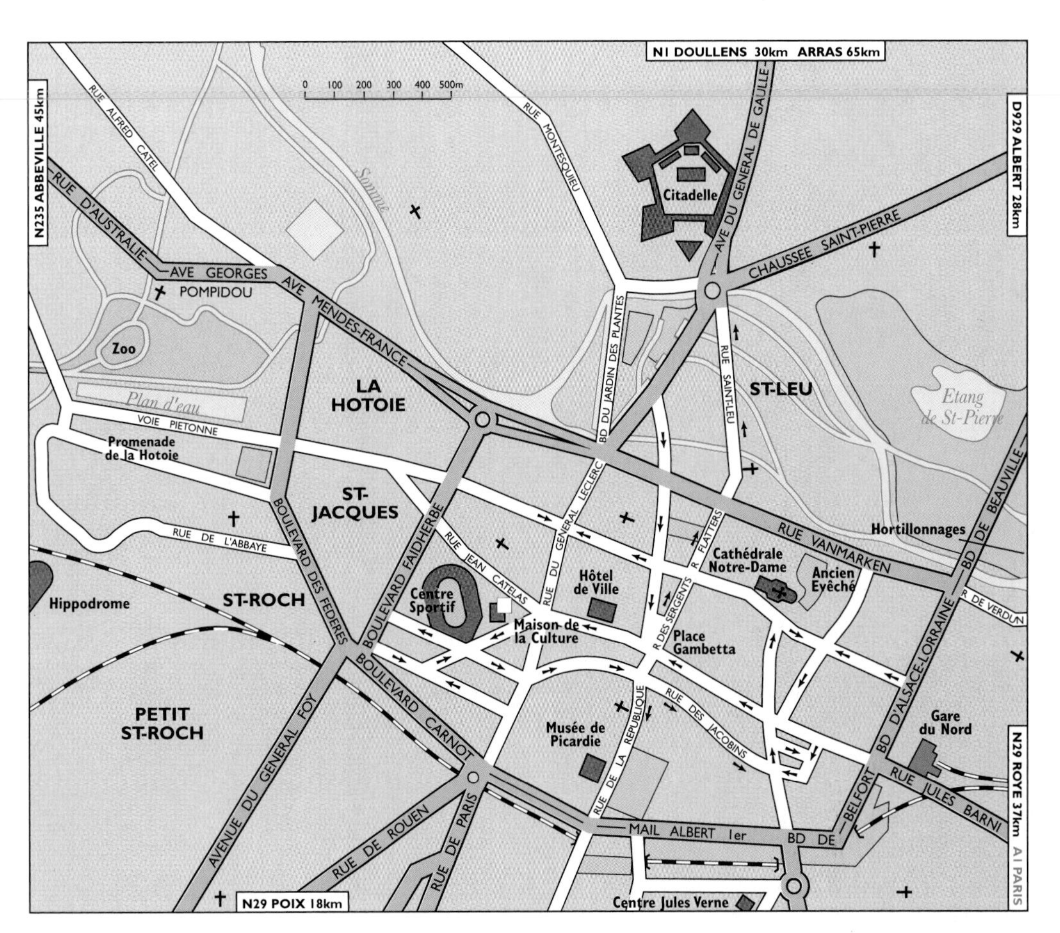

Left: Morning sunlight floods through the lancet windows into the soaring interior of Amiens Cathedral. The groin vaulting in the transepts is the earliest in France. There is some medieval glass in the rose windows, and 16th-century glass in the great rose window over the portal.

Right: Little gabled houses with coloured façades, where the market gardeners once lived, are characteristic of the old quarter around the Church of St-Leu. Water mills once powered by the river Somme can still be seen.

Rouen & the Caux

The
Normandy Coast

The white cliffs of Normandy mark the northern edge of the Caux Plateau – France's Alabaster Coast. In the shadows of steep cliffs lie quiet village resorts with long beaches, and pretty harbours shelter at the mouths of small rivers.

The little estuary town of Le Tréport looks across the Bresle River to Mers-les-Bains, over the border in Picardy. Beautiful beaches are the pride of both resorts, but Le Tréport boasts a heated swimming pool – a sensible contingency plan for a resort in so northerly a position. A tour inland takes you to the old town of Eu, a favourite holiday venue of England's Queen Victoria. It has an attractive Gothic church of St-Laurent dedicated to the 12th-century Irish archbishop, St Lawrence O'Toole.

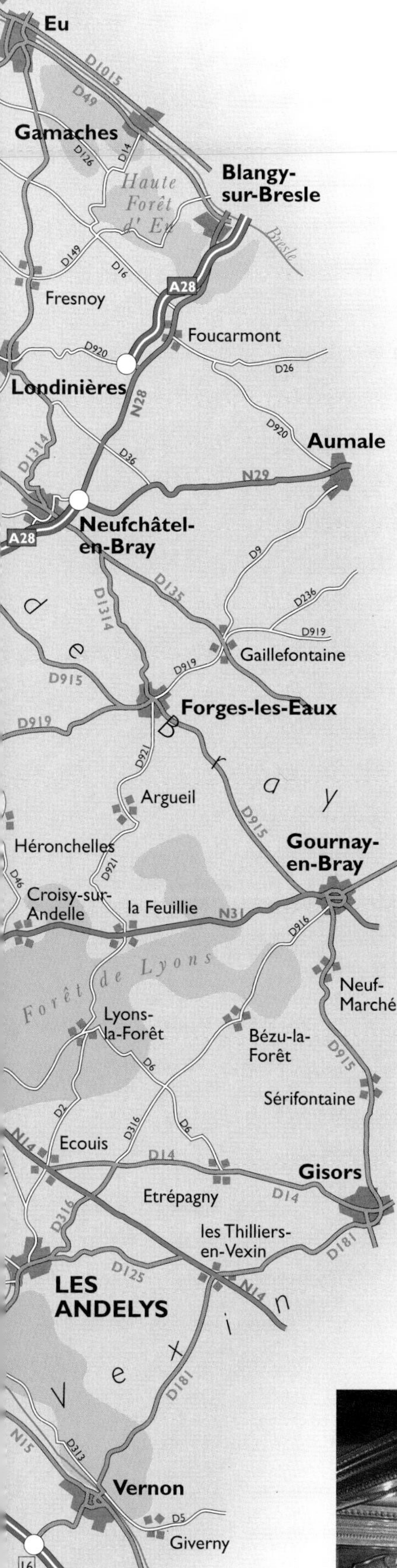

Bénédictine

Fécamp's 12th-century church is the only building surviving from a Benedictine monastery, founded in the 7th century to safeguard a relic of Christ's blood. At the beginning of the 16th century a Venetian monk, Dom Bernardo Vincelli, mixed 27 local plants and spices, and distilled an elixir with strengthening properties. A detail from the church's stained glass (right) shows the distiller-monks at work. The elixir was produced until the Revolution in 1789, when the monastery was destroyed and the recipe lost. It was rediscovered by chance in 1863. M. Alexandre Legrand, a local man, found among old family papers a recipe for distilling spirits that had belonged to the monks of Fécamp. He experimented until he had perfected the recipe, and marketed it as *Bénédictine* liqueur. You can visit Le Grand's distillery in Fécamp, an exuberantly decorated neo-Gothic building, which is also the Musée de la Bénédictine.

Below: The Café des Tribunaux in Dieppe.

Previous pages: The long, sandy beach at St-Valéry-en-Caux, sheltered by rampart-like cliffs. Insets: Rouen Cathedral and Le Havre's masterpiece by Niemeyer.

There are pleasant drives along the D49 beside the Bresle River, and the D126 through the beech forest of Eu. Return via the D16 through the Caux to the coast road, with panoramic views across the Channel.

Modern Dieppe manages the impossible: 19th-century charm and 1990s liveliness; Parisian weekenders and British holidaymakers; the quaint old Le Pollet fishermen's quarter and the super-efficient fishing port.

In Dieppe, capital of the Caux, is the much-loved Café des Tribunaux, a bar-café famous for its ice cream menu of unrivalled flavours, its wonderful Art Deco interior, and its history: Pissarro, Monet, Renoir, Gauguin, Whistler *et al* used to drink and talk there. Along the coast at Varengeville-sur-Mer, 10 km/6 miles to the west of Dieppe, is Les Moustiers, a country house designed by the English architect Edwin Lutyens with a garden by Gertrude Jekyll.

The Caux coast is a medley of varied sights and experiences. Varengeville-sur-Mer is buried in beech woods. Its cliffs are slashed by deep gorges descending to the sea. It is famous for its little Gothic church – now precariously balanced on the receding cliff edge – with a window by the painter Georges Braque, who lived nearby; and for the Renaissance Manoir d'Ango, with a round dovecot in the grounds, built for a lordly pirate.

Fronting Veules-les-Roses is a pebble-beach resort with its own casino; behind is an extraordinarily pretty medieval village of thatched, half-timbered houses overlooking a tiny, tinkling river. Sotteville has a stone staircase cut into the cliffs, leading down to the beach.

Le Havre, in its sheltered position on the Seine Estuary, is a centre for yachting and water sports. This once-picturesque old port suffered great damage in World War II and was bravely rebuilt in the 1950s in

Deauville (above) and Honfleur (right) are among the many attractive resorts and ports that are easily reached from Rouen and the Caux.

uncompromisingly modern style. Its cultural centre designed by Oscar Niemeyer, architect of Brasilia's main buildings, is a monument to its undaunted spirit.

To the south and south-west is the photogenic port of Honfleur, and the Côte fleurie. Here, cliffs give way to a chain of elegant resorts with long, wide sandy beaches. From Trouville to Cabourg, all are pricey in season and rather lifeless at other times of year. Cabourg, with its turn-of-the-century villas, is the most charming; Deauville is the largest and most glamorous, a short-break venue for film, stage and other personalities from Paris. In season it is a medley of polo events, regattas, balls and parties.

Dieppe

Few English people visit Dieppe for its beach, but, for the record, it has a good one. It is more than 1.6 km/1 mile long and very popular with French families at weekends.

English families visit Dieppe for the shopping, the markets, and the food. There is a Prisunic near the ferry, a Shopi that takes pounds sterling in the rue de la Barre, and the Mammouth hypermarket out on the Paris road. Celebrated food shops include a branch of Philippe Olivier's cheese shop; a marvellous Saturday market that takes over the town; and ultra-fresh fish, the day's catch sold on the quayside fish market.

Dieppe has a reputation for good cooking. Its repertoire ranges from some very special fish restaurants to true-blue English breakfasts at the Select Hotel on the rue de la Barre, and includes the best regional cooking, as well as classic and modern cuisine.

Oscar Wilde is said to have written *The Ballad of Reading Gaol* at a table in the Café suisse. Aubrey Beardsley took holidays in Dieppe. Walter Sickert painted it. Clémentine Hozier lived there before she met and married Winston Churchill. Georges Braque is buried in the clifftop cemetery of Varengeville 10 km/6 miles to the west. In Edwardian times and during the 1920s and 1930s, Dieppe was the fashionable cross-Channel holiday resort.

The 15th-century castle gives panoramic views along the coast; it has a good nautical museum plus a gallery of works by famous locals and residents – Braque, Sickert, Pissarro. At the gate of Les Tourelles on the seafront, the biennial Kite Festival takes place in September 1994, 1996, and so on. The town has two interesting Gothic churches, and Sea City, a museum of fishing. The Château de Miromesnil, 8 km/5 miles away to the south, was the birthplace of the French writer, Guy de Maupassant, and there is a medieval castle at Arques-la-Bataille, 6 km/4 miles south-east.

Normandy Coast Fact File

DIEPPE from **Calais** D925, D940, D40, N1 190 km/118 miles. **Postal zip code** 76204.
Tourist information **DIEPPE** Pont Jean-Ango, quai du Carénage. Tel 35 84 11 77. Fax 35 06 27 66. ***Open*** *Oct-Apr* 9am-noon, 2-6pm; *May-Jun, Sept* 9am-1pm, 2-7pm; *Jul-Aug* 9am-1pm, 2-8pm.
CAEN place St-Pierre, 14000. Tel 31 27 14 14. Fax 31 27 14 13.
DEAUVILLE BP 79, place de la Mairie, 14800. Tel 31 88 21 43. Fax 31 88 78 88. **LE HAVRE** Forum de l'Hôtel-de-Ville, BP 649, 76059. Tel 35 21 22 88. Fax 35 42 38 39. ***Open*** daily 8.45am-12.15pm, 2.30-6.30pm.

SIGHTSEEING
BAYEUX
La Telle du Conquest (or **Tapisserie de la reine Mathilde**) Centre culturel Guillaume-le-Conquérant, rue de Nesmond. Tel 31 92 05 48. ***Open*** *29 Apr-15 Sept* daily 9am-7pm; *16 Sept-15 Oct* daily 9am-noon, 2-6.30pm; *16 Oct-15 Mar* daily 9.30am-noon, 2-6pm; *16 Mar-28 Apr* daily 9am-12.30pm, 2-6.30pm. This famous tapestry depicting the Norman conquest of England is a unique document of the history of Normandy.
DIEPPE
Château de Miromesnil Tourville-sur-Arques, nr Dieppe. Tel 35 85 02 80. Guided tours *1 May-15 Oct* Mon, Wed-Sun 2-6pm.
Château-musée rue de Chastes. Tel 35 84 19 76. ***Open*** *June-Sept* daily 10am-noon, 2-6pm; *Oct-May* Mon, Wed-Sun 10am-noon, 2-5pm.
Les Moustiers Varengeville-sur-Mer (10 km/6 miles W of Dieppe). Tel 35 85 10 02. ***Open*** *15 Mar-15 Nov* daily 10am-noon, 2-6pm.
FÉCAMP
Musée de la Bénédictine 110 rue Alexandre-Legrand. Tel 35 10 26 00. ***Open*** *Jan-15 Mar* daily visits at 10.30am and 3.30pm; *16 Mar-May* daily 10am-noon, 2-5.30pm; *Jun-10 Sept* daily 10am-6pm.
LE HAVRE
Boat trips around the harbour *Easter-Sept.* Tel 35 42 01 31.

FOR CHILDREN
DIEPPE
Cité de la Mer (Sea City) 37 rue de l'Asile-Thomas. Tel 35 06 93 20. ***Open*** *Apr-Sept* daily 10am-noon, 2-7pm. *Oct-Mar* daily 10am-noon, 2-6pm. Aquariums, boat-building, fishing, ecology.

CAMPING
DIEPPE
Camping Vitamine chemin des Vertus. Tel. 35 82 11 11. ***Open*** *Apr-Oct.*
HONFLEUR
Camping de la Briquerie, Equemauville (from the D579 Pont-l'Evêque–Honfleur). Tel 35 89 28 32. ***Open*** *Apr-Sept.*
LE HAVRE
Camping de la forêt de Montgeon (access from harbour and SNCF station, cours de la République). Tel 35 46 52 39. ***Open*** *Easter-Sept.*

EATING AND DRINKING
BAYEUX
L'Amaryllis 32 rue St-Patrice. Tel 31 22 47 94. Menus from £9 to £20.
Le Lion d'Or 71 rue St-Jean. Tel 31 92 06 90. Fax 31 22 15 64. Menus from £12.50 to £40.
DIEPPE
A la Marmite dieppoise 8 rue St-Jean. Tel 35 84 24 26. From £10 to £26.
Le St-Jacques 12 rue de l'Oranger. Tel 35 84 52 04. From about £15.

Touring the Caux

A large slice of northern France's greenest province lies within easy reach of Calais. On its outer borders are the cheese-producing towns of Neufchâtel-en-Bray, Pont-L'Evêque and Livarot. It embraces the busy Seine and includes the coastal resorts (among them Veules-les-Roses, left) and ancient villages of the Caux.

The Pays de Caux is a chalk plateau within the triangle of land between Dieppe, Le Havre and Rouen. Its name comes from the Gaulish Caletes tribe, who occupied the area before the arrival of the Romans. Their capital was at Lillebonne, near the mouth of the Seine. Caudebec-en-Caux, nearby, was the old regional capital. Most wooden buildings in the old town were destroyed by fire in 1940, but some old houses survive in the main street, and the town still has its 15th-century church in Flamboyant Gothic style.

The Caux is a region of isolated, half-timbered farms, built into hollows for protection from the winds. There are many villages with thatched cottages, medieval churches, and old manors to discover on tours inland along pretty roads. The D10 from Veulettes-sur-Mer follows the Durdent Valley to the town of Barville, where the river forms a natural moat around the 17th-century Château de Cany, built on an island. The Durdent River flows on to the graceful 18th-century town of Héricourt-en-Caux. From Fécamp, now rather built-up, the D150 follows the Valmont River to the ruins of the 14th-century Abbaye de Valmont. The D3, branching off the N27 from Dieppe, runs alongside the river Scie to the ruins of an 11th-century Benedictine abbey at St-Victor-l'Abbaye, and to Clères, well worth visiting to see its unspoilt half-timbered houses and old market place. The 16th-century castle also has a bird sanctuary.

There are panoramic clifftop views and the remains of defensive castles along the rocky Caux coast. The cliffs are broken by coves sheltering small beaches or fishing ports, such as St-Valéry-en-Caux. To the south-west, the cliffs of Etretat, eroded by the sea into arches and needles, are one of the famous sights of Normandy.

The countryside between Dieppe and the Picardy border is networked with pretty roads: the D149 through the former royal hunting forest of Eu; the many roads leading into the Pays de Bray; and the D12 through the lush oak and beech forest of Eawy, bordered by the Varenne River, beloved of trout-fishing enthusiasts.

South-west of Rouen, the old river port of Pont-Audemer remained substantially undamaged after World War II. Nearby is the pretty town of Montfort-sur-Risle, and the 11th-century Bec-Hellouin Abbey, founded by Lanfranc, Archbishop of Canterbury during the reign of William the Conqueror. The ruins of this once-great seat of learning, which was destroyed during the Revolution, have been restored by monks who returned there in 1948.

South-east of Rouen is Les Andelys, one of the most photographed spots on the Seine, where the ruins of a great fortress, Château Gaillard, give magnificent views along the river. Near Les Andelys is Giverny, the home of the painter, Claude Monet. The garden has been recreated as he painted it. Other subjects of his paintings in his native Normandy are the Cathédrale de Rouen and the riverside village of La Bouille in the lovely Parc naturel de Brotonne. Towards Lisieux and the Pays d'Auge the countryside becomes still more lush, and the roads are bordered by countryside known as *bocage*, a patchwork of small fields surrounded by tall hedges. Signposted routes tour around the region's cheese-producing centres; and a Cider Route leads to farms where cider and calvados are produced on a small scale by traditional methods.

The port of Le Havre and the city of Caen were in the first line of fighting following D-Day 1944, and were almost completely destroyed. They were not restored, but rebuilt during the 1950s, and both have some outstanding modern buildings. Between the two stretch the most fashionable resorts in northern France – Deauville, Trouville, and the picturesque port of Honfleur.

The Seine Valley

As it reaches the end of its long journey from Burgundy to the sea, the Seine has carved wide valleys through the hilly countryside between Les Andelys and its estuary. Slowed by the weight of silt it carries, it has carved great loops around its flanking hills. From either bank rise the slopes of the Parc naturel de Brotonne, a wooded stretch of Normandy full of things to see and do.

Autoroutes to the south and departmental highways to the north whirl heavy traffic across the loops of the Seine between the two industrial ports of Le Havre and Rouen. From the Tancarville Bridge at the Seine mouth, as far as the forests of Roumare and La Londe outside Rouen, minor roads negotiate the Seine's meanderings through peaceful wooded hills. The area has remains of Celtic and Roman settlements – and it has been a natural haven for religious communities from the earliest days of Christianity.

West and east of the D81, there are spectacular views across the Seine Valley and the Brotonne natural park's 42,000 hectares/104,000 acres of dense beech and oak forest. Lillebonne is famous for its ancient Roman theatre and its castle, founded by William the Conqueror. A short drive away to the west on the D982 and A15 towards Le Havre is the little Romanesque church of St-Jean-d'Abbetot, decorated inside with wall-paintings.

Narrow roads and forest tracks penetrate the woods. For drivers, the tourist office has mapped out routes through the park. There is a 'Thatched Cottage Route' ('Route des chaumières') around the park's prettiest villages and the 'Route des fruits' takes you through fruit-growing villages around the forest of Jumièges. In spring, the orchards are a cloud of blossom; in the autumn villagers sell fruit from roadside stalls. Apple, cherry, and plum markets feature in the calendar of local activities. The 'Route des abbayes' guides you to the secluded ruins of abbeys founded at the dawn of European Christianity. The great Benedictine Abbaye de Jumièges founded in the 7th century was broken down and sold off during the Revolution. Near Lillebonne, the chapter house is still intact among the ruins of the 12th-century Cistercian Abbaye de Valasse, and at St-Martin-de-Boscherville, west of Rouen, the

Romanesque church of St-Georges-de-Boscherville remains from the Benedictine abbey founded by William de Tancarville in the 12th century. The 'Historic Route of Writers' ('Route des maisons des écrivains') guides visitors to the houses of Pierre Corneille, Victor Hugo, Gustave Flaubert, and other writers born along the Seine.

The occasional industrial site along the river interrupts the rural tranquillity – but the National Forest Office has signposted sites that are rich in wildlife. The natural park has absorbing museums of river life and history. An example, at La Haye-de-Routot south of the Forêt de Brotonne, is the 'Four à pain', a 19th-century communal bread oven, where bread is baked in the traditional way.

Abbeys Fact File

Abbaye de Jumièges ***Open*** *Apr-14 Jun* and *16 Sept-Oct* Mon-Fri 9am-noon, 2-5pm; Sat, Sun 9am-12.30pm, 2-6pm. *15 Jun-15 Sep* daily 9am-6.30pm. *Nov-Mar* Mon-Fri 10am-noon, 2-4pm; Sat, Sun 10am-noon, 2-5pm.
Abbaye de Valasse Gruchet-le-Valasse. Guided tours *Apr-Nov* 2nd and 4th Sun of month 2.30-5.30pm.
Eglise abbatiale St-Martin-de-Boscherville ***Open*** *Apr-Sept* daily 9am-noon, 2-7pm; *Oct-Mar* Mon-Tue and Thu-Sun 9am-noon, 2.30-5pm.
Lillebonne Roman amphitheatre. Guided tours by arrangement: tel 35 71 78 78.

River crossings

Bridges Pont de Tancarville (D910/N182/D279) toll about £2.50; Pont de la Brotonne (D490) toll about £2.50; Rouen (N238) free; autoroute A13-E05; Pont de Normandie, between Le Havre and Honfleur, to be opened in January 1995.
Ferries (bacs) Port Jérôme; D20 nr. Yainville; Duclair; Jumièges; La Bouille; Grand Couronne/le Val-de-la-Haye.

Marais Vernier

The *Marais Vernier* (below) is an area of drained marshland and peat bogs in what looks like a wasteland on the south side of the Tancarville Bridge. Peaceful 19th-century farmhouses, some with wells still in use, have spread along the roadsides. The farmland is used for pasture and for orchards – the village of Ste-Opportune-la-Mare has a cider museum. Long canals drain water into the Grande Mare Lake at the reserve's centre, which is now a protected area for wild flowers and other plants. Around it is a reserve for recently introduced Scottish cattle and Camargue horses.

Touring the Seine Valley affords an enjoyable variety of impressions and encounters. These include the manor house at St-Germain de Livet (main picture, below left) and, below, top to bottom, the ferry at Duclair, Victor Hugo's house at Villequier, and the Roman amphitheatre at Lillebonne.

Rouen

Rouen, the capital of Normandy, is a large port and big industrial city. At its heart is a medieval town with the beautiful Gothic cathedral of Notre-Dame, the famous subject of a series of Impressionist paintings by Claude Monet. And rising above the modern city suburbs are the green, wooded hills of the surrounding Forêt de Roumare.

The name of France's patron saint, Jeanne d'Arc, appears on buildings all over the old town. Near the railway station is the Tour Jeanne-d'Arc, part of the castle where the young Maid of Orléans was tried for heresy. To the west, in the rue Jeanne-d'Arc, is the tower in which she was imprisoned by the English. In the place du Vieux-Marché, part of the city's redevelopment after World War II bombing, the modern church of Ste-Jeanne marks the spot where in 1432, naked, with her head shaved, she was burned at the stake.

Around the place du Vieux-Marché are some fine reconstructed façades of old Norman half-timbered houses. Other old houses can be seen in the rue des Bons-Enfants, nearby. Leading off the place du Vieux-Marché is a street bridged by a 16th-century gatehouse bearing the famous clock face called the Gros-Horloge. Beside it, in the 14th-century belfry, is the clock's mechanism. Climb the belfry for a wonderful view of the towers and spires of Rouen's many surviving medieval churches.

Notre-Dame de Rouen is one of France's most beautiful cathedrals, despite its mixture of architectural styles. Begun in about 1170, this cathedral was completed in the 16th century. Its ornately sculpted West Front dates from this time. Wartime damage caused much of the south side of the church to be reconstructed. It has a Renaissance staircase in the north transept, 13th-century stained-glass and beautiful carved stalls in the choir. The ambulatory has effigies of several English kings, once rulers of this part of France. Buried in the Romanesque crypt is the heart of England's King Richard I, The Lion-Hearted.

The Musée des Beaux-Arts, one of several important museums in Rouen, has a number of Impressionist works (but Monet's paintings of Rouen cathedral are in the Musée d'Orsay in Paris). The Musée Le Secq des Tournelles (Museum of Ironwork), in a former Gothic church, is a favourite, full of shop signs and kitchen implements. Gustave Flaubert, author of *Madame Bovary,* was born in the 18th-century Hôtel-Dieu – the old hospital – now containing a museum of his life. And in the suburb of Le-Petit-Couronne, south of Rouen towards the Rouvray forest, is the 16th-century manor house where Pierre Corneille, the French dramatist, lived.

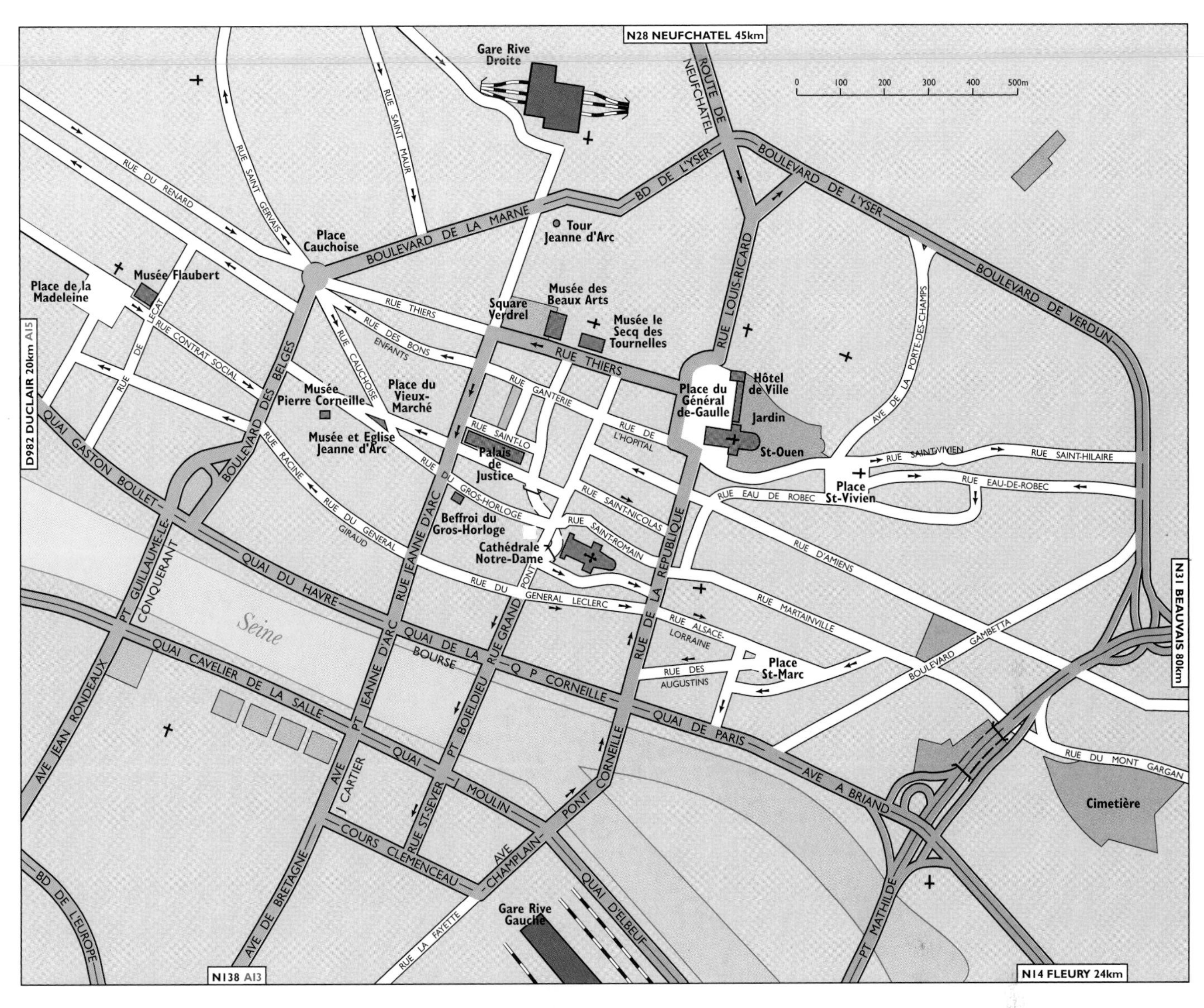

The one-handed Gros-Horloge (above) was originally the belfry clock, but was brought down to street level by popular demand in the 16th century.

Left: Rouen Cathedral.

Rouen Fact File

ROUEN from **Calais** N1, N28, A28, N1 215 km/134 miles.
Postal zip code 76000.
Tourist Information 25 place de la Cathédrale. Tel 35 71 41 77. Fax 35 98 55 50. ***Open*** *May-Sept* Mon-Sat 9am-7pm; Sun 9.30am-12.30pm, 2.30-6pm; *Oct-Apr* Mon-Sat 9am-12.30pm, 2-6.30pm.

SIGHTSEEING
Boat trips through the port *May, Jun* every Sat, *Apr, Jul-Sept* two Sats per month, from the quai de Boisguilbert, Jean Ango landing stage. Tickets can be booked at the tourist office.
Walking tours with official guides in English. Check with tourist office.
Beffroi du Gros-Horloge (bell tower beside the great clock) rue du Gros-Horloge. Check with the Musée des Beaux-Arts.
Cathédrale Notre-Dame place de la Cathédrale ***Open*** Mon 9am-noon, 2-7pm; Tue-Sat 7.30am-noon, 2-7pm; Sun 7.30am-6pm. Check with tourist office for times of guided tours, including crypt, Chapel of the Virgin, tombs. Illumination Sat, Sun from dusk.
Eglise Ste-Jeanne d'Arc place du Vieux-Marché. ***Open*** Mon-Thur 10am-12.15pm, 2-6pm, Fri, Sun 2-6pm.
Musée des Beaux-Arts (Fine Arts Museum) square Verdrel. Tel 35 71 28 40. ***Open*** Mon, Wed afternoon-Sun 10am-noon, 2-6pm. About £1.50. Guided tours Fri, Sun 2.30pm. About £3.50, under-18s free.
Musée Flaubert et d'Histoire de la Médecine (Flaubert and History of Medicine Museum) Hôtel-Dieu, 51 rue de Lecat. ***Open*** Tue-Sat 10am-noon, 2-6pm. About £2.50 adult, £1.50 child.
Musée Jeanne d'Arc (Joan of Arc Museum) place du Vieux-Marché. ***Open*** *May-15 Sept* daily 9.30am-6.30pm; *Oct-Mar* Tue-Sun 10am-noon, 2-6.30pm. About £2.50 adult, £1.25 child.
Musée Le Secq des Tournelles Rue J.-Villon. Tel 31 71 28 40.
Musée Pierre Corneille (Corneille's birthplace) 4 rue de la Pie. ***Open*** 10am-noon, 2-6pm, Mon, Wed afternoon-Sun.
Tour Jeanne-d'Arc (Joan of Arc Tower) rue du Donjon. ***Open*** Mon, Wed-Sun 10am-noon, 2-5.30pm.

CAMPING
Camping Municipal rue Jules-Ferry, Déville-les-Rouen (N 27 towards Dieppe, 5 km/3 miles NW of Rouen). Tel 35 74 07 59.

EATING AND DRINKING
Le Beffroi 15 rue du Beffroi. Tel 35 71 55 27. A restaurant in a half-timbered house. Menus from £12 to £35.
Le Bois Chenu 23 place Pucelle-d'Orléans. Tel 35 71 19 54. Menus from £10 to £20.
Dufour 67 rue St-Nicolas. Tel 35 71 90 62. Menus from £15 to £30
La Mer 41 place du Vieux-Marché. Tel 35 71 03 58. Seafooc restaurant, open until 11pm. Menus from £9 to £17.
Le Queen Mary 1 rue du Cercle. Tel 35 71 52 09. Brasserie-style food served until 11pm. Dining-room decorated like a 1930s transatlantic liner. Menus from £7 to £11.

Senlis & *the* Forests *of* South Picardy

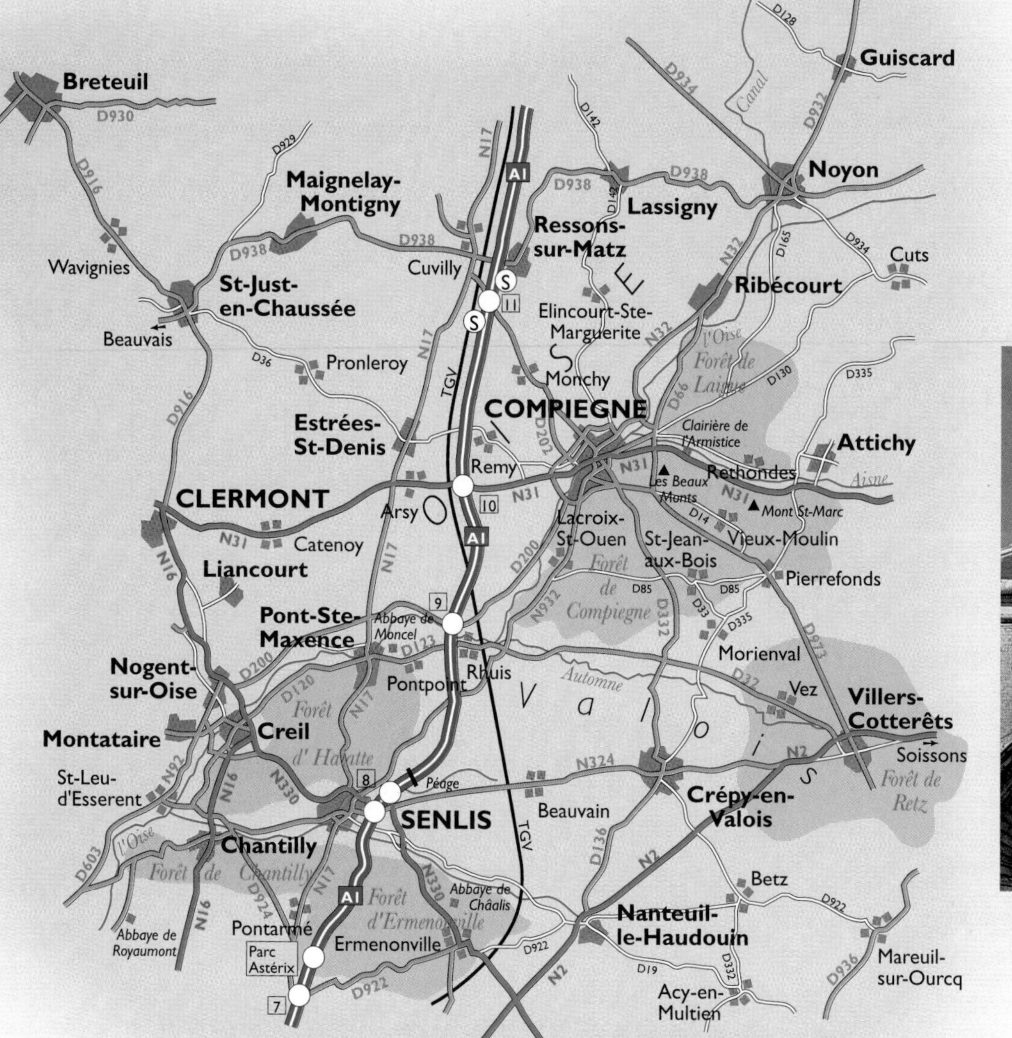

A detail from the gateway of the Château de Chantilly.

Touring *the* Oise

South of the vast, undulating expanses of the Picardy plateau, the Oise 'département' is leafy green, crowded with dense forests that conceal still lakes, and scattered with gracious, once royal towns in woodland settings. Compiègne's imposing summer palace was the seat of Napoleon III and his Empress, Eugénie. On the edge of Chantilly Forest is the great Château de Chantilly, built and rebuilt over centuries for scions of France's noblest families.

The dense forests of Hayatte, Chantilly and Ermenonville spread across the south and west of Picardy's Oise *département.* Add the vast expanses of the Forêts de Laigue and Compiègne to the north and the scattered Forêt de Retz around Villers-Cotterêts to the east, and you have some 48,500 hectares/120,000 acres of national forest, several rivers and hundreds of lakes, streams and ponds to explore by car and on foot.

The forest is richly varied. Around the border, low hills, called *monts*, give panoramic views across green canopies of hornbeam, chestnut, pine, lime, and birch. Beeches grow on the heights. There is a driving circuit around the beech plantations encircling the Mont St-Marc in the forest of Compiègne, and the D332 from Compiègne to Crépy-en-Valois has been named the 'Route du hêtre' (the beech route). Oaks grow on the lower sandy soils of the central forests and around Les Beaux Monts. In the oak stands just north of St-Jean-aux-Bois is the 800-year-old 'Chêne de St-Jean', the forest's oldest tree.

Previous page: The Château de Chantilly, magically reflected in its surrounding lake. An earlier château, designed by Chambiges for the Duc de Montmorency in the16th century, was demolished during the Revolution then rebuilt by Daumet in the 19th century for the Duc d'Aumale, son of King Louis-Philippe. His huge collection of works of art is displayed in the art gallery.

Forest pursuits

The National Forest information office on the D85 from St-Jean-aux-Bois to Pierrefonds has displays of forest flora, and a signposted tourist route caters for wildlife enthusiasts wanting to glimpse wild tulips or anemones, or spot a rare bee orchid.

Intersecting the forests at every point of the compass are paths for ramblers and cyclists. They are punctuated by picnicking spots and parking sites for drivers who want to stretch their legs along the two-hour walking circuits marked with yellow signs. Fisherfolk install themselves along the banks of the Oise as it meanders around the forests of Chantilly and Halatte, and fringe the woodland *étangs* (large ponds) of Ermenonville and Compiègne. Horses-in-training are a common sight on the sandy tracks around the equestrian town of Chantilly, but riding is popular all over these forested regions. Many forest roads were originally made for kings to hunt deer, wild boar, hare, and game birds.

Architectural treasures

Minor roads in the forests pass through pretty villages with ancient churches – Rethondes, in the vast forest of Laigue, with a church begun in Romanesque style; Vieux-Moulin in the Compiègne Forest, with a pretty classical church, and Rhuis near the forest of Halatte, with one of the oldest Romanesque churches in the region.

Christianity came early to this part of France, which is dotted with ancient abbeys. There are guided tours of the beautiful cloister, the refectory and the kitchens of the Cistercian Abbaye de Royaumont on the edge of the Chantilly Forest. The Abbaye de Moncel near Pontpoint in the forest of Halatte, dating back to the 14th century, has been restored, and you can tour the cavernous cellars, the refectory and the cloisters.

In the forest of Ermenonville, an avenue of plane trees leads you to the abbey of Châalis, founded by the Cistercians in the 12th century and sold as national property during the Revolution. Buildings designed by the 18th-century architect, Jean Aubert, now house a gallery of art and antiquities, but the huge, 13th-century transept arm is an evocative ruin.

Pierrefonds castle was originally built high on a hill on the eastern edge of Compiègne Forest. Seen from the D335 far below, its reconstructed medieval turrets and battlements are extraordinarily impressive. The keep of Vez, towering high on a rock on the *département* border, also looks quite intimidating from the pretty D32.

In this south-eastern corner of the Oise, the pretty valley of the Automne River runs through the region called the Valois, whose kings once ruled France. The great hall of the old Château de Crépy-en-Valois, its capital, which was sacked by the English during the Hundred Years War, houses the unique Musée de l'Archerie et du Valois

You can drive along minor roads through the South Picardy forests, hike along signposted forest paths, or cycle along marked tracks from St-Jean-aux-Bois.

(Museum of Archery and Valois). Behind the surviving ramparts are the remains of an 11th-century abbey. Between Crépy-en-Valois and Morienval are villages with ancient churches and gracious châteaux – a delight to explore by car.

Above: Pierrefonds, Louis d'Orléans' stronghold in the 14th century, looms from its hilltop. The castle, dismantled in 1616 by Richelieu, was reconstructed in the 19th century by Viollet-le-Duc for Napoleon III.

Left: Morienval is famous for its magnificent 11th-century Benedictine abbey church, with three Romanesque towers. Inside is the tomb of a crusader whose mummified body was brought back from Egypt.

Above: In a small museum beside the Armistice Clearing is the railway carriage in which France's Marshal Foch and General Weygand signed the Armistice in 1918. Bioscopes in the museum show unforgettable scenes of northern France during World War I.

Oise Fact File

Tourist information Comité départemental du tourisme de l'Oise, 19 rue Pierre-Jacoby, 60000 – Beauvais. Tel 44 45 82 12. Fax 44 45 16 19. ***Open*** Mon-Thu 8.30am-noon, 1.30-6pm; Fri-Sat 8.30am-noon, 1.30-5.30pm.
Crépy-en-Valois 7 rue de Soissons, 60800. Tel 44 59 03 97. ***Open*** Mon-Fri 1.45-6.15pm, Sat, Sun 9.30am-noon, 2-6.15pm.

SIGHTSEEING
Abbaye de Châalis Fontaine Châalis (off the N330 N of Ermenonville). ***Open*** Wed-Mon 9am-7pm.
Abbaye de Moncel off the D123 between Pontpoint and Pont Ste-Maxence. ***Open*** *Oct-Mar* 2-6pm.
Abbaye de Morienval on the D335 9 km/5 miles NE of Crépy-en-Valois (ask for the key at 2 place de l'Eglise, opposite the church).
Château de Pierrefonds on D335. ***Open*** *May-Aug* daily 10am-5pm; *Sept-Apr* daily 10am-noon, 2-5pm.
Clairière de l'Armistice (Armistice Clearing) Forest of Laigue, off N31, 6 km/4 miles E of Compiègne. **Musée de l'Armistice** ***open*** 9am-noon, 2-5.30pm.
Eglise de Vez off the D32 about 7 km/4 miles W of Villers-Cotterêts. ***Open*** *Apr-Oct* daily 2.30-6.30pm.

CAMPING
Tourist offices have details of campsites in the forests.
Chantilly
Camping A.T.C. route d'Apremont, 60300 – Aumont. Tel 44 60 00 42 (6 km/4 miles from Senlis). ***Open*** *15 May-15 Sept.*
Compiègne
Camping municipal de l'hippodrome avenue du Baron-Roger-de-Foultrait, 60200 (2 km/1 mile from town centre toward A1 motorway). Tel 44 20 28 58. ***Open*** *15 Mar-15 Nov.*
Ermenonville
Les Campéoles – 60950 (in Jean-Jacques Rousseau Park). Tel 44 54 00 08. ***Open*** all year.
Pierrefonds
Camping municipal rue de l'Armistice – 60350. Tel 44 42 80 83. ***Open*** *May-Oct.*

EATING AND DRINKING
Beauvais
Le Bellevue, 3 RN1 (Beauvais–Paris), Allonne. Tel 44 02 17 11. Fax 44 02 54 44. From about £25.
Le Chêne Bleu 171 av Marcel-Dassault. Tel 44 45 43 33. Fax 44 48 53 09. Menus from £11.
Hostellerie St-Vincent rue de Clermont. Tel 44 05 49 99. Fax 44 05 52 93. Menus from £9.
Elincourt-Ste-Marguerite
Château de Bellinglise route de Lassigny, (on D142 14 km/9 miles N of Compiègne): Tel 44 76 04 76. Fax 44 76 54 75. Renaissance château-hotel with menus from £23 to £45.
St-Jean-aux-Bois
La Bonne Idée 3 rue des Meuniers, (on the D33 and D85 11 km/7 miles SW of Compiègne, 6 km/4 miles W of Pierrefonds). Tel 44 42 84 09. Menus from £15 to £48.

Royal **Towns** *of the* **Oise**

Within a day's carriage-drive from Paris, fabulously wealthy nobles once resided in some of France's most magnificent châteaux. Many were built in medieval times as strongholds to defend the territories of feudal lords; others were designed in later centuries as sumptuous palaces. The largest and grandest are now museums, vast galleries of treasures collected by generations of former owners.

The Château de Chantilly is one of the most spectacular of all the great châteaux in the Oise. The oldest part is the Petit Château, first built in the 16th century by Bullant for the Duc de Montmorency, Constable of France. A new Grand Château was added later and renovated by the Prince de Condé in 1662. Destroyed during the Revolution, it was rebuilt in the 19th century. Its splendid encircling lake and gardens, originally laid out by André Le Nôtre – garden architect of Versailles – provide a most beautiful setting for the modern château. Inside, the Musée Condé is full of treasures collected by the Duc d'Aumale, Chantilly's last owner: Gobelins tapestries, Renaissance paintings, a mosaic pavement from Herculaneum, artefacts from Greece and Pompeii, 18th-century Chantilly porcelain. Among the thousands of rare, beautifully bound books in the *Cabinet des Livres* are some illuminated manuscripts, of which the most famous is the 15th-century *Les Très Riches Heures du duc de Berry*, containing exquisite illustrations showing aspects of daily life at that time.

Chantilly and Compiègne are both famous for their *hippodromes* or horse-racing circuits, and both towns are busiest during the racing season in June. Carriage-racing and other events take place outside the main racing season. France's National Stud is at Compiègne, and Chantilly's elegant 18th-century stables, Les Grandes Ecuries, the work of Jean Aubert, are now a Living Museum of the Horse (Musée vivant du Cheval), with displays of dressage and demonstrations of training throughout the year.

Top right: The Château de Chantilly is set in a magnificent park, with formal parterres, lakes, fountains and statuary (inset) laid out by André Le Nôtre, France's great garden architect.

Bottom: A display of dressage that is one of the daily events at Chantilly's unusual and memorable Musée vivant du Cheval.

Chantilly Fact File

CHANTILLY from **Calais** A1/D924 250 km/155 miles. **Postal zip code** 60500. **Tourist Information** 23 ave du Maréchal-Joffre, BP 233, 60631. Tel 44 57 08 58. Fax 44 57 74 64. ***Open*** Mon, Wed-Sat 9am-12.30pm, 2.15-6.15pm (*May-Sept* also open Tue 10am-noon, Sun 9am-noon).

SIGHTSEEING

Château and Musée Condé
Open *Mar-Oct* Wed-Mon, 10am-6pm; *Nov-Feb* Wed-Mon 10.30am-12.45pm, 2-5pm. About £4.50, gardens only £2.

Musée vivant du Cheval (Living Museum of the Horse) adjoining the **Grandes Ecuries** (stables) of the château. ***Open*** *Apr-Oct* Mon, Wed-Fri 10.30am-6.30pm; Sat, Sun 10.30am-6.30pm; *May-Jun* also open Tue 2-5.30pm; *Nov-Mar* Mon, Wed, Fri 2-4.30pm; Sat, Sun 10.30am-5.30pm. Riding displays all year Wed-Mon at 11.30am, 3.30pm, 5.15pm daily.

Hippodrome (Racecourse) ***Open*** 1st and 2nd Sun in Jun (Prix du Jockey Club and Prix de Diane). Check with tourist office for events and admission fees.

EATING AND DRINKING

Le Relais Condé 42 av du Maréchal-Joffre. Tel 44 57 05 75. A pretty woodland restaurant (closed Mon evening, Tue and public holidays). Menus from £20 to £32.

Relais du Coq Chantant 21 route de Creil. Tel 44 57 01 28. Imaginative cooking. Menus from £13 to £35.

Imperial Compiègne

By contrast with Chantilly's parkland splendour, the 18th-century Château de Compiègne, court residence of Napoleon Bonaparte and the Emperor Napoleon III, is an urban palace, a monumental neo-classical building of the Second Empire, with formal gardens extending to the forest's edge – but close to the centre of Compiègne. Guided tours take you round the luxurious, silk-hung apartments of Marie-Antoinette, the sumptuous *chambre* and *boudoir* of the Empress Eugénie, and the chandeliered ballroom. The palace also contains a museum of furniture and artefacts from the Second Empire, and a transport museum, with a display of carriages and coaches, bicycles, and the first classic cars.

Compiègne is a historic town, founded by the Romans and a stopping point on the Roman road from Beauvais – famous for its lofty Gothic cathedral – to Soissons in the Aisne *département*. Frankish kings resided here, and Jeanne d'Arc was wounded and captured while defending the city from an attack by the Burgundians in 1430.

The town was badly damaged during World War II, and extensively rebuilt, but several old half-timbered houses and the late-Gothic and early Renaissance town hall were unharmed. In the town hall is an unusual museum of some 12,000 model soldiers; in the Musée Vivenel an outstanding collection of Greek vases.

Compiègne Fact File

COMPIEGNE from **Calais** A1 217 km/135 miles.
Postal zip code 60200.
Tourist information place de l'Hôtel-de-Ville, BP 9. Tel 44 40 01 00. Fax 44 40 23 28. ***Open*** Mon-Sat 9.30am-12.15pm, 2-7pm; Sun 9.30-12.30pm, 2.30-5pm. The tourist office will arrange guided tours and publishes a leaflet giving details of boat tours on the rivers Oise and Aisne.
Parking place du Général-de-Gaulle, outside the gates of the National Palace. A tourist office map shows parking places.

SIGHTSEEING
Château place du Général-de-Gaulle. Tel ***Open*** *Apr-Sept* Wed-Mon 9.15am-6.15pm; *Oct-Mar* Wed-Mon 9.15am-4.30pm. About £3.
Hôtel de Ville (Town Hall) place de l'Hôtel-de-Ville. An impressive late-Gothic and early-Renaissance building dominated by a bell-tower housing an ancient bell, 'la Bancloque'. Not open to the public.
Musée de la Figurine historique Hôtel de Ville. ***Open*** *Mar-Oct* Tue-Sat 9am-noon, 2-6pm, Sun-Mon 2-6pm; *Nov-Feb* Tue-Sat 9am-noon, 2-5pm, Sun-Mon 2-5pm. Interesting audiovisual reconstruction of the Battle of Waterloo.
Musée Vivenel 2 rue d'Austerlitz. ***Open*** *Mar-Oct* Tue-Sat 9am-noon, 2-6pm, Wed and Sun 2-6pm; *Nov-Feb* Tue-Sat 9am-noon, 2-5pm, Wed and Sun 2-5pm.

EATING AND DRINKING
Le Bistrot de Flandre 2 rue d'Amiens. Tel 44 83 26 35. Menu at £11 (£13.50 at weekend).
Les Jardins d'Eugénie 17 rue Legendre. Tel 44 40 00 88. A brasserie with terrace room serving quality food. Menus from £12 to £30.

The Château de Compiègne.

Senlis

It is the quiet charm of this lovely old cathedral town, as well as its closeness to the royal forests, that makes Senlis a favourite weekend retreat for Parisians. In high summer visitors crowd its little squares and tour its narrow streets on foot or 'en calèche' – in horse-drawn carriages. But in September Senlis regains the timeless tranquillity appropriate to a town founded before the Romans conquered Gaul.

The 78-m/255-ft tall spire on the south tower of Senlis' 12th-century cathedral rises above the rooftops and is visible far across the forested countryside.

Senlis began as an *oppidum* – a fortified town – built by a Celtic tribe called the Silvanecti on a wooded hillock at the confluence of the rivers Aunette and Nonette. The conquering Romans destroyed their fort in the 1st century AD, and built a new town there. Their arena and Temple of Hercules were excavated in the 19th century and you can see them today in the place des Arènes. But in the 3rd century the Roman town was ransacked by warring Barbarians.

One of Senlis' greatest monuments remains its best-kept architectural secret. After the Barbarian invasions, the Romanised Gauls of the region rebuilt the old Roman town, surrounding its high south-eastern side with a wall 8 km/5 miles long, flanked by 28 towers. Part of the walls can be seen near the ruins of the royal castle – and as you explore the convoluted streets of the old town, you catch sight of them at the ends of alleys and between buildings. It is harder to spot the 16 great towers that remain, hidden among a hotch-potch of ancient dwellings built into and around them. They are the most complete example of Gallo-Roman fortifications extant today.

The Musée d'Art et d'Archéologie (Museum of Art and Archaeology) in the 13th-century former episcopal palace beside the cathedral displays treasures dating from Roman and Carolingian times. A unique Museum of Hunting (Musée de la Vénerie) occupies part of the Château Royal and the adjoining 16th-century Hôtel des Trois-Pots. But the real appeal of Senlis is found more by exploring its old squares and alleys and discovering the Renaissance and classical *hôtels* or mansions in its cobbled streets, than by visiting its museums and galleries. The rue des Cordeliers on the site of a former 15th-century convent has particularly fine examples of townhouse architecture.

Exploring the old town

Eleventh-century houses still stand among the Renaissance and neo-classical buildings along the rue de Beauvais. Off the rue Vieille-de-Paris is a delightful old post-house with a polygonal tower in its courtyard. The 13th-century cloisters of a former monastery abutting the Gallo-Roman wall now form the garden of a commercial bank in the rue du Châtel. At the crossing of these three roads, is the lovely place Henri-IV with the 15th-century town hall, marking the town centre.

The place de la Halle is an exquisite asymmetrical square. Cafés and useful shops occupy the lower storeys of venerable houses with quaintly serpentine walls. Hidden among the old buildings clustering along the Gallo-Roman wall run ancient cobbled alleys and little stone stairways leading up to the ramparts.

Senlis is full of surprises. The Romanesque Church of St-Frambourg, a former royal chapel, was used as a garage until bought by Cziffra, the celebrated pianist, and converted into a concert hall. St-Aignan, begun in the 11th century, is now a cinema, and the Gothic Church of St-Pierre is now a conference centre. On the 18th-century Hôtel Dufresnoy at 20 rue Bellon is a plaque announcing that it was from this building that Marshal Foch and General Weygand set out to sign the armistice that ended World War I.

Rings of trees, first planted in the 19th century when the town's medieval ramparts were destroyed, surround Senlis. Beyond them, wooded suburbs merge into the ancient forests of Halatte in the north and Pontarmé and Ermenonville in the south, making Senlis a good centre for excursions to the castles and abbey churches of the southern Picardy countryside.

Senlis Fact File

SENLIS from **Calais** A1/D940 232 km/144 miles. To **Chantilly** D924 10 km/6 miles; to **Compiègne** D932 32 km/20 miles; to **Paris** A1 44 km/27 miles.
Postal zip code 60302.
Tourist information place du Parvis-Notre-Dame, BP 24. Tel 44 53 06 40. Fax 44 53 29 80. ***Open*** *Feb-14 Dec* Wed-Mon 10am-noon, 2.15-6.15pm.
Parking off cours Boutteville, beside the city wall; off rue de Bordeaux; off rue St-Pierre.

SIGHTSEEING
Walking tours *Mar-Oct* Sat and Sun at 3pm. The tourist office publishes a map of the main sights within walking distance.
Horse-drawn carriages from place de la Cathédrale *Apr-Sept* Mon, Wed-Thu, Sat-Sun 10.30am-12.30pm, 3-7.30pm; Tue, Fri 3-7.30pm. *Oct-Mar* Mon-Sun 3-7pm.
Ancienne Abbaye St-Vincent (not open to the public, but can be seen from the rue de Meaux).
Arènes gallo-romaines place des Arènes. Group guided tours by arrangement with tourist office.
Chapelle royale St-Frambourg Place St-Frambourg. Check with Fondation Cziffra Tel 44 53 39 99.
Musée d'Art place Notre-Dame. ***Open*** *all year* (except *11-31 Jan*) Mon, Wed afternoon-Sun 10am-noon, 2-6pm.
Musée de la Vénerie (Museum of Hunting) place Notre-Dame. Guided tours available *11 Jan-19 Dec* at 10 and 11am, and at 2, 3, 4 and 5pm

FOR CHILDREN
Parc Astérix A1 S of Senlis, NE of Paris. Tel 44 62 34 34. ***Open*** *10 Apr-Sept* daily 10am-6pm (check closing days and prices with tourist offices).
Parc Jean Richard to the N of Ermenonville village, off the D330. ***Open*** *Easter-Sept* (tel 44 54 00 96 for opening hours and prices, or ask at tourist offices). The Amusement Park has a 'Sea of Sand', a simulated desert with camels, and a 'Redskin Valley'.

EATING AND DRINKING
Les Gourmandins 3 place de la Halle. Tel 44 60 94 01. Menus from £15 to £28.
Le Vieux Logis 105 rue du Général-de-Gaulle, Fleurines (6.5 km/4 miles N of Senlis on N17). Tel 44 54 10 13. A Michelin-starred restaurant noted for seasonal game dishes. (***Closed*** *Nov-Mar* Sat lunch, Sun evening, Mon). Menus from £25.

Religious events and other festivities in the old centre of Senlis (above) enliven the area around the cathedral and neighbouring churches, some of which now have a civic use.

Tiny cobbled streets (right) and winding alleys radiate from the centre of Senlis towards the ancient Gallo-Roman walls.

Parc Astérix

Hugely popular since it opened at the end of the 1980s is the humorous Parc Astérix, based on the comic book characters created by Goscinny and Uderzo: Astérix the Gaul and his sidekick, Obélix.

The Via Antica is Cartoonland, where scaled-down replicas of buildings discovered by Astérix and Obélix on their cartoon journeys around the globe are gathered into one town. In the Cité romaine, you can watch gladiatorial fights and chariot races, experience the fall of the Styx, and take part in a Gaulish Carnival.

In Astérix village, the Gauls hold daily at-homes in their replica houses, and run boat trips to neighbouring river villages. In the rue de Paris you take a voyage back through the capital's past, with D'Artagnan-style swordfights and with drives through Parisian streets in replicas of early cars. You can also ride on the Trans'Arverne railway, take a 'Grand Splatch' in the fairground, or play with dolphins in the Grand Lac. Then there's the Relais gaulois where you can refuel and hear Radio Menhir FM report all.

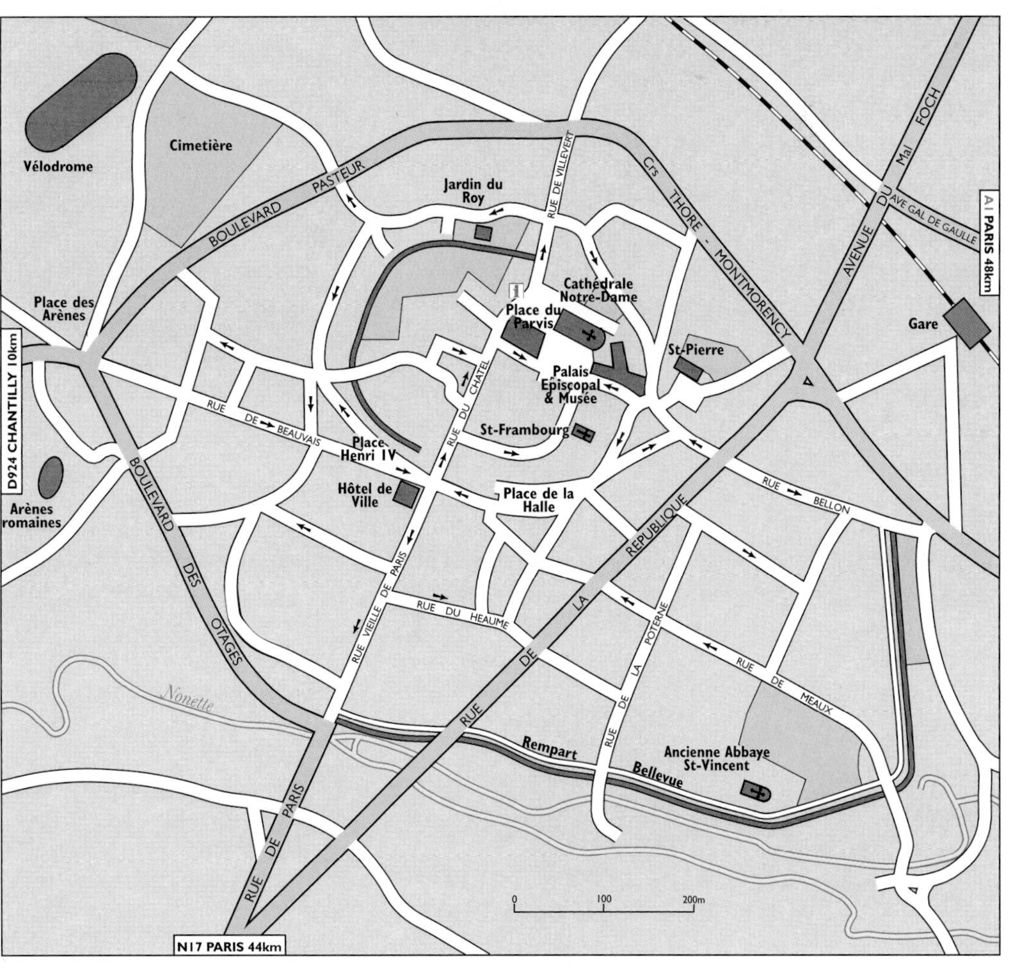

MUSÉE NATIONAL
PICASSO

YVES SAINT LAURENT
variation

Paris

The **sights** *of* **Paris**

Paris in April, or at any other time of year, is a joy, where the art, the Eiffel Tower, the markets, the museums, the food, the architecture, the pavement cafés, Notre-Dame, the clothes, the Louvre, the nightlife can all seem romantic – and the city is so centralised that, if you wish, you can get a taste of them all in a single day.

Paris's most famous landmark was built by a French engineer, Gustave Eiffel, for the great exhibition held in 1889 to celebrate the centenary of the 1789 Revolution. Like most modern architecture, it was widely disliked when it was first built, and it survived only because it was converted into a useful mast for telecommunication aerials. Expect a long queue for the lift, but also expect to be rewarded for the wait by a 67-km/42-mile view from Level 3 on a clear day – and a dazzling Parisian cityscape at night. There is an expensive restaurant on Level 1 and some cheaper ones on Level 3.

South-east of the Eiffel Tower spreads the Champ-de-Mars – site of a battle in 52 BC between the Romans and the Parisii, the Celtic tribe that inhabited the area. A short walk north-east is Les Invalides, a classical masterpiece by the architects Libéral Bruant and, later, Jules Hardouin-Mansart. It was built as a home for veteran soldiers and contains a huge army museum. In the crypt of the church at its centre is Napoléon's tomb.

North-west of the tower, across the Seine, is the Parc du Trocadéro – surrounded by cafés and restaurants – and the Palais de Chaillot. This complex has a theatre, concert spaces, and the Cinémathèque française, which shows a daily programme of film classics. It also has a cinema and photography museum; a naval museum, a museum of anthropology, and a museum of French architecture.

Arc de Triomphe and Champs-Elysées

Built as a tribute to Napoléon's military victories (and commissioned in 1806 by Napoléon himself), the Arc de Triomphe's role as a war memorial was extended in 1920

Previous pages: The place de la Concorde, with images of Paris inset.

Opposite: The Eiffel Tower is a prominent feature in the Parisian night-time cityscape – and its Level 3 platform makes a perfect vantage point for a dazzling view of Paris before and after dark.

Below: The Glass Pyramid, by I. M. Pei, in the courtyard of the Louvre, is one of the brilliant touches of modernist style that characterise Paris in the 1990s.

Revolutionary Paris

The first revolutionary stirrings took place in the quarter around the Champs-Elysées and the Louvre. In the gardens of Richelieu's Palais-Royal, owned by Louis XVI's cousin, Louis-Philippe d'Orléans, Parisians protested against the royal reaction to their National Assembly. The Comédie Française now occupies a part of the Palais. There is nothing to see of the Bastille prison in the place de la Bastille, which was destroyed by the mob.

Louis XVI, Marie-Antoinette and the Dauphin were taken by the revolutionaries from Versailles to the Palais des Tuileries, north of the Louvre. This was destroyed during the Paris Commune in 1871, but the gardens, laid out by Le Nôtre, survive. The keep of the Knights Templars' fortress, where the royal family was imprisoned in August 1792, was destroyed. But the name remains in the unspoilt Quartier du Temple, where Robespierre lived in the rue de Saintonge. Danton lived in the Odéon quarter on the Left Bank.

The condemned were imprisoned in the Conciergerie on the Ile de la Cité – you can see Marie-Antoinette's cell. From there they were driven in tumbrils (open carts) to the guillotine, set up in what was then the place de la Révolution, now place de la Concorde.

when the body of an unknown soldier was buried there, and an eternal flame lit to commemorate the dead of World War I. You reach the arch via a subway beneath the traffic. At the top is a museum, but the view from there is the main attraction.

The Champs-Elysées, the broad avenue between the Arc de Triomphe and the place de la Concorde, was built for Queen Marie de Medici, regent mother of Louis XIII, in 1616 as a tree-lined vista from the palace of the Louvre. The Champs-Elysées has unfortunately become a tourist trap in recent years, lined with tacky fast-food outlets and chainstores. But the trees and gardens laid out by the 17th-century designer André Le Nôtre between the place de la Concorde and the Louvre, the Jardin des Tuileries, give it an aspect of grandeur. It is still the location of great national events and ceremonies such as the Bastille Day procession.

The Champs-Elysées is part of a processional route called La Voie Triomphale, or 'Triumphal Way', which extends north-westwards from the Louvre – once a royal palace and now a world-renowned museum housing Michelangelo's *Mona Lisa* amongst other treasures – 6 km/3.5 miles to the extraordinary Arche de la Défense, a hollow cube in glass and white marble. The ride up to the 112-m/367-ft roof belvedere has been a great attraction since La Défense was completed at the beginning of the decade.

Notre-Dame and the Ile de la Cité

When the Cathédrale de Notre-Dame was completed in 1250, it was a landmark visible from far around. Built in less than 100 years on an island in the Seine, it was the first Gothic cathedral on a monumental scale, an audacious 100-m/328-ft high. It became a model for cathedral-building throughout Europe.

Climb the towers for a close-up of the gargoyles and the golden figures ascending the fleche to heaven – and a long-distance view across Paris. Go inside and see the wonderful medieval stained glass of the rose windows, the great pillars, the high vaults, the crypt – or just wander around and get a feel for the place.

Notre-Dame deserves to be seen from every angle, so walk around the Ile de la Cité and look at the carvings on the West Front, and the flying buttresses at the back.

There is plenty to see and do here and around the Ile de la Cité. This is the very heart of France. In the square in front of the cathedral is an underground museum in which you can see parts of the original cathedral on the site, the excavations of a city wall built by the people after the Romans left, and other finds from the Roman city. All distances in France are measured from a spot in front of the cathedral's west door.

Street entertainers often perform on the Petit Pont de la Cité, which connects Notre-Dame with the left bank. There are lovely walks along the Seine. At weekends, a delightful market, a mixture of antiques and food stalls, spreads along the water's edge in the direction of the Gare d'Austerlitz. On the other side of the bridge, in the place Louis-Lépine, is the fragrant daily flower market, with a bird market opposite.

Any café with a view of Notre-Dame is guaranteed to be expensive, but the cafés in the busy streets behind the waterfront tend to be cheaper, and the stalls in the riverside market very good value.

Art Nouveau *métro* entrance by Guimard.

Street market near the Porte de Vanves.

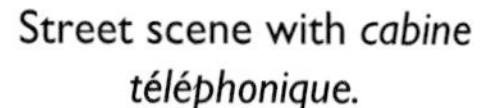

Street scene with *cabine téléphonique*.

Notre-Dame on the Ile de la Cité.

Left **Bank,** *Right* **Bank**

The Seine divides Paris into left and right banks ('rive gauche' and 'rive droite'). The Left Bank is café society, bookshops, cheap restaurants, ancient history, and innovative clothes. The Right Bank is haute-couture and designer wear, museums, chic cafés and tea-rooms, avant-garde art galleries, commerce, government, and the red-light district. To really appreciate what makes the difference, you need to get to know the Parisian 'quartiers', from Montmartre in the north to the Latin quarter in the south, and west to east from Les Halles to La Bastille.

The Beaubourg

The Pompidou Centre – also called Centre Beaubourg – is one of the popular spots in Paris. There are queues for the exterior escalators, which take you up to the café terrace, and a view across Paris. Inside, there is a cinema showing rare and art films, dance, theatre, and music spaces, and Paris's premier gallery of modern art on the fourth floor. This specialises in 20th-century works, with collections ranging from post-Impressionism through Fauvism, Cubism, Abstract Expressionism and contemporary movements, plus galleries of photography and prints.

Outside on the plaza, singers, mime artists, buskers, musicians and other street entertainers perform to the crowds. In the streets around the Beaubourg are dozens of small private art galleries.

Everyone spoke Latin when Paris's Roman arena (now a park) and Cluny Baths were built in the 1st century BC. But what gives the Latin Quarter its distinctive atmosphere is another ancient institution, the Sorbonne. France's first university, the oldest still in existence, was founded in the 12th century as a theology school. Students spoke Latin there right up to the Revolution. This is old Paris: the Church of St-Séverin has a Romanesque tower, and St-Julien-le-Pauvre was built in the 13th century.

Latin Quarter and the Left Bank

The Latin quarter should be browsed around. The small streets around the Sorbonne are full of bookshops, small art shops, and cinemas. The Panthéon seems out of place – a grandiose funerary monument, the resting place of French luminaries such as Voltaire, Jean-Jacques Rousseau, and Victor Hugo.

The Left Bank's artistic tradition is commemorated in the Musées Zadkine (in the Russian sculptor's former studio) and Rodin. The most beautiful gallery in the quarter is the Musée d'Orsay, in a converted railway station, specialising in 19th-century art.

The area around the rue Mouffetard, one of the oldest streets in Paris, seems like a small village in the heart of the French capital with its truly Parisian open-air market and narrow winding streets.

But the Left Bank isn't all history. Around the boulevard St-Germain is one of the city's best areas for established and new young designer fashion, hats, jewellery and modernistic interior design.

Montmartre

Paris's highest point is the 127-m/417-ft hill or *butte* of Montmartre, with the landmark dome of the 18th-century Sacré-Cœur on top. The balcony of the 83-m/272-ft high dome is the city's tallest architectural eyrie. The streets around the Sacré-Cœur, the place du Tertre, and other obvious tourist spots give Montmartre its reputation as Paris's biggest tourist trap. The squares and steep cobbled alleys, little parks and pleasant cafés away from the tourist

A painting on view in the Musée Picasso.

Hat shop in rue des Saints-Pères on the Left Bank.

Sculpture in the Musée Picasso.

Flower market near Notre-Dame.

The dome of the 18th-century Sacré-Cœur in Montmartre is Paris's highest point. Its 83-m/272-ft high balcony gives fine views.

spots retain much of their original character.

You can see the Bateau-Lavoir, where Picasso lived and painted, and the Lapin agile, the 19th-century cabaret frequented by Renoir, and the Moulin Rouge, advertised by Toulouse-Lautrec, and visit Utrillo's old studio.

This area is also full of surprises. You can get to the base of the Sacré-Cœur by cable-car. Montmartre has Paris's last-remaining commercial vineyard. It has one of Paris's oldest Gothic churches, the former Abbey Church of St-Pierre-de-Montmartre, founded in 1147. Its museum, in an 18th-century manor, has reconstructed Montmartrian rooms. In its cemetery are buried Degas, Nijinsky, Offenbach, and the French romantic composer, Hector Berlioz.

Left: Pigalle, red-light zone and hip new residential district. Paris is rediscovering its neo-classical architecture and traditional *brasseries*.

Pigalle

Berlioz lived in Pigalle, Paris's traditional red-light zone of peep shows and hostess joints south of Montmartre. Pigalle is alive all night. Since the late 1980s, its traditional brasseries and increasing numbers of 'straight' nightclubs and bars have attracted nocturnal Parisians from all over the city. Beware! The sleaze persists and customers are just as likely to be ripped off over the price of drinks in sex dives as in any other city. But Paris has been rediscovering the neo-classical aesthetics of the area around the rue Chaptal, with its tea-rooms; the traditional brasseries of the boulevard de Clichy; the food shops along the rue des Martyrs, and the fascinating Museum of Romantic Life.

Les Halles

Paris's centuries-old food market was moved to the cleared site of the old Cemetery of the Innocents in the centre of town as part of a new-look Paris planned by the Prefect of the Seine *département*, Baron Haussman, in the late 19th century. Its glass and steel market *halles* became the centre of an atmospheric quartier. In the 1970s the market was moved again, out to the suburbs, and the Forum, four glass-roofed, underground levels of shopping centre, replaced the *Halles*.

Now Les Halles is Paris's chic district, a 24-hour area full of shops and bars and things to do. The Forum has museums: a waxworks; a holography museum. It also has the Forum Horizon cinema, plus hundreds of shops. In the old streets around are designer clothes boutiques, aromatic food and wine stores around the (16th-century) Church of St-Eustache. This is also the quarter of the Beaubourg and cafés to see and be seen in.

Le Marais

Beautiful 17th-century houses characterise Le Marais, Paris's traditional Jewish area. The quarter centres on the place des Vosges, the capital's first square, former residence of Victor Hugo and Madame de Sévigné. There are antiques shops and designer boutiques beneath the arches around the square.

Today this elegant quarter is one of the city's trendiest shopping areas for clothes, accessories, and home furnishings, especially around the rue des Francs-Bourgeois. Kosher delis and restaurants cluster around the rue des Rosiers. Le Marais has some of Paris's most visited cafés, tearooms, and bars. It also has the Musée Picasso.

The sites and monuments of the Revolution take you all over Paris. Many of the old working-class areas where revolutionaries lived and events took place – Temple, Odéon, La Bastille – are now favoured Parisian domiciles. La Bastille, for example, site of barricades in the 1790s, has become the new artists' quarter in the 1990s and is the site of avant-garde art galleries, young designer ateliers, and great traditional restaurants.

Day trips *from Paris*

There is a rich choice of spectacular and entertaining places to see within easy reach of Paris, all readily accessible by car or by train.

There's as much to see around Paris as there is within the city. The Ile de France has some of France's most regal châteaux – Fontainebleau, Vaux-le-Vicomte, and the Palais de Versailles. The Basilique St-Denis, in St-Denis, was the first-ever Gothic building. The list of other interesting destinations is almost endless so just a few are described below.

The Palace of Versailles

Louis XIV's vast palace and grounds, 17 km/10 miles south-west of Paris, are too much to take in on one visit. The palace was begun in the 1660s on the orders of the king, who was determined to create a palace more magnificent than Vaux-le-Vicomte, the great château his Finance Minister, Nicholas Fouquet, had built. Architects Louis Le Vau, and later Jules Hardouin-Mansart, landscape gardener André Le Nôtre, and the painter Charles Le Brun, were brought in to convert a former hunting lodge into a residence for king and court.

Tours cover the sumptuous Hall of Mirrors; the bedchamber where Louis XIV died and where Louis XVI and Marie-Antoinette faced the mob in 1789; the private apartments of Marie-Antoinette; the room where the Swiss Guards confronted the revolutionaries; and the apartments of Louis XV, Madame de Maintenon, Madame du Barry, and Madame de Pompadour.

Versailles' formal gardens alone merit a day trip. Another could be spent at the Grand Trianon, a small palace to which Louis XIV would retreat from the tedium of the court; the Petit Trianon, former residence of Madame du Barry; and the Hameau, a miniature farm.

Vaux-Le-Vicomte

Le Vau's masterpiece of Baroque architecture is 46 km/ 26 miles south-east of Paris. The château deserves to be seen from Le Nôtre's beautifully restored gardens. Among the most impressive rooms are the domed Grand Salon and the Chambre du Roi. The furnishings are the result of careful restoration by Alfred Sommier, an industrialist who bought the building in 1875. The château is best seen on one of the candlelit evenings, and the gardens on Saturdays when the fountains are playing.

Fontainebleau

The Palais de Fontainebleau is only one of the attractions of Fontainebleau, 70 km/43 miles south-east of Paris. The other is the Forêt de Fontainebleau, a favourite weekend retreat for Parisians. It has strange rock formations and is ideal for walks and horse or cycle rides. In the 16th century, King François I began the conversion of a former hunting lodge, into a royal palace, employing Italian artists and artisans. The palace is a medley of styles. Its most imposing external feature, the horseshoe-shaped staircase, dates from the mid-17th century, and inside are Renaissance frescoes in the Galerie François I and the Salle de Bal.

EuroDisney

Sail away on a Mississippi riverboat. Tour the solar system on the Orbitron. Explore Sleeping Beauty's Castle, with turrets and drawbridge, and a sleeping dragon in the Dungeon. Spend a weekend in Wonderland in one of northern France's most magical theme parks.

Just an hour out of Paris and four hours' drive from Calais, the EuroDisney Resort, its theme hotels and campsites, and Golf EuroDisney, cover some 20 square kilometres/8 square miles of the Marne Valley.

Topiary and sculpture (inset) grace Fontainebleau's grounds, which include a maze and the Jardin Anglais laid out for Napoléon I.

La Truffière: quietly excellent food from the south-west of France in an unassuming Left Bank restaurant.

Eating in Paris

From chef Alain Senderens' culinary wizardry at the Right Bank **Lucas-Carton**, to **Chartier**'s classic soup kitchen in Pigalle; and from the Left Bank's macrobiotic **Le Grenier de Notre-Dame** to the historic **La Coupole**, quality, variety and atmosphere are the combined attractions of eating out in Paris. Noted restaurant critics complain about falling standards, but the capital has more than 100 Michelin-starred restaurants, and dozens of award-winning chefs and dishes. Newcomers to eating out in Paris might bear in mind that some Parisian restaurants serve poor food at inflated prices, but if a moment's observation tells you that a streetside café looks clean and bustling, and smells good, plunge in and experiment (after you've checked the menu prices). Otherwise, use a restaurant guide, such as Gault Millau's *Best of Paris*. Eating and drinking trends change in Paris as elsewhere. To keep abreast of them, check with *Pariscope*, the weekly magazine detailing Parisian life (with a section in English), or check with a Parisian friend.
Look forward to a succession of weekend breaks if you want to discover Paris's eating places. Don't miss the specialist food and drink shops — such as **Truffles** in place de la Madeleine, 8^{e}, which specialises in the sweet, as well as the savoury, varieties; and **La Ferme St-Hubert**, a cheese shop that doubles as a restaurant, in rue Vignon.

Fresh food stalls set up in itinerant markets all over the city, on Tuesday to Sunday mornings. Left: a *charcuterie* stall in the permanent food market on the rue Mouffetard in the Latin Quarter.

Paris Fact File

PARIS from **Calais** A26, A1, 290 km/180 miles.
Tourist information 127 av des Champs-Elysées, 8e. Tel 1 49 52 53 54. Fax 1 49 52 53 00. ***Open*** daily 9am-8pm (except *1 May*).
Gare du Nord, 18 rue de Dunkerque, 10e. Tel 1 45 26 94 82. ***Open*** *May-Oct* Mon-Sat 8am-9pm; *Nov-Apr* Mon-Sat 8am-8pm. Museum card about £8 for 1 day, £15 for 3 days.

SIGHTSEEING
Boat trips *bâteaux-mouches* from the Pont de l'Alma pier on the Right Bank, 7^{e}. Tel 1 42 25 96 10. Daily every half hour 10am-11.30pm. About 1½ hrs. About £4 adult, £2 child. Also lunch and dinner cruises.
L'Arc de Triomphe place de l'Etoile, 8^{e}. ***Open*** *Apr-Sept* daily 10am-5.30pm; *Oct-Mar* daily 10am-5pm. ***Closed*** on public holidays. About £4.
Centre Georges Pompidou place Beaubourg, 4^{e}. Tel 44 78 12 33. ***Open*** Mon, Wed-Fri noon-10pm; Sat-Sun 10am-10pm. ***Closed*** *1 May*.
Conciergerie 1 quai de l'Horloge, 1er. ***Open*** *Apr-Sept* daily 9.30am-6.30pm; *Oct-Mar* daily 10am-4pm. ***Closed*** *1 Jan, 1 May, 1* and *11 Nov, 25 Dec.* About £3.25.
La Grande Arche 1 parvis de la Défense, 92040 Paris-la Défense. ***Open*** *summer* Mon-Fri 9am-7pm, Sat-Sun 9am-8pm; *winter* Mon-Fri 9am-6pm, Sat-Sun 9am-7pm. About £5.
Les Invalides Esplanade des Invalides, 7e. ***Open*** daily 10am-5pm. ***Closed*** *1 Jan, 1 May, 1* and *11 Nov, 25 Dec.* About £5. Napoléon's tomb can be seen in the Eglise du Dôme.
Musée Carnavalet 23 rue de Sévigné, 3e. ***Open*** Tue-Sun 10am-5.40pm. Museum of the history of Paris. About £3.50.
Musée national du Louvre cour Napoléon, 1er. ***Open*** Mon, Wed-Sun 9am-6pm (Museum), 9am-10pm (Pyramid). About £2.50 after 3pm and on Sun, £5 before 3 pm Mon-Sat.
Musée de l'Orangerie des Tuileries place de la Concorde, 1er. ***Open*** Mon, Wed-Sun 9.45am-5.15pm. ***Closed*** *1 Jan, 1 May, 25 Dec.* About £3.50.
Musée d'Orsay 1 rue de Bellechasse, quai Anatole France, 7e. ***Open*** *summer* Tue-Sun 9am-6pm; *winter* Tue-Sun 10am-6pm. ***Closed*** *1 Jan, 1 May, 25 Dec.* About £4.50.
Musée Picasso 5 rue de Thorigny, 3e. ***Open*** Mon, Wed-Sun *summer* 9.30am-6pm, *winter* 9.30am-5.30pm. ***Closed*** *1 Jan, 25 Dec.* About £3.25.
Musée Auguste-Rodin Hôtel Biron, 77 rue de Varenne, 7e. ***Open*** Tue-Sun 9.30am-4.45pm. ***Closed*** *1 Jan, 1 May, 25 Dec.* About £3.50.
Thermes de Cluny (Cluny Baths) 6 place Paul-Painlevé, Paris 5e. Tel 1 43 25 62 00. ***Open*** Mon, Wed-Sun 9.15am-5.45pm. ***Closed*** *1 May* and *25 Dec.* About £3.50.
Tour Eiffel Champ-de-Mars, 7e. ***Open*** daily *summer* 9am-midnight, *winter* 9.30am-11pm. About £1.50 stairs to level 2, £2.50 lift to level 1, £4.50 lift to level 2, £7 lift to level 3.

CAMPING
Camping-caravaning du Bois de Boulogne (Porte Maillot, Bois de Boulogne exit from the Paris ring road, then follow the signs). Tel 1 45 24 30 00. ***Open*** all year.

FOR CHILDREN
EuroDisney on A4 motorway 28 km/17 miles E of Paris. Take A26 from Calais (from Boulogne reach A26 via N42 to St-Omer)/ A1 direction Paris/A104 after Roissy/A4 to EuroDisney exit. Tel in UK 0171 753 2901. ***Open*** *15-23 Apr, 10 Jun-10 Sept, 23 Dec-1 Jan* daily 9am-11pm: one-day pass £31 adult, £22 child (3-11 yrs); *11 Feb-14 Apr, 24 Apr-9 June, 9 Sept-6 Nov* daily 10am-6pm: one-day pass £28 adult, £19 child (3-11 yrs); *7 Nov-22 Dec, 2 Jan-10 Feb* Mon-Fri 10am-6pm, Sat 10am-8pm: one-day pass £22 adult, £16 child (3-11yrs)

EATING AND DRINKING
Au Pied de Cochon 6 rue Coquillère, 1er. Tel 1 42 36 11 75.
Chartier 7 rue du Faubourg-Montmartre, 9e. Tel 1 47 70 86 29. From about £8.
La Coupole 102 boulevard Montparnasse, 14e. Tel 1 43 20 14 20. From about £14 to £28.
Le Grenier de Notre-Dame 18 rue de la Bûcherie, 5e. Tel 1 43 29 98 29. From about £10.
Lucas-Carton 9 place de la Madeleine, 8e. Tel 1 42 65 22 90. From £47 (lunch) to £232 (lunch and dinner).
La Truffière 4 rue Blainville, off place de la Contrescarpe, 5e. Tel 1 46 33 64 74. Truffle menu-dégustation £33, special carte-menu £24 (dinner).
Le Vieux Bistro 14 rue du Cloître Notre-Dame, 4e. Tel 1 43 54 18 95. From about £38.

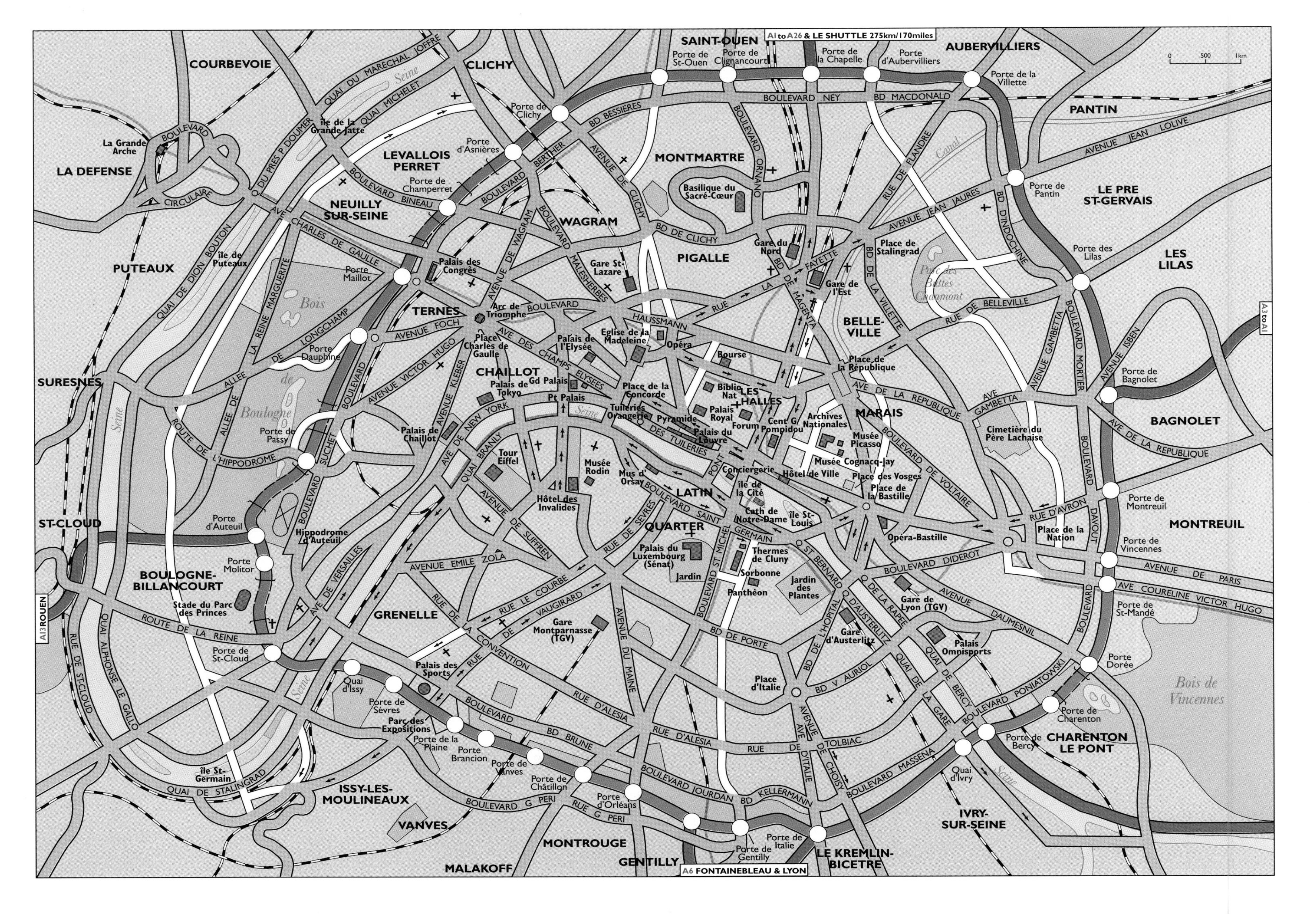

A1 to A26 & LE SHUTTLE 275km/170miles
A3 to A1
A6 FONTAINEBLEAU & LYON
A13 ROUEN
0 500 1km
COURBEVOIE
CLICHY
SAINT-OUEN
AUBERVILLIERS
PANTIN
LE PRE ST-GERVAIS
LES LILAS
BAGNOLET
MONTREUIL
Bois de Vincennes
CHARENTON LE PONT
IVRY-SUR-SEINE
LE KREMLIN-BICETRE
GENTILLY
MONTROUGE
MALAKOFF
VANVES
ISSY-LES-MOULINEAUX
BOULOGNE-BILLANCOURT
ST-CLOUD
SURESNES
PUTEAUX
LA DEFENSE
NEUILLY SUR-SEINE
LEVALLOIS PERRET
MONTMARTRE
PIGALLE
WAGRAM
TERNES
CHAILLOT
BELLE-VILLE
MARAIS
LES HALLES
LATIN QUARTER
GRENELLE
La Grande Arche
île de la Grande Jatte
île de Puteaux
île St-Germain
Porte de St-Ouen
Porte de Clignancourt
Porte de la Chapelle
Porte d'Aubervilliers
Porte de la Villette
Porte de Pantin
Porte des Lilas
Porte de Bagnolet
Porte de Montreuil
Porte de Vincennes
Porte de St-Mandé
Porte Dorée
Porte de Charenton
Porte de Bercy
Quai d'Ivry
Porte de Italie
Porte de Gentilly
Porte d'Orléans
Porte de Châtillon
Porte de Vanves
Porte Brancion
Porte de la Plaine
Parc des Expositions
Porte de Sèvres
Quai d'Issy
Porte de St-Cloud
Porte Molitor
Porte d'Auteuil
Porte de Passy
Porte Dauphine
Porte Maillot
Porte de Champerret
Porte d'Asnières
Porte de Clichy
Bois
de
Boulogne
Hippodrome d'Auteuil
Stade du Parc des Princes
Palais des Sports
Palais des Congrès
Arc de Triomphe
Place Charles de Gaulle
Palais de Tokyo
Palais de Chaillot
Gd Palais
Pt Palais
Tour Eiffel
Hôtel des Invalides
Musée Rodin
Mus d'Orsay
Palais de l'Elysée
Eglise de la Madeleine
Place de la Concorde
Tuileries
Orangerie
Pyramide
Palais du Louvre
Palais Royal
Opéra
Bourse
Biblio Nat
Forum
Cent G Pompidou
Archives Nationales
Musée Picasso
Musée Cognacq-Jay
Hôtel de Ville
Place des Vosges
Place de la Bastille
Opéra-Bastille
Conciergerie
île de la Cité
Cath de Notre-Dame
île St-Louis
Thermes de Cluny
Sorbonne
Panthéon
Palais du Luxembourg (Sénat)
Jardin
Jardin des Plantes
Gare Montparnasse (TGV)
Gare St-Lazare
Gare du Nord
Gare de l'Est
Gare de Lyon (TGV)
Gare d'Austerlitz
Palais Omnisports
Place d'Italie
Place de la Nation
Place de la République
Place de Stalingrad
Basilique du Sacré-Cœur
Parc des Buttes Chaumont
Cimetière du Père Lachaise
Canal
Seine
QUAI DU MARECHAL JOFFRE
QUAI MICHELET
DU PRES P DOUMER
BOULEVARD
CIRCULAIRE
QUAI DE DION BOUTON
AVE CHARLES DE GAULLE
BOULEVARD BINEAU
BOULEVARD BERTHIER
BD BESSIERES
BOULEVARD NEY
BD MACDONALD
BOULEVARD ORNANO
AVENUE JEAN LOLIVE
RUE DE FLANDRE
AVENUE JEAN JAURES
BD D'INDOCHINE
AVENUE DE CLICHY
BD DE CLICHY
BOULEVARD MALESHERBES
AVENUE DE WAGRAM
BOULEVARD HAUSSMANN
RUE LA FAYETTE
BD DE MAGENTA
BD DE LA VILLETTE
RUE DE BELLEVILLE
AVENUE GAMBETTA
BOULEVARD MORTIER
AVENUE ISBEN
AVE DE LA REPUBLIQUE
AVE GAMBETTA
BOULEVARD DE VOLTAIRE
RUE D'AVRON
BOULEVARD DAVOUT
AVENUE DE PARIS
AVE COURELINE VICTOR HUGO
BOULEVARD DIDEROT
AVENUE DAUMESNIL
BOULEVARD PONIATOWSKI
QUAI DE BERCY
QUAI DE LA RAPEE
QUAI DE LA GARE
QUAI D'AUSTERLITZ
BD DE L'HOPITAL
QUAI ST BERNARD
BD V AURIOL
RUE DE TOLBIAC
AVENUE DE CHOISY
AVE D'ITALIE
BOULEVARD MASSENA
BD KELLERMANN
BOULEVARD JOURDAN
BOULEVARD BRUNE
BOULEVARD G PERI
RUE G PERI
RUE D'ALESIA
AVENUE DU MAINE
BD DE PORTE
BOULEVARD ST MICHEL
BOULEVARD SAINT GERMAIN
RUE DE SEVRES
RUE DE VAUGIRARD
RUE LE COURBE
RUE DE LA CONVENTION
AVENUE EMILE ZOLA
AVENUE DE SUFFREN
AVE DE VERSAILLES
QUAI BRANLY
AVE DE NEW YORK
AVENUE KLEBER
AVENUE VICTOR HUGO
AVENUE FOCH
AVE DES CHAMPS ELYSEES
QUAI DES TUILERIES
PONT
BOULEVARD SUCHET
ROUTE DE L'HIPPODROME
ALLEE DE LONGCHAMP
ALLEE DE LA REINE MARGUERITE
ROUTE DE LA REINE
QUAI ALPHONSE LE GALLO
RUE DE ST-CLOUD
QUAI DE STALINGRAD

L'ARBRAMOUCHE

Laon & *the* Aisne

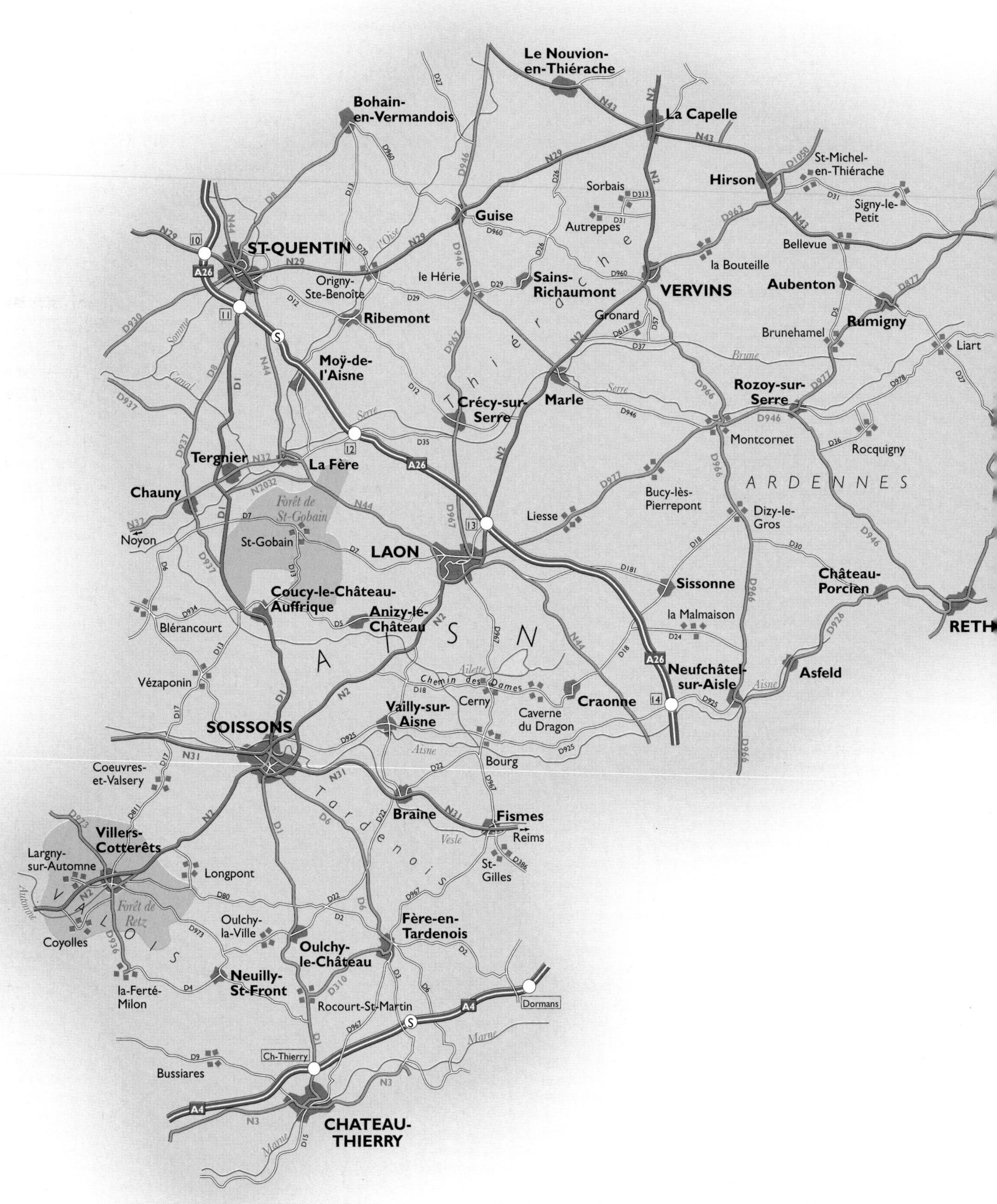

Previous page: From the medieval ramparts of Laon's Upper Town rise the towers of its great Gothic cathedral, a landmark across the Aisne's vast central plains. Laon is famous for the animal scuptures that decorate its façade – a goat, horses, even a rhinoceros and a hippopotamus (inset) are depicted on the West Front. Outdoor theatre is often perfomed in the square outside the old Bishop's Palace, now the Palais de Justice (inset).

Exploring *the* Aisne

Stretching between the forests of the Valois and the chalk slopes of Champagne, and from the wooded hills of the Ardennes to the borders of Paris, the Aisne 'département' is varied touring country. Winding roads cross the central plains, passing through little villages, each with a protective château, medieval church or ruin of an ancient abbey. Longpont in the Valois has a château built into the ruins of an 11th-century Cistercian abbey. West of Laon, the forest of St-Gobain hides the remains of the first monastery of the aescetic, charitable Premonstratensian order.

In the Aisne's south-western corner, the old village churches of Largny-sur-Automne and Coyolles mark the point where the peaceful valley of the Automne River (see also page 45) crosses the border from the Oise. It bubbles through the Valois to the charming town of Villers-Cotterêts, where Alexandre Dumas, creator of *The Three Musketeers*, once lived.

Nine km/five-and-a-half miles south of Villers-Cotterêts is La Ferté-Milon, the steep canalside town where Jean Racine, France's great dramatist, was born. Between the two spreads the forest of Retz, the largest woodland region in the lovely Aisne.

Flowing east to west across the central plain is the Aisne, one of the *département*'s three great rivers. The Oise meanders across the north-western corner, and the Marne creates a cool valley in the southern vineyard areas. South of Laon is the Ailette Valley, with its 162-hectare/400-acre lake for fishing, water sports – or just picnicking beside.

Along the south-eastern border with Champagne runs the Tardenois, a region dotted with Romanesque village churches – many surprisingly unharmed by the fighting that ravaged this region in summer 1918. The village of Oulchy-la-Ville, on the D22, has an exquisite 12th-century church, and nearby is the church of Oulchy-le-Château, inside the walls of a castle built for the Counts of Champagne.

The Tardenois extends through the Champagne vineyards into the *département* of Marne, where the D386 leads you via the medieval churches of Fismes and St-Gilles along a 65-km/40-mile driving route through wooded hills and valleys sprinkled with abbeys, churches and castles.

A peaceful day's fishing on the river is an attractive alternative to exploring the charming valley of the Aisne River by car. Check with the tourist office for details of regulations and fishing permits for the rivers in South Picardy.

Cathedrals

The Aisne was a focus of activity during the age of cathedral-building that began about 1150 in and around the Ile de France. Laon, begun in 1155, and Notre-Dame in Paris (see page 56) are the two earliest pure Gothic churches. Soissons Cathedral has a Romanesque choir, a very early Gothic south transept, and a later Gothic north transept and tower. The town's huge Abbey Church of St-Jean-des-Vignes, now in ruins, was founded in the 11th century; its façade resembles that of Reims Cathedral, just over the Aisne/Marne border. Noyon, just over the Oise border in the west, has a beautiful cathedral in Transitional style which houses a library of precious books and illuminations. The west tower of the Basilica of St-Quentin in the north is partly Romanesque, but the glory of this late-Gothic building is its Flamboyant Gothic Lamoureux porch.

The fortified church at Rozoy-sur-Serre.

Aisne Fact File

Tourist information Comité départemental du tourisme de l'Aisne, 1 rue St-Martin, BP 116, 02005 – Laon Cedex. Tel 23 26 70 00. Fax 23 20 49 80.

LA FERTÉ-MILON

Musée Jean Racine 2 rue des Bouchers. ***Open*** *1 Apr-11 Nov* Sat-Sun 10am-12.30pm, 3-5.30pm.

LONGPONT

Abbaye de Longpont (Cistercian abbey ruins). Tel 23 96 01 53. ***Open*** *15 Mar-15 Nov* Sat-Sun 10.30am-noon, 2.30-6.30pm (weekday visits may be arranged for groups).

SOISSONS

Abbaye de St-Jean-des-Vignes. ***Open*** Mon-Sat 9am-noon, 2-6pm; Sun 10am-noon, 2-6pm. About £1 adult, child free.

Cathédrale daily 8.30-11.45am, 2.30-5.30pm. An original painting by Rubens can be seen ('L'adoration des bergers'). Free.

VILLERS-COTTERÊTS

Musée Alexandre-Dumas rue Desmoustiers. Tel 23 96 23 30. ***Open*** Mon, Wed-Sun 2.30-5pm. ***Closed*** last Sun of every month and on public holidays.

Touring *the* Thiérache

The historic Thiérache, in the north-east corner of the Aisne, is one of the most varied parts of this region, with its rolling hills, remains of ancient forests, wooded river valleys, and most memorable, its fortified medieval manors and churches.

The Thiérache is a sleepy region of undulating, wooded hills, spanning the valleys of the rivers Oise, Brune and Serre. It extends northward from Montcornet roughly to Le Nouvion-en-Thiérache and La Capelle, west to Guise, and east into the Ardennes.

Capital of the Thiérache is Vervins, a fortified hilltop town founded by the Romans in the 1st century AD, with narrow cobbled streets overlooked by 17th-century houses contained within the remains of the medieval town walls.

Strategically sited on France's northern border, the Thiérache was a focus of military activity between 1515 and the 17th century, when the House of Habsburg under Charles V fought for French territory, and the region was plagued by internal and external wars.

The villagers of the Thiérache, under constant threat of invasion and pillaging, turned to their churches for protection. New churches were built, sited on high vantage points within or on the outskirts of villages, and built with deep foundations, thick walls of brick and stone, and stout doors, strong enough to withstand attack. They were given lookout towers and belltowers, from where a watch could be kept for attack and the village warned of danger. The nave doubled as a donjon, big enough to house every villager – with food stores and stoves for cooking and heating, stables, and stalls for cattle.

But for its spire, the church at Gronard on the D613 south of Vervins looks like a small castle. Its tiny porch is dwarfed by the high walls of its keep, and flanked by two enormous towers, their walls pierced by arrow slits. North-east of Vervins, La Bouteille on the D963 has a church with walls buttressed with stone and brick, and four pepperpot towers. At Sorbais on the pretty D313 is a church with a machicolated keep, and at Autreppes, close by, is a church with chimneys which once belonged to fireplaces where villagers under siege could cook.

In the Aisne alone there are 60 of these fortified churches, and more across the border in the Ardennes Thiérache. It is easy for anyone driving through the region to explore a few, as well as to discover some of the many beautiful monasteries and castles in this little-known part of France.

A Romanesque church, fortified with a huge tower in the 16th century, dominates Vervins, capital of the Thiérache.

Thiérache Fact File

VERVINS from **Calais**
A1-A26/N29/D29/D960
225 km/140 miles. **Tourist information** Maison de la Thiérache, 43 rue du Général-de-Gaulle, 02260 – La Capelle. Tel 23 97 84 75. Fax 23 97 21 44. ***Open*** Mon-Fri 9am-12.30pm, 2-6pm, Sat 9-noon, 3-7pm; *Easter-Sept* open also on Sun 3-7pm.

SIGHTSEEING
Coucy-le-Château-Auffrique
Abbaye de Prémontrés in the St-Gobain forest. ***Open*** Mon-Fri 10am-noon, 2-5pm. Tel 23 23 66 02. Parts of this abbey (now a hospital) can be visited.
Château. Tel 23 52 71 28. ***Open*** *Jun-Sept* daily 9am-noon, 2-6pm; *Oct-May* Mon, Wed-Sun 10am-noon, 1.30-4pm.
Château-Thierry
Musée Jean-de-la-Fontaine 12 rue Jean-de-la-Fontaine. Tel 23 69 05 60. ***Open*** *Apr-Sept* Mon, Wed-Sat 10am-noon, 2-6pm, Sun 10am-noon, 2-5pm. *Oct-Mar* Mon, Wed-Sat 10am-noon, 2-5pm. Special exhibitions celebrating the writer's tricentenary in 1995.
Guise
Château. Tel 23 61 11 76. ***Open*** *Apr-Jun* daily 9am-noon, 2-6pm. *Jul-Aug* daily 9am-noon, 2-7pm. *Sept-Mar* daily (except Christmas day) 9am-noon, 2-5pm .
Marle
Musée des Temps barbares et parc archéologique. ***Open*** *15 Apr-15 Oct* Mon, Wed-Sun 3-7pm. Museum of life in the Dark Ages.
St-Michel-en-Thiérache
Abbaye *Open* *May-Oct* Mon-Fri 2-6pm; Sat-Sun 2.30-6.30pm.
Musée de la Vie rurale et forestière (Museum of Rural life and Forestry) 34 blvd Savart. ***Open*** *May-Oct* Mon-Fri 2-6pm; Sat-Sun 2.30-6.30pm.

FOR CHILDREN
La Bouteille
Vallée des Cerfs (deer park). Tel 23 97 49 60. Check for directions and opening times.
Le Nouvion-en-Thiérache
Parc de l'Astrée A lakeside/forest recreation site (check with tourist office).

EATING AND DRINKING
Laon
Les Chenizelles 1 rue du Bourg. Tel 23 23 02 34. Menus from £9.
Noyon
Le Cèdre 8 rue de l'Evêché. Tel 44 44 23 24. Menus from £10.
Le St-Eloi 81 blvd Carnot. Tel 44 44 01 49. Menus from £16.

You can walk around Coucy-le-Château's walls (above); their towers were built for Enguerrand III, Sire de Coucy, in the 13th century.

Fortified towns of the Aisne

The Aisne is encircled by a ring of towns built on sites that have been fortified since ancient times. Château-Thierry, on the river Marne in the south of the Aisne, was a fortified settlement of the Gauls. Charles Martel, king of the Franks, built a castle on the site in 710, but the impressive rings of walls and towers that remain were built on the hilltop site for the Counts of Champagne in the 14th century. In the town below, the Tour Bahlan, part of the town's 15th-century defences, is now the belfry. The town was the birthplace of Jean de la Fontaine, writer of fables.

The ancient fortifications of Soissons were destroyed long ago, but huge towers and ramparts still surround Coucy-le-Château-Auffrique, on the D1 to the north. They were raised in the 13th century, when this modest town was one of France's great defensive sites, the seat of the Sires de Coucy. A road scales the ramparts and enters the huge ring of walls through the medieval city gates. Today, the walls contain the old castle keep – blown up by the retreating Germans in 1917 – the modern town, and its Gothic church. A famous story of the city relates how the first Frankish king, Clovis, never forgave one of his warriors who broke the treasured Vase of Soissons – and many years later broke the warrior's head in revenge.

Dominating the Oise Valley is Guise, a fortified town on the edge of the Thiérache. There are tours around the maze of galleries and underground rooms at the base of the keep of the old castle, begun in the 11th century for Duke Gauthier. Centuries later, the town was enclosed within a massive brick fortress. It also has a gigantic brick church – its west front more like a castle donjon than the entrance to a place of worship.

Rumigny (below) in the Ardennes *département*, is one of the Thiérache's many fortified, moated manors, built in 1546.

Laon

Gazing across the plains from each corner of Laon's great west towers are massive medieval carvings of the oxen that hauled the building stone 10 km/6 miles from the quarries south of the city.

The old churches, streets and houses of Laon's Upper Town crowd the roughly triangular summit of a hill that was first fortified by the Romans.

Its first cathedral was built in the 5th century, when Laon became a bishopric. Today its medieval successor, the glorious Cathedral of Notre-Dame, crowns the rock, its towers rising 56 m/180 ft above the town. Begun in 1155 and completed in 1230, it is one of France's two great cathedrals in early Gothic style. Today, far below, the modern suburbs of the lower town spread across the plain.

According to legend, an ox fell exhausted while hauling building stone across the plain from the quarries of the Chemin des Dames, and up the steep hill to the cathedral building site; it was replaced by a divine ox, which appeared from the heavens. This is the reason for the famous medieval carvings of oxen at the corners of the cathedral towers.

You don't need to understand architecture to enjoy looking at the carvings on the building's façade. Things to look at inside include the beautiful rose windows filled with medieval glass at the west and east ends, and in the north transept, the lantern tower at the central crossing, the peaceful 13th-century cloister, and the chapter house, the medieval meeting house of the bishop and clergy.

Other things to see

The 13th-century Bishop's Palace (now the Palais de Justice) beside the cathedral, may be visited. The restored Church of St-Martin dominates the west end of the upper town. It was built in 1150 in Transitional style. The Hôtel-Dieu, to the north, built on the site of a former abbey, was badly damaged during World War II, but a hospital ward, the abbot's lodgings, and the cloister make an interesting visit. In the garden of the city museum is the exquisite, octagonal Chapelle des Templiers, begun in 1134.

Laon's narrow streets with their rows of 18th-century houses are a pleasure to walk through – but the city's impressive 13th-century ramparts, their towers and gates, make the most rewarding walk, with spectacular views across the surrounding chalk plains.

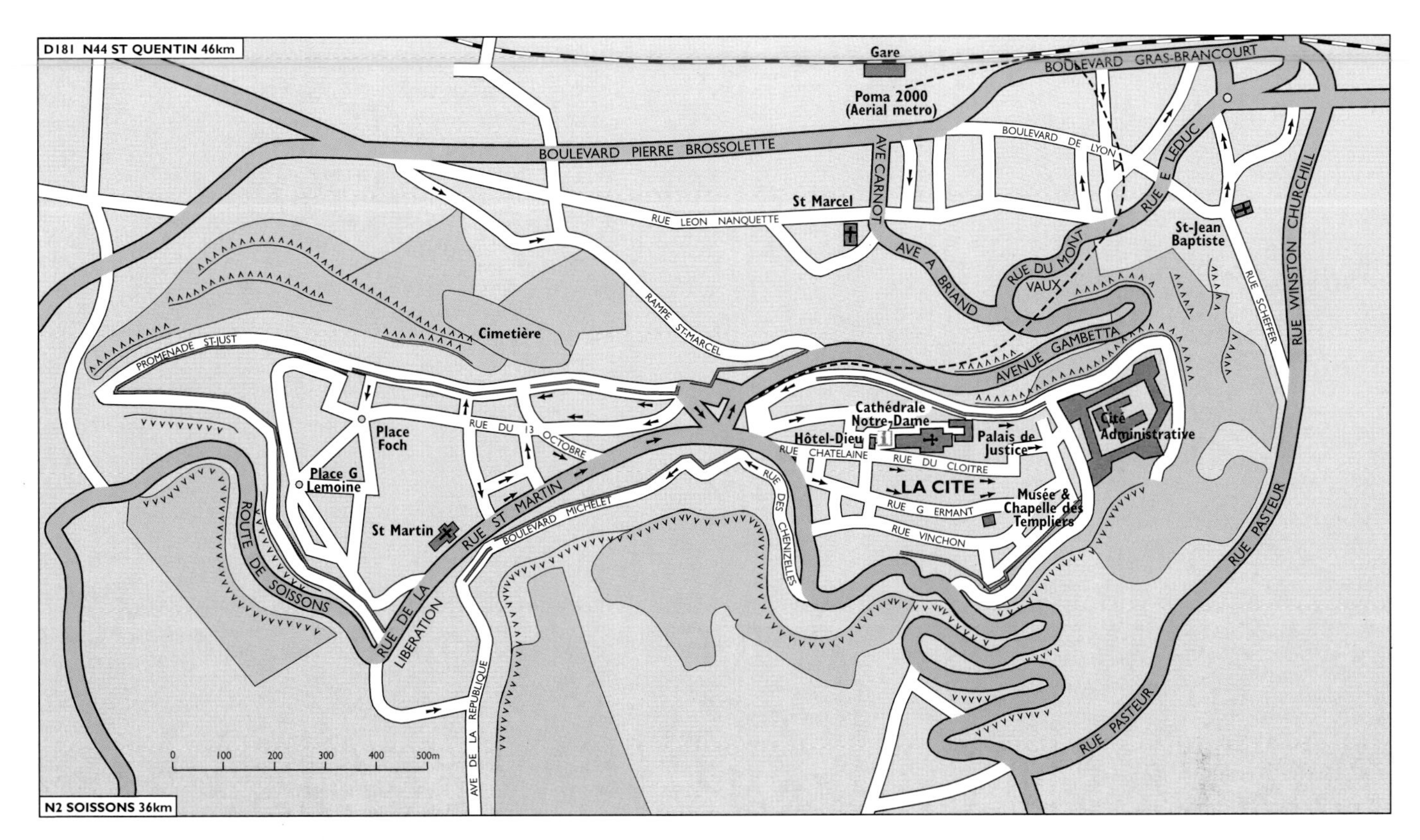

Laon Fact File

LAON from **Calais** A26 197 km/123 mi. **Postal zip code** 02000. **Tourist information** place du parvis. Tel 23 20 28 62. Fax 23 20 68 11. ***Open*** *Jun-Sept* Mon-Sat 9am-7pm, Sun 10am-7pm; *Oct-May* Mon-Sat 9am-12.30pm, 2-4.30pm, Sun 10am-1pm, 2-5pm.
Parking small parking lots in Upper Town. Large car park at railway station: place de la Gare, also terminus of **Poma 2000** aerial metro *Sept-Jul* Mon-Sat 7am-8pm; *Aug* Mon-Sat 7am-8pm, Sun 2-8pm.

SIGHTSEEING
Walking tours the tourist office publishes a map of walking tours in the Upper Town.
Cathédrale Notre-Dame parvis de la Cathédrale. ***Open*** *Apr-Aug* 8am-7pm; *Sept-Mar* 8am-6.30pm. Guided tours *Apr-Oct* Sat-Sun 3pm.
Chapelle des Templiers (Chapel of the Knights Templar) and **Musée d'Archéologie** 32 rue Georges-Ermant. ***Open*** *Apr-Sept* Mon, Wed-Sun 10am-noon, 2-8pm; *Oct-Mar* Mon, Wed-Sun 10am-noon, 2-5pm. ***Closed*** *1 Jan, 1 May, 14 Jul, 25 Dec.*
Palais de Justice (chapels) place Aubry. ***Open*** Mon-Fri 10am-noon, 2-5.30pm.

OUT OF TOWN
Chemin des Dames
(D18 hill road, 24 km/15 miles S of Laon) The road is an ancient hilltop route of the Gauls, paved in 1770 for the daughters of Louis XV to visit the Ailette Valley. It is now a site of memorials to World War I battles fought along it. Visits Mon, Wed-Sun.
Caverne du Dragon (in the stone quarries near the Ferme d'Hurtebise). ***Open*** Mon, Wed-Fri 10.30am-noon, 2.30-6pm; Sat, Sun 10.30am-noon, 2.30-6.30pm. Subterranean fortress. Audiovisuals, some in English. About £2 per adult, 50p per child.

CAMPING
Camping rue Jean-Pierre-Timbault, Lower Town.

EATING AND DRINKING
Crêperie Agora rue des Cordeliers. A café-restaurant close to the cathedral serving a wide range of snacks and meals.
La Petite Auberge 45 blvd P.-Brossolette. Tel 23 23 02 38. Country cooking with gourmet touches.

Below left: Street entertainment gives Laon a carnival atmosphere in summer. Below right: A shop in the old town.

Reims & Champagne Country

Touring *the* **Champagne countryside**

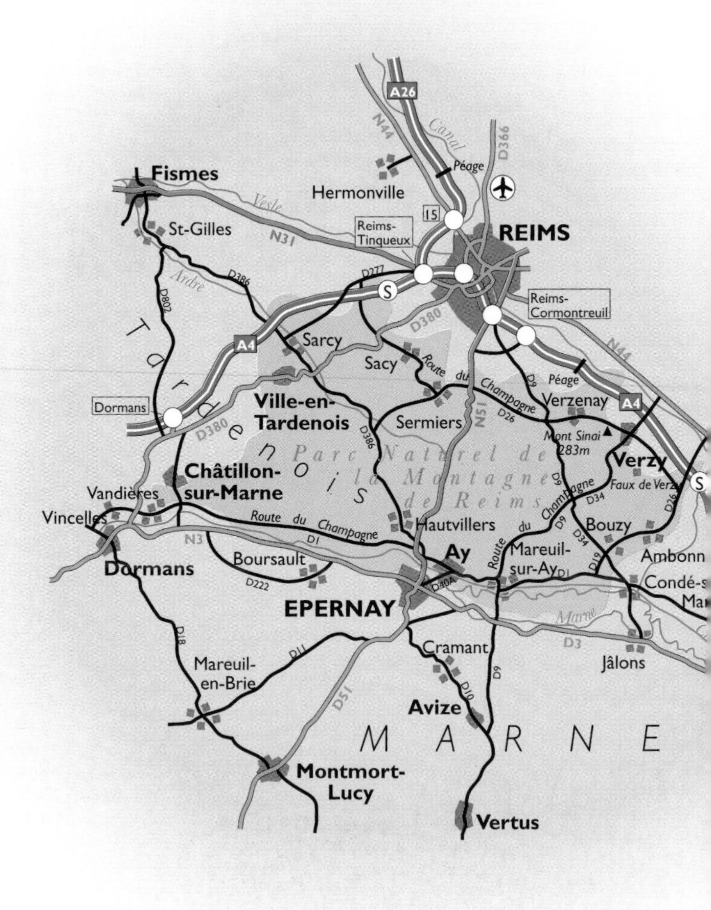

From Reims to Epernay, the air over Champagne is charged at harvest-time with the strong, sweet smell of 'must' – the newly pressed grape juice. Visit this region in September to catch that special atmosphere – and at any other time of year to visit the champagne houses, taste their famous wine, and explore the villages, with their castles, abbeys and exquisite Romanesque churches.

The region that gives champagne its name, Champagne-Ardenne, is wide-ranging. Its borders stretch a long way north, south and west of the renowned vineyard area, from the open plains of the south-west planted with crops and vegetables, to the forest of the Ardennes in the north-east.

The production of France's most prestigious wine centres on a range of low, vine-planted hills on the Côte d'Ile de France between the Tardenois and the Brie Plateau and the long chalk plain of Champagne sèche, capped by broad expanses of ancient forest. Minor roads – the D386 from Fismes along the Vesle River; the D9 from Reims; the D34 down to the Marne; the D19 and D26 around Bouzy in the east – give spectacular views across the wooded Champagne countryside.

Only wine made from vines planted within the strictly delineated 34,000 hectares/84,000 acres of the *vignobles*, or vineyard area, of Champagne, and prepared according to a carefully defined process, can, by law, be called champagne. In fact, the *vignobles* begin outside Champagne, in the Tardenois on the south-eastern border of the Aisne *département*.

But the heart of the region, where the best grapes grow, focuses on an area centring on the Montagne de Reims outlined by the Marne River in the south and a curved

Previous pages: The Parc naturel de la montagne de Reims is a nature reserve covering 50,000 hectares/123,550 acres between Reims and Epernay, and stretching as far west as Châtillon-sur-Marne and east as Verzy. It is crossed by a network of picturesque roads and tracks, and pinpointed with magnificent panoramas across the Champagne countryside. The harvest, or *vendanges*, usually takes place in September. Workers pick the grapes by hand (inset).

line drawn between Vincelles, Reims, and Ambonnay in the west, north and east respectively. Some of this land is owned by the famous *maisons de champagne* (champagne houses), which produce most of the wine; but most of it is owned by thousands of small growers, called *vignerons*, many with tiny landholdings. Some sell their grapes to the *maisons*, but some produce their own champagne. Along the roadsides, and in the stone-built villages and towns that dot the area, are signs directing you to visit the *caves* (cellars) of these small producers.

What to see

As well as the vineyards, there are forests and rivers to explore. You can drive through the forest to the Montagne's second highest point, 283 m/928 ft, marked by the Mont Sinaï observatory, from where there are splendid views across the vineyards. In the woods above the wine-producing village of Verzy nearby are the 'Faux de Verzy', a group of old, strangely twisted beech trees. There are picturesque drives along the Marne.

For drivers, the tourist office has signposted a long touring circuit, the 'Route touristique du champagne', covering the area from Reims to Villenauxe-la-Grande, via Epernay, Dormans and Vertus.

Below: The Romanesque church at the village of Hermonville, north of Reims, has a galleried porch typical of churches in the Champagne region.

A rose planted at the end of every row of vines helps experts detect vine disease because the symptoms show up first on the leaves of the rose.

The tower of the Maison de Castellane contains a museum showing the champagne-making process. The bottle room has a unique collection of labels.

The tourist route takes you to almost every point of interest in the Champagne area – so it can be rewarding to follow it for half an hour or so, and investigate just a few of the places marked.

The route begins in Reims, at the cathedral, where stained-glass windows depict the activities of wine-production. It tours the vineyards and their many attractive villages and small towns – Sermiers, with its village fountain and old washhouse; Vandières with its Romanesque church and castle. The route passes through every village famous for its vintage – Ambonnay, for example, Cramant and Avize, and Bouzy, famous for an exquisite still red wine it produces in small quantities.

Many of the area's châteaux and abbeys are in private hands, but you can visit the former Benedictine Abbaye de Hautvillers by appointment with Moët et Chandon in Epernay. Here, in the 17th century, the monastery's cellarer, Dom Pérignon, is said to have created the wine we know today as champagne by mixing different grapes, experimenting with double fermentation and also making the basic local wine more bubbly.

When to go

Visit Champagne at any time of year and there are always interesting things to see. In spring, the vines are carefully tended as the first delicate leaves form. A check is kept on the temperature, and the vines are heated – by steam, or spraying – if there is a hint of frost. In summer the vines produce tiny pale flowers.

The height of the season is the harvest, or *vendanges*. The date is fixed by local agreement, usually 100 days after flowering. The baskets for collecting the grapes are now often replaced by plastic containers, and the traditional carts by lorries and tankers. But mechanical picking is not permitted, so every year temporary workers are hired to pick the grapes carefully by hand.

After the harvest, the vineyard and its woodlands turn a magnificent brown and gold and the workers prepare the land for the normally mild Champagne winter.

The **story** *of* **Champagne**

To the south and east of Reims are the gently rolling, green and gold, vine-covered hills and valleys of Champagne. Deep beneath them are tunnels, tens of kilometres long, quarried out of the chalk hills by the Romans. Today they are cold stores for the region's unique wine during its long, crucial fermentation period.

Recently acquired vineyards of the Maison Mumm, in Reims, are around the windmill of Verzenay (below) on the Montagne de Reims in the heart of the Champagne vineyards. The black Pinot noir grapes grown here produce a clear white wine with a round, ripe flavour. There is a museum of antique champagne-making equipment in the Mumm *caves* in the rue du Champ-de-Mars in Reims, where Mumm's *Vinotèque* has bottles dating back 100 years. Tastings at the end of the tours may give visitors a chance to try new champagnes.

A stained-glass window depicting vine-growing and wine-making scenes in Reims cathedral.

Champagne is a northerly vine-growing region. The success of its vines is said to be partly due to its own, pleasant, microclimate – so that, unusually, the Montagne de Reims yields exceptionally good wine from the grapes grown on its northern, as well as its southern slopes. The Montagne is planted with Pinot noir (black) grapes, which are the basis of the flavour of champagne. Meunier (black) grapes from the vines planted on the southern slopes of the Vallée de la Marne give body to the champagne. South and east of Epernay is the Côte des Blancs, planted with white Chardonnay grapes, which add youth and freshness to the blend.

The champagne houses have their headquarters in Epernay and Reims and it is here that the wine is blended and fermented in underground cellars, or *caves.* Many of the *caves* make use of the old Gallo-Roman chalk quarries beneath Epernay and Reims, extending for kilometres into the countryside around – those of Moët et Chandon in Epernay are 28 km/17 miles in total length. The *caves* of Taittinger in Reims, just north of the place des Droits-de-l'Homme, occupy part of the cellars and crypt of the former Abbey of St-Nicaise.

Many of the *maisons* – large and small – run tours, usually at times that are advertised outside their buildings. Some charge a small fee; others require you to make an appointment before visiting. Tours are usually on foot – though the houses of Mercier, in Epernay and Piper Heidsieck, in Reims, run tours by electric train. Each tour includes a talk, and visitors are sometimes shown the champagne-making processes. All tours end with a tasting – perhaps of a new, young champagne, and a chance to buy (prices are not usually substantially lower than in a good discount wine warehouse in the UK).

Epernay

The champagne *maisons* of Epernay are all to be found on the long avenue du Champagne, off the central square, the place de la République. The largest is Moët et Chandon at No. 20, whose founder was born at Epernay. Moët own the cloisters and vines of the Abbaye de Hautvillers on the Montagne de Reims, where the

The underground *caves* give perfect conditions for the champagne's second fermentation. Especially strong bottles are used, so that they will not explode as the pressure inside builds up.

blending process is said to have originated, and the house of Mercier in Epernay, and Ruinart in Reims.

Epernay is an ancient town, founded in the 5th century AD on an area of former swamp, drained by the Romans and occupied by a group of tanners, who settled along the banks of the Cubry River. In medieval times the town was owned by the Counts of Champagne, and it later became part of the Kingdom of France.

But in World War I most of Epernay, like Reims, was destroyed, and the town was heavily bombarded in World War II. Little reconstruction or restoration was carried out, so for this reason, Epernay has fewer tourist attractions than Reims (see pages 76-77). There is only the 16th-century gateway of St-Martin, the façade of the House of Louise of Savoie – and the magnificent 19th-century mansions of the champagne houses. But in the Maison de Castellane off the rue du Champagne is a museum of champagne-making.

Champagne File

EPERNAY from **Calais** A26/N51 294 km/183 miles.
Postal zip code 51202.
Tourist information 7 avenue de Champagne, 51201. Tel 26 55 33 00. Fax 26 51 95 22. ***Open*** *Easter-15 Oct* Mon-Sat 9.30am-12.30pm, 1.30pm-7pm, Sun 11am-4pm; *16 Oct-Easter* Mon-Sat 9.30am-12.30pm, 1.30pm-5.30pm.

CHAMPAGNE CELLARS
Listed below are the largest houses in Epernay and Reims. They run tours of their cellars and museums, often with tastings. Other champagne houses can be visited in the Vallée de la Marne, the Côteaux du Sézannais and the Côte des Blancs.
De Castellane 57 rue de Verdun, Epernay. Tel 26 5515 33. ***Open*** (tour, *caves*, champagne museum) *Easter-Oct* daily 10-11.15am, 2-5.15pm. About £2 adult, £1.50 child. Inclusive fee for butterfly garden, tour, *caves*, museum about £3.50.
Heidsieck 51 blvd Henry-Vasnier, Reims. Tel 26 84 43 44. ***Open*** *Mar-Nov* Mon, Thu-Sun 9-11.45am, 2-7.15pm.
Moët et Chandon 18 av de Champagne, Epernay. Tel 26 54 71 11. ***Open*** *Apr-Oct* Mon-Sat 9.30-11.30am, 2-4.30pm, Sun 9.30-11.30am, 3.30-3.45pm; *Nov-Mar* Mon-Fri 9.30-11.30am, 2-4.30pm.
Mumm 34 rue du Champ-de-Mars, Reims. Tel 26 49 59 70. ***Open*** *Mar-Oct* daily 9-11am, 2-5pm; *Nov-Feb* Sat-Sun 2-5pm. About £2.50. Tours in English to Mumm Museum, *vinothèque*, *caves*, tasting room and shop.
Taittinger 9 place St-Nicaise, Reims. Tel 26 85 45 35. ***Open*** Mon-Fri 9.30am-noon, 2-4.30pm, Sat-Sun 9-11am, 2-5pm.

CAMPING
Allée de Cumières (beside the Marne). Tel 26 55 32 14. ***Open*** *Apr-Sept.*

How champagne is made

Mechanical harvesting is strictly forbidden in Champagne, but the grapes are pressed mechanically and efficiently these days, as quickly as possible after they have been picked to conserve the fresh qualities of the must, or juice. From every 150 kg/330 lb of grapes, 100 litres/180 pints of must are extracted.

Must, fermenting agents and sugar are fermented in large casks for several months. After this first fermentation, the wine is blended. Tasters take years to train – not everyone is capable of learning. They work in teams to decide on the *cuvée*, the blend of different wines that will determine the taste of the mature champagne. Every house guards its secret of the proportions that give its champagne its unique taste.

If the wine produced by one harvest is particularly good, it can be declared a 'vintage' year. Bottles labelled 'vintage' with the date must be based exclusively on wine produced that year.

Once the *cuvée* has been prepared, the bottles are filled and a small quantity of a natural fermentation medium and a little sugar are added. The bottles are corked, and stored upside-down in racks in the cool, dark, underground *caves*.

The second fermentation must, by law, take a minimum of one year, but most champagnes ferment for longer, and vintages take three to five years. During the second fermentation, sediment collects inside the bottle. This is disturbed by turning each bottle (mechanically, usually, but still sometimes by hand), or *remuage,* once every day over a period of several weeks. The sediment is dislodged and falls on to the inside of the cork. In a process called *dégorgement*, the bottle is uncorked, the old cork, the sediment and a little wine are removed, the bottle is topped up with new wine and a small quantity of yeast, corked, and left to rest at its pre-determined level of sweetness or dryness before shipping.

An old champagne press (above) marks the entrance to the *maison* Mumm in the rue du Champ-de-Mars in Reims.

EATING AND DRINKING
Les Berceaux 13 rue des Berceaux, Epernay. Tel 26 55 28 84. ***Closed*** Sun evening. A restaurant and wine bar in an old coach house. Menus from £12.50 to £40.
La Briquèterie 4 route de Sézanne, Vinay (on N51 7 km/ 5 miles S of Epernay). Tel 26 59 99 99. ***Closed*** 23-29 Dec. Exceptional cooking from an imaginative chef whose restaurant occupies an old inn. Menus from £16 to £48.
Royal Champagne Champillon-Bellevue (on N2051 5 km/ 3 miles N of Epernay). Tel 26 52 87 11. Outstanding food by a chef who formerly worked with Guérard and Boyer. Menus from £23 to £50.

Reims

The stately Gothic cathedral rises proudly above the modern city of Reims, its richly carved façade contrasting starkly with the bare walls of the city's modern buildings.

Reims was one of France's earliest Christian towns. Its bishopric, founded in AD290, became an archbishopric in AD744. The city grew and flourished around its cathedral which was to become the coronation cathedral of most of the kings of France after the 12th century. In 1429, Charles VII of France, the *dauphin* (heir apparent), was crowned there in the presence of Jeanne d'Arc who had succeeded in defeating the English both at Orléans and Reims, thus enabling him to accede to the throne.

When Reims was virtually obliterated by shelling during World War I, its population was reduced from 117,000 to 25,000, but its cathedral miraculously survived, to become the focus of the postwar city. The cathedral, begun in the early 13th century, replaced an earlier building destroyed by fire. The city's oldest church is the Basilique St-Remi, built in the 11th century over the tomb of St-Remigius, the archbishop who baptised Clovis in 496.

Clearing the debris after World War I uncovered remains of Reims' Roman predecessor. Part of the 12th-century former Benedictine Abbaye de St-Remi is now the city's archaeological museum. The Cryptoporticus – a vaulted passage with openings in the walls, leading to the Forum – has been uncovered and can be seen in the place du Forum. Marooned on a road island is the Porte de Mars, a Roman triumphal arch dating from the 3rd century, which also escaped bombing.

Reims has a good Musée des Beaux-Arts (Fine Arts Museum), with works from the 15th to 20th centuries, including 27 paintings by Corot and several Impressionist paintings. The town also has some interesting houses – the restored Gothic Maison des Comtes de Champagne, the Renaissance Hôtel de la Salle, and the 17th-century Hôtel de Ville. But people visit Reims mainly to see its cathedral and to visit the cellars of the champagne houses in the underground tunnels beneath the city – many of which served as bomb shelters during the last wars. The *maisons* are grouped in two major areas of town: around the rue du Champ-de-Mars, in the north; and either side of the boulevards Diancourt and Pommery in the south.

The modern city, though lively, is scarcely picturesque, but it is excellent for shopping, cinemas, and nightlife. It is the starting point for exploring Champagne – and for discovering the outstanding regional cuisine in its many excellent restaurants.

The magnificent towers of the cathedral dominate the skyline of modern Reims.

Reims Fact File

REIMS from **Calais** A26 269 km/168 miles. **Postal zip code** 51100. **Tourist information** 2 rue Guillaume-de-Machault. Tel 26 47 25 69. Fax 26 47 23 63. ***Open*** *Easter-Jun, Sept* Mon-Sat 9am-7.30pm, Sun 9.30am-6.30pm, *Jul-Aug* Mon-Sat 9am-8pm, Sun 9.30am-7pm; *Oct-Easter* Mon-Sat 9am-6.30pm, Sun 9.30am-5.30pm.
Parking place Drouet-d'Erlon, blvds Général-Leclerc and Foch.

SIGHTSEEING
Cathédrale Notre-Dame (***Open*** daily 7.30am-7.30pm) and the **Palais du Tau** place du Cardinal-Luçon. ***Open*** *16 Mar-Jun, Sept-14 Nov* daily 9.30am-12.30pm, 2-6pm; *Jul-Aug* daily 9.30am-6.30pm; *15 Nov-15 Mar* Mon-Fri 10am-noon, 2-5pm, Sat-Sun 2-6pm. About £3. The palace, built in 1690 by Jules Hardouin-Mansart and Robert de Cotte, is the cathedral museum. The Salle du Tau is the coronation banqueting hall.
Basilique St-Remi rue Simon. ***Open*** 8am-7pm. **Museum** ***Open*** Mon-Fri 2-6.30pm, Sat, Sun 2-7pm. About £1 to tour buildings of the former abbey, now a museum of tapestries.
Cryptoportique place du Forum ***Open*** *15 Jun-15 Sept* Tue-Sun 2-6pm. Admission: apply at St-Remi Museum. Free.
Musée des Beaux-Arts 8 rue Chanzy. ***Open*** Mon, Wed-Sun 10am-noon, 2-6pm. About £1.50.
Musée le Vergeur 36 place du Forum. ***Open*** Tue-Sun 2-6pm. About £2 (guided tours only). The history of Reims, with furniture, porcelain, paintings.
Salle de Reddition (World War II Surrender Room) Collège technique de Reims, 10 rue Franklin-Roosevelt. ***Open*** Mon, Wed-Sun 2-6pm. ***Closed*** on public holidays. US General Eisenhower's HQ in 1945. On 7 May, in the Map Room, the Germans signed their surrender.

CAMPING
Airotel de Champagne av Hoche (route de Châlons). Tel 26 85 41 22. ***Open*** *Easter-Sept.* (For other periods call Tel 26 88 37 89.)

EATING AND DRINKING
L'Assiette champenoise 40 av Paul-Vaillant-Couturier. Tel 26 04 15 56. Menus from £40 to £62.
Boyer (les Crayères) 64 blvd Henry-Vasnier. Tel 26 82 80 80. One of France's celebrated restaurants. Menus from £56.
Le Paysan 16 rue de Fismes. Tel 26 40 25 51. From about £9.

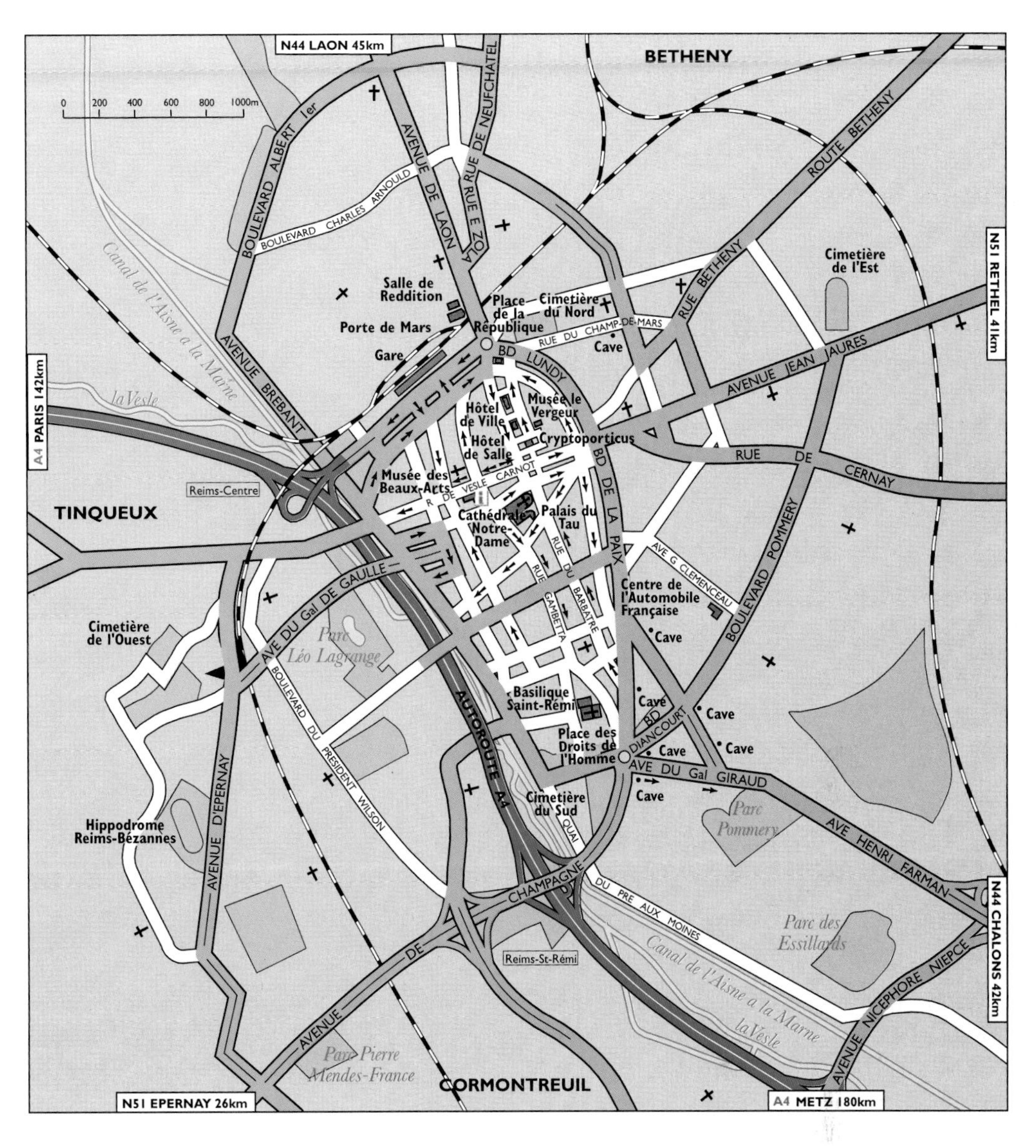

Reims cathedral

Reims Cathedral is France's finest example of mature Gothic architecture. Begun in 1211, it took almost 300 years to finish – yet it has a perfect unity of style. It has no transepts, but has a widened nave, aisles, and east end to provide space for coronations. Note the 500 delightful carved figures on the portals (right) – especially the famous smiling Angel of Reims; the palisade of elegant flying buttresses supporting the nave; and, inside, the impressive spaciousness of the 139-m/456-ft long, 38-m/125-ft high nave, and the exceptionally beautiful medieval stained glass (inset), which was removed and stored during the wars. The Palais du Tau displays some of the cathedral's carvings.

The **Fields** *of* **War**

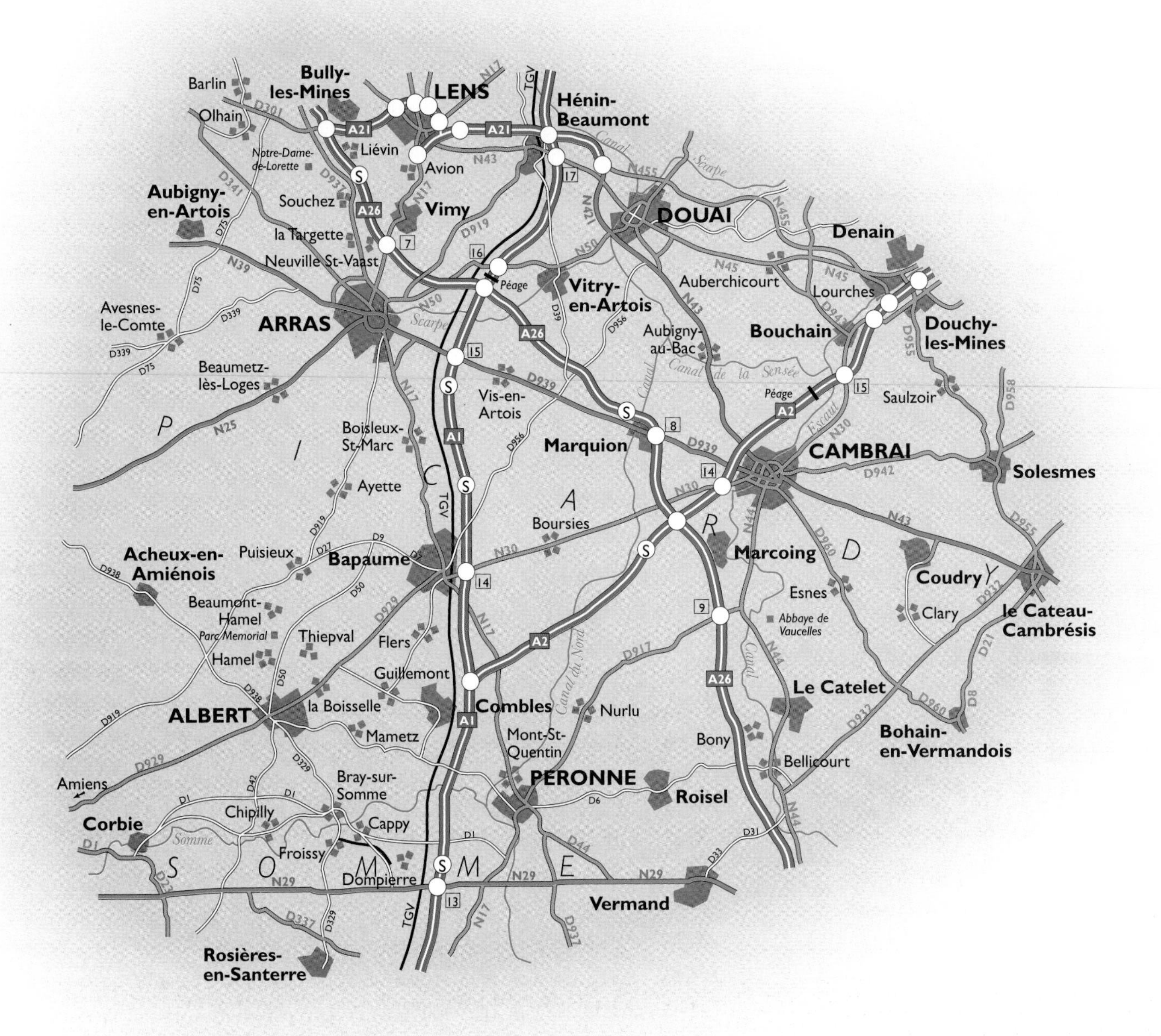

Touring *the* **battle sites**

under Constable d'Albret. In Azincourt village a museum and cinema detail the strategy of the short but crucial battle on 25 October, 1415, in the Hundred Years War between England and France for control of Normandy.

Precisely positioned cutouts of English archers kneel beside rural roads around the fields of Azincourt, near Hesdin. Longbows drawn, they point their arrows at cutouts of French knights, eternally riding towards them into ambush. In the 1980s, little more than a cross and plaque marked the site of the battle of Agincourt. Now, an orientation table shows the exact positioning of Henry V's English forces, and those of the French army

Warfare and tourism seem uneasy partners. Tourism departments across France and Belgium have therefore been surprised at the resurgence of interest in the sites and strategies of distant battles, such as Crécy and Agincourt (see page 26). Six decades or so after World War I, visits to 1914-18 battlefields were expected to have diminished. Instead, battlefield tours are the fastest-growing branch of tourism in northern Europe.

Previous pages: East of Amiens, the Villers-Bretonneux cemetery and memorial to Australian soldiers killed during World War I. The ranks of gravestones overlook the now-peaceful fields of the Somme Valley, formerly the scene of such carnage that they can truly be described as The Fields of War.

Sites of World War I

World War I came to Picardy on 31 August, 1914, when the German army reached Amiens. In September, French and British armies halted the German advances through France and Belgium. In October, the armies dug themselves in, to form a Western Front of trenches stretching across north-eastern Belgium and France as far as the Swiss border. At Hamel, Camp Terre-Neuve has been preserved with its shell holes and trenches as it was left in 1918.

The Somme front stretched roughly north-south across the region, passing 6 km/4 miles east of Albert. It hardly moved for almost four long years. Beside the fields that were fought over, you sometimes see shells and grenades found by farmers, left for the Mine Clearance Service. They destroyed 75.5 tonnes even as recently as 1985. There are still two cement entrances to a German underground shelter in a field at Guillemont.

The Somme

In 1916, the Allies launched the Battle of the Somme, an offensive by troops from Britain and its Empire and France to try to break the trench warfare deadlock. The attack began at 7.30am on July 1, with the simultaneous explosion of several huge mines. 'Lochnagar', the crater left by the mine near the village of La Boisselle, has been preserved. On the hilltop at Thiepval is the monument designed by the architect Sir Edwin Lutyens to 73,367 British dead, 58,000 of them on the first day of battle.

In manpower terms, the offensive was a disaster. Some 600,000 men were lost by each side. The Allies gained little ground. From Albert, a signposted route, the 'Route du souvenir', guides you to the principal sites: the slope of Beaumont-Hamel, with its shell holes, from where the Scots Highlanders followed the sound of their bagpipes; the Bois des Troncs, taken and lost 18 times in 7 days; the memorial to the 3rd Welsh Division in Mametz Wood; the Ulster Tower, commemorating the 36th Irish Division near Hamel; Delville Wood, taken by the South Africans, and its new museum; the Memorial Park to the Newfoundland Regiment, with undisturbed trenches, and a blackened tree stump marking the German lines.

Pas-de-Calais

Two towers on the skyline, visible from far away across the Pas-de-Calais, mark a piece of Canadian territory in France. On 9 April, 1917, Canadian artillery and infantry advanced on Hill 145, the highest point of the 14-km/9-mile Vimy Ridge, one of the key points in the German defence system. In two days, 100,000 soldiers of the Canadian Corps succeeded where all earlier attempts had failed. Trenches, shell holes and underground passageways, where the troops rehearsed for months before the attack, can all be seen, overshadowed by the bleak and imposing Vimy Ridge Memorial to the battle.

Below: The 18th-century Augustinian abbey church on Mont St-Eloi was destroyed by shelling in World War I and left unrestored as a powerful symbol of wanton destruction on French soil.

流芳百世
A GOOD REPUTATION
ENDURES FOR EVER.
劉子有
No 47739

There is scarcely a town or village in the area covered by this book without a memorial and a fighting tale to tell, and everyone finds a museum or plaque or monument that is especially evocative. A soldier comforts a wounded horse on a monument at Chipilly to 250,000 horses killed in the fighting. Froissy, near Cappy, still has a narrow-gauge railway line like the one that supplied the battlefields, and a steam railway museum. Near the memorial to French soldiers at Notre-Dame-de-Lorette, in the village of Souchez, is a graveyard of Moslem, Hindu and Buddhist soldiers, with a beautiful memorial gateway in wrought iron. At Mont St-Quentin is the memorial to the 2nd Australian Division – restored, because it was destroyed shortly after it was built, during World War II.

Annual services and ceremonies are held on or near days commemorating key dates during World War I in almost all battlefield sites in France and Belgium.

Battlefields of World War II

The beaches of Normandy, to the north-west of Caen are a long day's drive from Calais but still within the scope of an extended weekend trip. Caen and Le Havre make ideal bases for exploring the battlefields of World War II.

Left: Hundreds of military cemeteries (inset, top left) dot the landscape of the Somme, where poppies flourished in the disturbed ground after the war ended. One memorial (top right) commemorates the thousands of carrier pigeons that took messages across the lines. Eroded shell holes of Camp Terre-Neuve at Hamel (centre) commemorate the British and Scottish Divisions and the Royal Newfoundland Regiment who fought there. A Chinese gravestone (bottom) from the cemetery of Chinese and Indian war graves at Ayette is a telling reminder that soldiers from all parts of the world also fought in the bitter trenches that spread their deadly web over the fields of this embattled part of Europe.

Battlefields Fact File

ALBERT from **Calais** A1-D929 145 km/90 miles. **Postal zip code** 80300. **Tourist information** **ALBERT** 9 rue Gambetta, BP 82. Tel 22 75 16 42. Fax 22 75 11 72. ***Open*** *Apr-Sept* Tue-Sun 9am-noon, 3-6.30pm. **AMIENS Comité départemental du tourisme de la Somme** 21 rue Ernest-Cauvin, 80000. Tel 22 92 26 39. Fax 22 92 77 47. ***Open*** daily 8.30am-12.30pm, 1.30-5.30pm. **PÉRONNE** 31 rue St-Fursy, 80200. Tel 22 84 42 38. ***Open*** Mon-Sat 3-5pm.

BATTLEFIELD TOURS
Major & Mrs Holt's Battlefield Tours Golden Key Building, 15 Market Street, Sandwich, Kent, UK CT13 9DA.
Middlebrook-Hodgson
48 Linden Way, Boston, Lincolnshire, UK PE21 9DS.

MUSEUMS
NEUVILLE ST-VAAST La Targette (D937 Arras–Béthune). 1914-18 and 1939-45 museum. Tel 21 45 15 80. ***Open*** daily 9am-8pm.
PÉRONNE Historial de la Grande Guerre place du Château. Tel 22 83 14 18. ***Open*** *18 Jan-Apr* and *Oct-19 Dec* Tue-Sun 10am-6pm; *May-Sept* daily 10am-6pm. About £6.
SOUCHEZ (ABLAIN–ST-NAZAIRE) Musée Notre-Dame-de-Lorette. Tel 21 45 15 80. ***Open*** daily 9am-8pm.
VIMY RIDGE (MÉMORIAL CANADIEN) ***Open*** *1 Apr-15 Nov* guided tours 10am-noon, 2-5pm. Call Tel 21 45 15 80. About £2.50 adult, £1.25 child.

WAR GRAVES INFORMATION
American Memorial Commission 02420 – Bony. Tel 23 66 22 81.
Commonwealth War Graves Commission in France rue Angèle-Richard, 62217 – Beaurains. Tel 21 71 03 24.
Secretary of State for Veterans, War Cemeteries Service, regional office, 3 route de Choisy, 60200 – Compiègne. Tel 44 40 06 90.
Service for the Care of German Cemeteries rue de Nesle prolongée, 80320 – Chaulnes. Tel 22 85 47 57.

FOR CHILDREN
Château d'Olhain (Tel 21 27 94 76) and **Olhain Leisure Park** Fresnicourt-le-Dolmen (on the D57, 20 km/12 miles NW of Arras, W of Souchez). Tel 21 27 91 79. ***Open*** *Apr-Sept* daily 8am-9pm, *Oct-Mar* daily 8am-5pm. Adventure-story castle, with towers, moat and drawbridge.
Azincourt Museum Town Hall, Azincourt village. Tel 21 04 41 12. ***Open*** *Easter-25 Oct* daily 10.30am-6pm, *26 Oct-Easter* daily 11am-5pm. Information about the 'Route touristique et historique du Drap d'Or' (Field of the Golden Cloth) from the Museum. Guided tour and map of the battlefield also available.

Below: Memorial to an ancient battle: the orientation table at the battle site of Azincourt, showing the battle formations of the medieval swordsmen (inset) and archers.

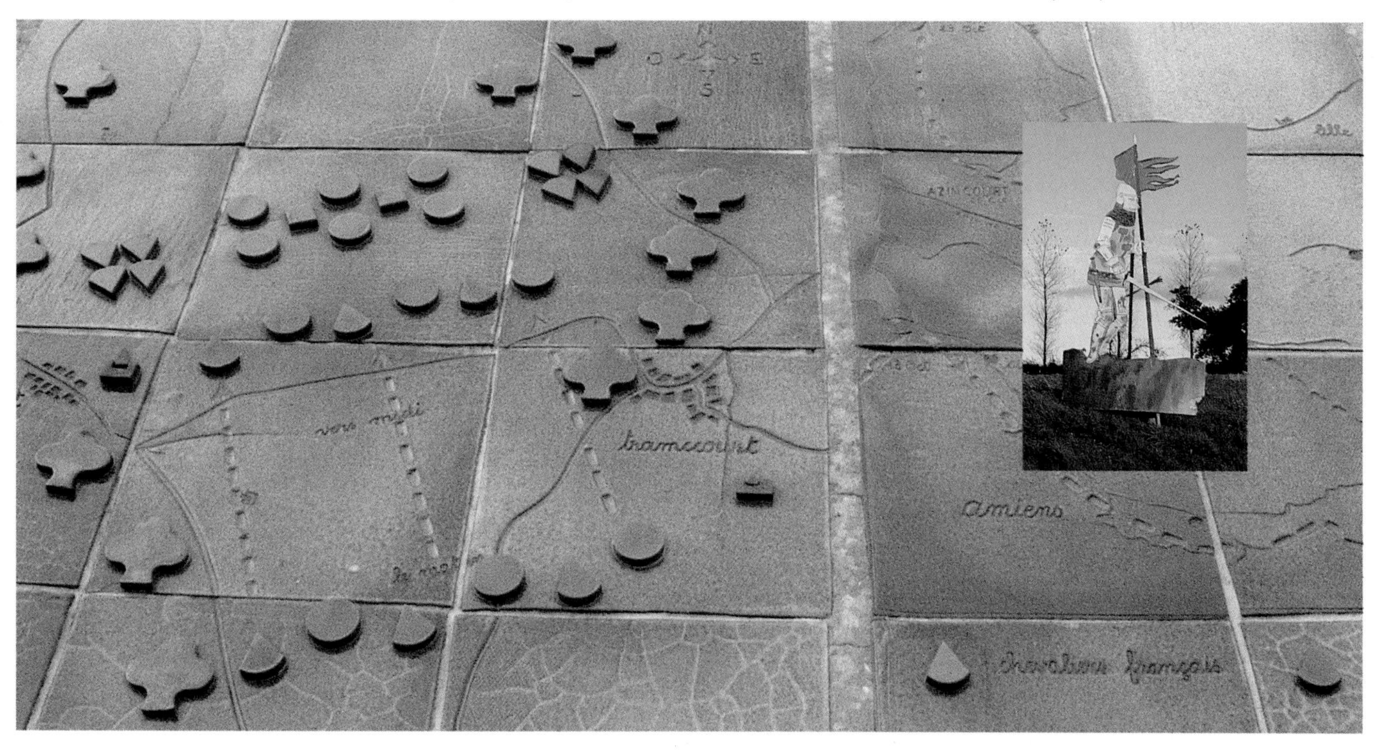

Cambrai

Cambrai was the site of the first full-scale tank battle, carried out by British forces against the Germans who had occupied the city in 1914.

The battle of Cambrai began in the early hours of 20 November, 1917, when some 400 British tanks, supported by a force of more than 250 aircraft, crossed the Hindenburg Line of German fortifications, 10 km/6 miles to the south-west. The British made great advances for the first 24 hours, but the Germans counter-attacked on 30 November, and less than three weeks later the British had lost close on 200 tanks and all the advantage. Tanks had been used for the first time in warfare in the Battle of the Somme in 1916 at the village of Flers, and neither the technology nor its support had been perfected. Primitive tank design and inadequate support, communications, and back-up were, therefore, the reasons for the failure.

World War I buffs make excursions to the sights and memorials of the first-ever tank battle, and to trace the route of the Hindenburg Line. Battlefield tours also visit the American Memorial and cemetery at Bellicourt and Bony, where, in the Second Battle of Cambrai in 1918, more than 1,000 American troops were cut off after breaking through the German front.

Before surrendering Cambrai, the Germans mined the city and set fire to the town centre, destroying the town hall, its archives, and many other buildings.

Cambrai was badly damaged again in World War II, but this ancient riverside town retains enough character and places of interest to make a pleasant short stay. A good place to start exploring is the tourist office, in the Maison espagnole, the town's oldest building, dating from 1595, when Cambrai was under Spanish rule. Pride of the city is the 18th-century Eglise St-Géry, a former monastery chapel, with a beautiful interior enhanced by Rubens' painting *The Entombment*. The 76-m/250-ft tower is one of three belfries in this town; there is a tower on the 18th-century Cathédrale de Notre-Dame, and the town belfry, formerly the tower of a 15th-century church.

Cambrai's city museum has a good collection of Dutch, Flemish and Fauvist paintings, but the most important art gallery in the region is the Musée Matisse at Le Cateau-Cambrésis, 22 km/14 miles to the south-east, birthplace of Henri Matisse, founder of Fauvism. About 12 km/ 7 miles to the south, the fine chapter house and scriptorium remain standing among the ruins of the Cistercian Abbaye de Vaucelles.

Today Péronne, 33 km/20 miles to the south-west, is a tranquil town on the lagoons of the Somme. It was almost destroyed during World War I. The recently opened Historial de la Grande Guerre is an impressive new Museum of the Great War, with five exhibition rooms, beginning at Europe in 1914, progressing to an audiovisual room showing rare film footage of the Battle of the Somme, and finishing with the aftermath of the war.

La Terrine has been a *charcuterie* since before World War I. Inside is a photograph of it in 1918, one of only three houses left standing in rue des Liniers, Cambrai.

Exploring further

There are many other centres of battlefield exploration: at Verdun; along the Marne; on the Normandy coast; at Ypres in Belgium; and at Arnhem in the Netherlands.

Arras and Cambrai Fact File

ARRAS from **Calais** A26 100km/62 miles. **Postal zip code** 62000. **Tourist information** Beffroi, Hôtel de Ville, place des Héros. Tel 21 51 26 95. Fax 21 71 07 34. ***Open*** *15 May-Sept* daily 9am-6pm; *Oct-14 May* Mon-Sat 9am-noon, 2-6pm, Sun 10am-noon, 3-6.30pm. **Parking** station car park; place Victor-Hugo; off the NE corner of Grand'Place.

CAMBRAI from **Calais** A26 140km/88 miles. **Postal zip code** 59400. **Tourist information** 48 rue de Noyon. Tel 27 78 36 15. Fax 27 74 82 82. ***Open*** Mon-Sat 9am-noon, 2-6pm. **Parking** place Aristide-Briand, town centre.

SIGHTSEEING

ARRAS

Ask at the tourist office for details of guided tours (for individuals or groups) around the town and to also Vauban's Citadel nearby.

Abbaye de St-Vaast/Musée des Beaux-Arts 22 rue Paul-Doumer. Tel 21 71 26 43. ***Open*** *Apr-Sept* Mon, Wed-Fri 10am-noon, 2-6pm, Sat 2-6pm, Sun 10am-noon, 3-6pm; *Oct-Mar* Mon, Wed-Fri 10am-noon, 2-5pm, Sat 10am-noon, 2-6pm, Sun 10am-noon, 3-6pm.

Hôtel de Ville (Town Hall), **Beffroi** (Belfry), and **Les Boves** place des Héros. ***Open*** *15 May-Sept* daily 9am-6pm; *Oct-14 May* Mon-Sat 9am-noon, 2-6pm, Sun 10am-noon, 3-6.30pm.

CAMBRAI

Eglise St-Géry rue St-Aubert, Cambrai.

CAMPING

Arras municipal campsite off the N17, S of Arras. Tel 21 71 55 06. ***Open*** *Apr-Oct.*

EATING AND DRINKING

ARRAS

L'Ambassadeur place de la Gare. Tel 21 23 29 80. A pleasant railway buffet serving simple dishes. ***Closed*** Sun evening. Menus from £16 to £ 25.

La Brouette 14 rue St-Aubert. Tel 21 71 14 00. A cellar restaurant. From £10.

La Faisanderie 45 Grand'Place. Tel 21 48 20 76. An outstanding restaurants, in an elegantly renovated cellar. From £25.

La Rapière 44 Grand'Place. Tel 21 55 09 92. A cellar restaurant. From £10.

Le Victor Hugo 11 place Victor-Hugo. Tel 21 71 84 00. From about £25.

Arras

Centred on majestic open market squares, surrounded by Flemish façades, the proud city of Arras has been almost entirely rebuilt from the rubble created by the devastation of two world wars.

From Arras's fine flamboyant Gothic Hôtel de Ville , visitors are guided down to *Les Boves*, a network of cellars and underground tunnels spreading beneath the town centre. The first caves were cut into the chalk hillside on which Arras is built before the end of the first millennium. Some chambers have Romanesque arches, or Gothic vaulting; some have fine pillars and tiled floors. The people of Arras sheltered in these caverns when the Dukes of Burgundy took possession of the town in 1384; when it was captured by the Prince of Orange; again in 1479, when it was taken by Louis XI; when it was taken by the Spanish, retaken by Richelieu in 1640, and attacked again by the Spanish in 1655. They last became a refuge from attack by the Germans in World War I, when they were used as a barracks and a clearing hospital for British troops defending the city.

Above *Les Boves* spread the two enormous cobbled squares of central Arras, a tribute to the aesthetic sensitivity of city aldermen, who between 1670 and 1780 permitted building only to approved designs. The squares are surrounded by gabled, Flemish brick-and-stone houses, their façades resting on pillars, forming an arcaded walk at pavement level. The oldest house, No. 47 Grand'Place, called 'The Three Leopards', has a stepped gable and a 15th-century watchtower.

Arras was created a bishopric in the early centuries AD. Its first cathedral, destroyed by the Vandals in the 5th century, was rebuilt in the 12th century, only to be sold during the Revolution and demolished in 1812. St-Vaast, built as a chapel for a Benedictine monastery, was consecrated to replace it in 1833. It is a neo-classical building, begun in 1773 by Contant d'Ivry, architect of the Madeleine Church in Paris. The Revolution interrupted its building in 1793, and bombing destroyed it in 1914-18. The restored building reopened in 1934.

Its Roman predecessor was destroyed by the barbarians in the 5th century AD, and since then Arras has been destroyed and rebuilt time and again. World War I trenches were dug into the great squares, and one-third of their 155 surrounding houses were bombed. From the top of the painstakingly reconstructed *beffroi* (belfry) you can see across the town to Vauban's great 17th-century *citadelle*, built to protect the city from the Spanish. In the farther distance lie the more recent battlefields of 20th-century wars: Vimy Ridge, Notre-Dame-de-Lorette, and the Hindenburg Line.

Famous in the Middle Ages as a textile-manufacturing town, in particular for woollen cloth, Arras became especially renowned for its high-warp tapestries, competing with the town of Tournai, now in Belgium.

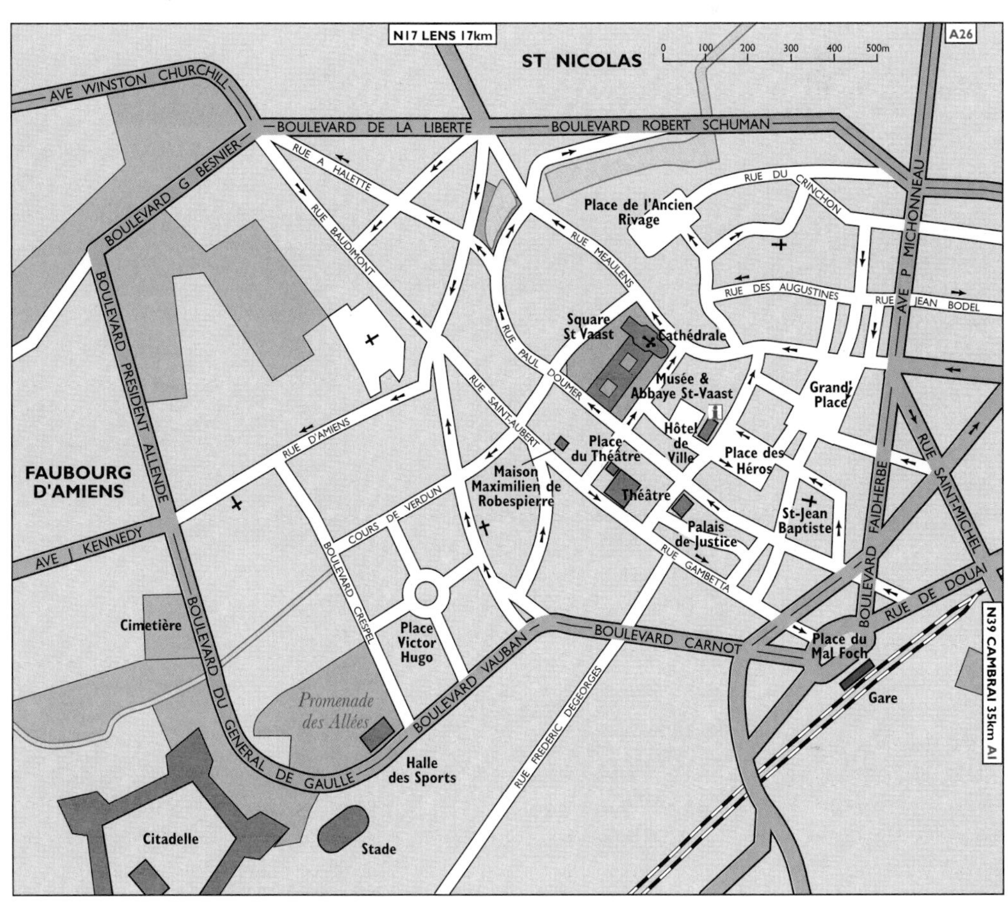

The oldest of the 17th-century gabled houses (below) surrounding the Grand'Place and Petite Place in Arras is now an attractive hotel. There are shops and cafés in the covered pavement arcades.

Bruges & Northern Belgium

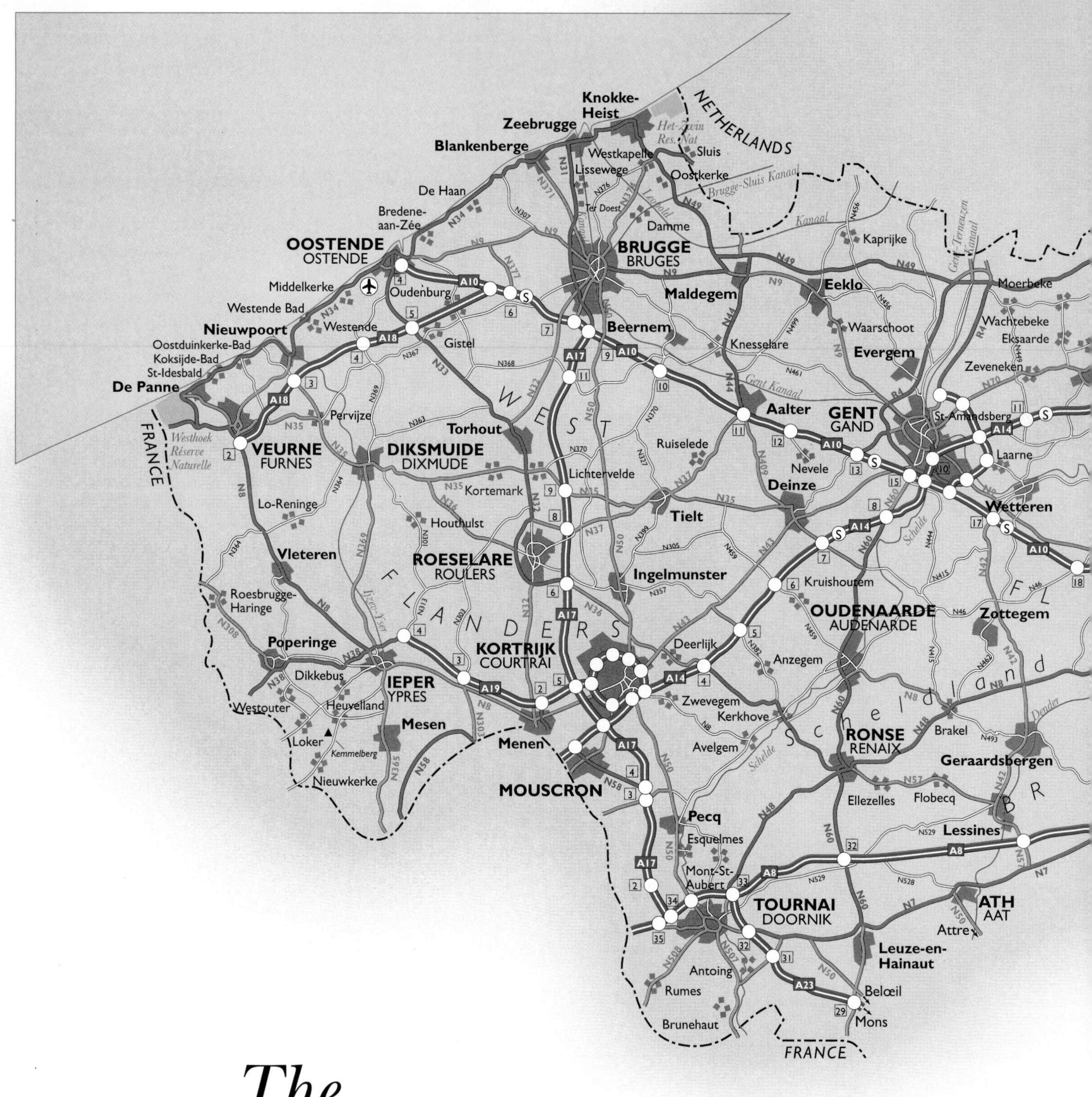

The Flanders coast

By contrast with the cliffs and shingles of Britain's southern seaboard, the coast of Flanders – only 70 km/44 miles from end to end – is fringed with sands so long and wide in places that beaches away from the resorts seem almost empty, even on hot August days.

Belgium has put its biggest and busiest seaside resorts on show, just inside its borders. De Panne, near France, is large and popular enough to draw crowds for occasional big-name rock concerts on the beach in summer. But high rise is minimised and there are over 4 km/2 miles of wide beaches and wooded dunes to walk along and ride through, stretching westward into France and east to the broad sands at Oostduinkerke-Bad.

Previous pages: Bruges is as beautiful in daylight as at night, when buildings and monuments are spotlit. Insets: It is equally famed for its buildings, such as the Church of Our Lady, its lace and its breweries.

Brush screens make effective windbreaks, and sand dunes double as sun traps along the Belgian coast (right).

The resort the Belgians like to be seen in is Knokke-Heist near the Dutch border, an 11-km/7-mile chain of beaches and promenades, but with a sprawl of apartment blocks and retirement suburbs behind. Prices in Knokke are so high the Belgians reputedly go to shop there just to impress their friends. The resort has a casino, discos, night clubs, and a long list of sports facilities – international-standard golf courses, water-skiing centres, bowling alleys, and courts for racquet sports.

Best beaches

West of Ostende (Oostende in Flemish) the sands narrow, and many resorts are backed by high-rise developments, but from Ostende eastward the tower blocks and promenades disappear and the beaches widen. Bredene-aan-Zee has a seafront of broad dunes undulating down to the shore, and is popular with campers. De Haan, north-east of Ostende, is a gem, the resort a miscellany of turn-of-the-century villas and the seafront a nature reserve of long, empty sands and wild, grassy, wooded dunes.

Oostduinkerke-Bad and Knokke-Heist have seawater swimming pools on the beach for those who don't want to walk far out to sea to swim at low tide. Nieuwpoort and Ostende have heated outdoor pools, and all resorts have indoor pools for when the wind blows cold off the sea. (The Belgian coast claims more days of sun, less rain, and closer proximity to the outer edges of the Gulf Stream than southern Britain. But note the ingenious windbreaks on the beaches: natural grasses, canvas screens, wooden chalets ...) Belgium may have better beaches, but on the weather stakes it levels with Britain.

Dune country

The Flanders coast begins and ends with a nature reserve, and there are at least ten others in between, all trying to conserve a different type of dune landscape, flora and fauna. The oldest is the Calmeybos, part of the Westhoek reserve beside the French border. Maurice Calmeyn was a Belgian botanist who in 1903 began to experiment with plants with roots that would bind the dunes and prevent erosion. His experimental plantation is now a woodland of salt- and wind-resistant trees. Nature treks along the reserves' marked paths, aided by maps and leaflets from the tourist office about plants, birds and animals to spot, are a favourite activity all along the coast.

Ostende

Uninterrupted sands (left) stretch from Westende to Ostende ('Eastend'), and farther eastwards, giving Ostende 8 km/5 miles of beaches. The port is Belgium's natural centre for cross-country rail and motorway networks, and transport links along the coast. It also has shipbuilding and other industries – yet despite all this, it's a surprisingly nice town and a pleasant place to spend a day.

Attacks during successive wars destroyed the medieval town, but in the 19th century, Ostende was adopted as the King of Belgium's royal residence, and became one of Europe's most fashionable resorts. The James Ensorhuis at Vlaanderenstraat 27 was the home and studio of the artist, James Ensor, whose father was English and mother was from Ostende. His paintings also hang in the Fine Art museum. He was buried outside the Onze Lieve Vrouw ter Duinen Kerk, Ostende's oldest building, dating partly from the 14th century.

Strolling along Ostende's gracious Albert I Promenade is as popular a pastime as in the town's aristocratic past. Favourite local sports are horse-racing in season at the Wellington Hippodrome and fishing from the pier – where there are no smelly burger bars, just the scent of the sea mingling with the aroma of good Belgian coffee served in a little café at the end. Judging by the abundant restaurants and cafés, Ostenders do nothing but eat. The town has at least one Michelin-starred restaurant, and although cuisine quality is not always high by Belgian standards, in the cheaper places, fish, especially mussels cooked every way and always served with chips, are a safe bet here as elsewhere on the coast.

Ostende is famous for its Carnival in March – the *Bal du Rat Mort*, named after a Montmartre cabaret, is one of the biggest and grandest carnival balls in Europe – and for its October beer festival. The town is also the coast's focus for evening entertainment, with discos and night clubs (and a red-light district – inevitable in an international port). The casino is a cultural centre, staging opera, ballet, classical music, and various concerts. And there's gambling, from 3pm daily.

Ostende Fact File

OSTENDE (Flemish **Oostende**) from **Calais** N1/N39 91 km/57 miles. To: **Bruges** N9 24 km/16 miles; **Gent** A10 59 km/37 miles; **Ypres** N33/ N369 50 km/ 30 miles; **Brussels** A10 107 km/67 miles; **Antwerp** N49/N9 115 km/72 miles.
Postal zip code 8400-Oostende
Tourist information Monacoplein 2. Tel 059 70 11 99. Fax 059 70 34 77.

CAMPING
De Haan
Camping Holiday Village (turn off A10 Gent-Ostende road towards De Haan and follow signs). Tel 059 23 63 41.
Knokke-Heist
Camping de Vuurtoren (on N300, on SW edge of town). Tel 050 51 17 82. ***Open*** *Mar-Oct.*
Westende
Camping Zon end Duin (signposted from town). Tel 058 23 50 51.
K.A.C.B. Camping (leave N34 Ostende-Blankenberge road at NE edge of Bredene and follow signs). Tel 059 23 7343.

FOR CHILDREN
There are extensive facilities and entertainments on the beaches and in the resorts (contact the local tourist offices for details), plus several leisure parks:
Meli Recreational Park, De Pannelaan (Adinkerke-De Panne). Tel 058 42 01 54. ***Open*** daily *Apr-Sept* from 9.30am. An amusement park with over 30 attractions, including a fairground, a bowling alley and a zoo. All-in ticket about £10 per visitor.
Ostende: Maria Hendrika-park with fish ponds, playing fields and boating lakes.
Paelsteenveld outside **Bredene**. Recreation park with a children's playground and sports.
Sand train – a railway over the dunes from **De Panne** to **Dunkerque**, France, through the Westhoek nature reserve. **Trips** *Jul, Aug* 10am Sun and public holidays, from Adinkerke, De Panne. Returns 6pm. Contact the tourist office for details.
Velodrome at **Blankenberge**. ***Open*** *Easter-15 Sept.* About 75p. Crazy cycling on a board track.

Belgium's *medieval* cities

Tiny Belgium is graced with a higher concentration of well-preserved medieval towns than any other European country. Their origins were vastly different. Tournai, first a Roman fort on the military road from Cologne, became the royal capital of the Franks. Gent grew up around two abbeys founded in the seventh century. Antwerp began as a Viking fortress, and Ypres as a stopping point on a trade route.

After the 9th century, Flanders became increasingly prosperous as the natural focus for a rising trade in wool with England. Merchants built new markets, wharves and warehouses beside ecclesiastical palaces, abbeys and fortresses, and gradually replaced the old buildings with great guildhouses, magnificent churches, and protective ramparts. Over succeeding centuries, as trade expanded, the medieval town achieved its finest flowering in Flanders.

Medieval merchants' houses mix with more modern buildings in Gent. Some of the oldest date from the 13th century.

Gent

Children with an interest in the gruesome are fascinated by the tour of the dungeons beneath the keep of Gent's spectacular fortress. Its name, *'s Gravensteen*, meaning 'the Gravestone' is the apt Flemish name for the Castle of the Counts. Its grey walls enclose a chilling medieval prison and adjoining torture chamber. Instruments of torture in the museum range from thumbscrews and branding irons to a rack and a guillotine.

The cellars are the oldest part of the 9th-century castle of the Counts of Flanders. It was built by the first count as the seat of the ruling dynasty of an increasingly independent Flanders. The tour takes in the 12th-century gateway and towering ramparts – with lookout turrets, machicolations (holes through which boiling oil was poured over attackers) and latrines (reeking openings in the walls, overhanging the moat).

Guided boat trips along the central canals tour around the castle's looming walls. The quay, nearby in the old city port, is overlooked by the decorative gabled guildhouses and town houses built along the Graslei and Kornlei by rich merchants. Another trip takes you along the Gent-Bruges Canal, dug through the marshes during the 13th century to bring English wool from Bruges.

A good way to get to know the charming old town is to follow the walks mapped out by the tourist office (conveniently located in the flamboyantly decorated Stadhuis). They take you through the chain of central market squares to the winding narrow streets of Petershol, the old 17th-century Flemish quarter east of the castle, and along the canals to the south and west.

The 14th-century belfry, with pealing chimes and carillon, is the central landmark. It dominates St Baaf's square, while St Baaf's Cathedral, Gent's finest church, begun in the 15th century, is tucked into its eastern corner. The church contains outstanding works of medieval art, including Van Eyck's huge masterpiece, the *Adoration of the Mystical Lamb.* In the nearby late Gothic St Michielskerk are works by Gaspard de Crayer and others, and the collections in the Museum voor Schone Kunsten (Fine Arts Museum) include masterpieces by Hieronymus Bosch and Pieter Brueghel the Younger.

Character and nightlife

Gent, capital of East Flanders, still rivals Bruges – as an art town. But it is also Belgium's second port, a major producer of flowers, and a thriving university city – a voluble café society operates into the small hours among its many architectural treasures. Gent has more than 20

Belgian belfries

Belfries in the Low Countries have their origins in the very foundations of the towns they guard, when rulers granted the 'right to a bell'; the city charters used to be stored in the lower storey of Gent's belfry. The 12th-century belfry of Tournai, now being restored, is the region's oldest.

On the spire of Gent's 14th-century belfry is a gilded copper dragon (below), eternally on guard – dragons reputedly never sleep – from its vantage point 65 m/214 ft above the city. Built on to the belfry is the former city gaol, and the draughty watchmen's rooms inside the belfry once served as civic meeting places and refuges at times of attack. One is now a small museum of belfry life, with rows of retired bells on shelves, and the skeletal remains of a once-daunting medieval dragon.

The guided tour takes you in a glass lift to Level 3, where the machinery that clicks and whirrs the *carillon* (bell) into action is explained; and Level 4, where 17th-century Triomfante bongs out the time every 15 minutes. A spiralling stone staircase leads to the balcony and a magnificent view over Gent, and on to the vertiginous heights of the *carillon*, where 51 bells, most cast in the 16th century, chime snatches of Mozart and other tunes to the crowds in the square below. The *carillon* can work automatically, but a *carillon* player gives regular concerts in summer from a small bellside gallery.

Gent Fact File

GENT (French **Gand**, English **Ghent**) from **Calais** A18/A10 146 km/93 miles.
Postal zip code 9000-Gent
Tourist information Stadhuis Botermarkt. Tel 092 24 15 55. Fax 092 25 62 88 ***Open*** daily *7 Nov-14 Apr* 9.30am-4.30pm; *2 Apr-7 Nov* 9.30am-6.30pm.
Parking Burgemeester Braunplein (W of belfry); 20BF coins, max. 2 hours. Vrijdagmarkt (two streets N of Stadthuis). Tourist office map shows city car parks.

CAMPING
Camping Blaarmeersen Zuiderlaan 12, 9000-Gent (leave A10 Brussels-Ostende road at Gent-West/Drongen exit, follow Drongen road 5 km/3 miles towards Gent). Tel 092 21 53 99. ***Open*** *Mar-15 Oct.*

SIGHTSEEING
Guided walking tours leave tourist office 2.30pm daily *Apr-Oct.* About £3/2 hrs.
Horse-drawn carriages from St Baaf's square *Easter-Sept* daily 10am-7pm. About £6 per carriage/30 mins.
Boat trips from Kornlei/Graslei quay *Apr-Oct* daily 10am-7pm every 15 min. About £2.50 adults, under-12s free/35 mins.
's Gravensteen (Castle of the Counts of Flanders) Geldmunt. ***Open*** daily 9am-5.15pm (last ticket 4.30pm). About £1.50, children 75p, under-12s free. **Guided tours**. The museum of torture has some grisly illustrations and is unsuitable for young and nervous children.

FOR CHILDREN
Puppet theatres: Museum of Folklore Kraanlei 65 in the Petershol district. About £1 adults, 50p children 6-12s, under-6s free.

theatres. Most productions are in Flemish, but there are puppets, mime and cabaret. It has five cinemas, often showing films in English; numerous nightclubs and discos, and good, up-to-date live music. Plus, of course, hundreds of restaurants, streetside cafés, and excellent beer bars.

Ypres

At 9pm on summer evenings, the *carillon* in the immense square belfry above Ypres' Cloth Hall peals out over the Grote Markt. In the northern areas of the Low Countries, belfries were never ecclesiastical buildings, with bells to call people to church. They were watch towers – their bells used to summon the locality to arms or warn of disaster – and symbols of municipal autonomy and pride. Obvious targets for an enemy, they were always rebuilt when damaged or destroyed.

In the 600 years of its history, Ypres' belfry survived half a dozen major wars and countless attacks on the city, finally to be destroyed by the German artillery bombardment which devastated the entire town in November 1914. The Cloth Hall and belfry were rebuilt, a faithful copy of the original, in the 1930s.

In 1201, when Ypres' Cloth Hall was begun, the medieval textile cities of the Low Countries competed in building sumptuous civic buildings. The Cloth Hall, 135 m/440 ft long and decorated with carvings, spires, and its immense central tower, outshone all. When completed in 1304 it was Europe's outstanding secular building. You can best appreciate the imposing façade – with sections of the original on the lower storey – from the pavement cafés around the vast, restored Grote Markt.

Rebuilding and restoration after attack has been a fact of life in the Low Countries since towns were founded there. St Martin's Cathedral was only completed during its post-World War I restoration – the cloister dates from the 12th century; the cathedral was reconstructed to its original plan in the 1930s – and the spire, planned for centuries ago but never built – was added then. Many other old buildings were reconstructed after 1918, making modern Ypres a pleasant base for its major tourist industry: exploring the surrounding memorials and battlefields of World War I.

Ypres Fact File

YPRES (Flemish **Ieper**) from **Calais** N1/N225/A25/N38 96 km/60 miles.
Postal zip code 8900-Ieper
Tourist information Stadhuis (E end of Cloth Hall) Grote Markt. Tel 057 20 07 24. ***Open*** *Apr-Sept* Mon-Fri 9am-5.30pm, Sat, Sun 9.30am-5.30pm; *Oct-Mar* Mon-Sat 9am-5pm, Sun 11am-4pm.
Parking on Grote Markt.

SIGHTSEEING
Guided tours by arrangement. Ask at the tourist office or telephone 057 20 26 23.
Signposted tour for cars: **Hop Route** through hop-growing area to National Hop Museum Gasthuisstraat 71, Poperinge ***Open*** *Jul-Aug* daily 2.30-5.30pm; *May, June-Sept* Sun 2.30-5.30pm. About £1.

FOR CHILDREN
Bellewaerde Amusement Park 5 km/3 miles E of Ypres off E17 (take A19 exit towards Ypres, then exit 3). Tel 057 46 86 86. ***Open*** *Apr-June, Sept* daily 10am-6pm; *Jul-Aug* daily 9.30am-7pm. About £7 (check with tourist office for changes). Flanders' biggest amusement park, with a zoo, a jungle, a lake, a river with rapids and a pirate boat, and special events.

The Ypres Salient

At the start of World War I in August 1914, the Germans surprised the Allies by invading neutral Belgium. Belgian, French and British resistance was quickly overcome, but in October the Allies established a front along the Yser River. The Germans concentrated on attacking the British lines around Ypres, but failed to break through, and both sides dug in. There followed nearly three years of trench warfare along a front established between Nieuwpoort on the Belgian coast and the Swiss border. Attacks focused on two salients (bulges) in the German lines around Ypres and Verdun. The deadlock broke after a renewed offensive in June 1917 by British and Commonwealth troops on Mesen, south of Ypres, and by French, British and US forces in France.

More than 150 cemeteries and dozens of memorials to divisions and regiments, battles, individuals, and the courageous Belgian resistance cover the countryside for miles around Ypres. The tourist office publishes a driving tour of a 40km/25mile '14-18' Route around the north-east area of the Salient.

No tour should miss the Salient Museum in the Ypres Stadhuis; the city's moving Menin Gate Memorial to the armies of the British Empire and their dead, or the simple but intensely poignant Sanctuary Wood Trenches Museum (off the N8) where a length of trench (below) has been left undisturbed since the war ended, with bomb craters and blackened, shattered trees in the surrounding wood. A small museum in a shed shows mud- and rust-encrusted articles that have been found in the ground. Evocative photographs and bioscopes convey something of the horrific reality of the futile deaths of millions of men and horses, and the devastation of Ypres and vast stretches of Belgium.

Above: Decorative details on many of the older buildings in Antwerp reflect its wealthy history as a trading centre.

Antwerp

Belgium's second largest city, and capital of the province of the same name, Antwerp (Antwerpen in Flemish, Anvers in French) seems an unlikely tourist spot. But modern development has been confined, sensitively, to the outskirts, and the old town retains much of its Flemish Renaissance character.

At the end of the Middle Ages, Antwerp was a small frontier town clustering around an ancient fortress – the Steen – on the right bank of the river Schelde. As silt blocked Bruges' river route to the sea, Antwerp rose to prominence, because its broad river outlet allowed it to take over as Flanders' principal port. Merchants, guilds and financiers moved there, initiating a golden age of prosperity. The new guildhouses, churches, abbeys, and mansions they commissioned were built in the Flemish Renaissance style, strongly tinged with Baroque.

The town became an artistic centre. Pieter Paul Rubens, court painter to Antwerp's ruler in the 17th century, led an elite of Flemish artists living and working there, including Jacob Jordaens and Pieter Brueghel the Younger. Their major works are in the city's museums.

Art and architecture

The Stadhuis (Town Hall), the Beurs (Stock Exchange), the Vleeshuis (House of the Guild of Butchers), and the gabled guildhouses around the complex of cobbled central squares, are among the town's many civic buildings dating from this period of expansion. Antwerp's graceful Cathedral of Our Lady survives from the medieval town. It is Belgium's largest and one of its most notable Gothic cathedrals.

Three religious paintings by Rubens hang in the cathedral, and there are others in the 17th-century Huis Rockox, the house of the Antwerp burgomaster, a friend of Rubens. A late work hangs in the Rubens Chapel in the Gothic St Jacobskerk, where the artist is buried; and his sketches are displayed in the Rubenshuis, where he lived and painted. There are works by Rubens, van Dyck, Jordaens, and many other artists in the Maagdenhuis, a former orphanage, the 16th-century St Pauluskerk and the Mayer van den Bergh Museum; and major collections in the Museum voor Schone Kunsten (Fine Arts Museum). The Ridder Smidt van Gelder Museum has collections of decorative arts; and the Plantin-Moretus Museum has early printing machines, books and prints.

Pickles on display in all shapes of bottles, are among the specialities found in Antwerp's central shopping area.

Atmosphere and nightlife

There are boat trips along the Schelde and around the docks, walks and cafés along the waterfront, a beach on the river's right bank, wide squares in the old town, and parks and gardens dotted here and there. But Antwerp is an industrial port, seedy in places, with a red-light district (predictably in Schipperskwartier, the dock area), and is hard to drive around, not a summer holiday resort. Its cultural vivacity and its nightlife are its social attractions – and it is lively into the small hours, all year round.

The tourist office produces events lists of theatre productions, ballet and contemporary dance, opera and music, modern art and photography. There are good cafés and beer bars around Grote Markt and Groenplaats – Groene Ongenoegen at Jeruzalemstraat 9 claims the longest beer list in Belgium, including the local dark Bolleke Koninck. Discos and nightclubs centre on the station area, around Statiestraat.

Like every international port, Antwerp's restaurants represent a high proportion of the world's cuisines, and the quality is high. You find French and Belgian haute cuisine; Flemish mussel dishes, (especially around Suikerrui); Spanish tapas bars; Italian, South American, African, and vegetarian food; and eateries from the Orient (there is a Chinatown on Van Wesenbekstraat). Ask at the tourist office for details.

Antwerp Fact File

ANTWERP (Flemish **Antwerpen**, French **Anvers**) from **Calais** N1/N39/A18/A10/N44/N49 201 km/126 miles. To **Ostende** N9/N49 115 km/72 miles; **Bruges** N49/N9 91 km/56 miles; **Gent** A14 53 km/33 miles; **Tournai** N48/N60/A14 120 km/75 miles; **Brussels** A19 47 km/25 miles.
Postal zip code: 2000-Antwerpen
Tourist information Grote Markt 15. Tel 03 232 01 03. Fax 03 231 19 37.
Open Mon-Sat 9am-6pm; Sun 9am-5pm. **Centraal Station** Koningin Astridplein
Open Mon-Fri 8.30am-8pm; Sat 9am-7pm; Sun 9am-5pm. Tel 03 204 20 40.
Parking between Gilderkamersstraat and Kaasstraat near tourist offices; opposite the station. A tourist office map shows parking around town.

SIGHTSEEING
Walking tours tourist office publishes signposted themed walks such as the Rubens Walk.
Guided walks cost about £20 for a group for 2 hrs – contact the tourist office.
Horse-drawn carriages operate *Easter-May* weekends noon-6pm; *Jul-Aug* daily 11am-7pm. Check with tourist office.
Boat trips on the Scheldt from a quay near the Steen *Apr-Sept* daily 10am-4.30pm. About £3.75/1 hr; £5/2 hrs. Check with tourist office for details of trips to the docks and other destinations.

FOR CHILDREN
Royal Puppet Theatre Van Campen Lange Nieuwstraat 3 – one of four puppet theatres. Details from the tourist office.

CAMPING
Stedelijk Kampeerterrein Jan van Rijswijcklaan (on S side of city, look for Crest Hotel; access via ring road exit 5). Tel 02 38 57 17. ***Open*** *Apr-Sept.*

Tournai Fact File

TOURNAI (Flemish **Doornik**) from **Calais** N1/N225/A25/N27/N7 142 km/89 miles; to **Bruges** N50/A17 94 km/59 miles; **Gent** N50/A14/N60/N48 67 km/42 miles; **Ostende** A10/N50/A17 109 km/68 miles; **Ypres** N38/A19/A17/N7 75km/47 miles; **Antwerp** A14/N60/N48 120 km/75 miles; **Brussels** N7/A7 81km/51 miles.
Postal zip code 7500-Tournai
Tourist information rue du Vieux Marché-aux-Poteries 14 (opposite belfry). Tel 069 22 20 45. Fax 069 21 62 21. ***Open*** Mon-Fri 9am-7pm; Sat-Sun 10am-1pm, 3-6pm.
Parking place St-Pierre near the cathedral. A tourist office map shows parking zones and lists tariffs.

SIGHTSEEING
Walking tour tourist office maps give marked routes in the centre and outskirts.
Horse-drawn carriages operate from 2pm weekends only *Easter-June* and Tue-Sun *Jul-Aug.* About £10 per tour (max. 5).
Boat trips from quay near the Pont des Trous *May-Aug* daily 11am, 2.30-4.15pm. About 75p adults, 40p children.

EATING AND DRINKING
The tourist office publishes a list of restaurants (French, Flemish, Italian, Vietnamese) and bars.
Bistro de la Cathédrale 15 Vieux Marché-aux-Poteries. Tel 069 21 03 79. ***Open*** daily 10am–11pm. A bistro specialising in Flemish food, with a list of 50 beers.
Le Pinacle 1 Vieux Marché-aux-Poteries. ***Open*** daily 10am-1am or later. A beer bar with a long list, serving snacks.

Tournai Cathedral (opposite, right) miraculously escaped damage from the bombing that flattened the Grand-Place. It is built of grey Tournai marble, which influenced the Tournai school of architecture and sculpture.

Tournai

The Schelde River, on which Antwerp's prosperity turned, begins its course through Belgium in the south, at the village of Brunehaut on the French border, marked by a menhir, a prehistoric standing stone. It meanders through the hilly *pays blanc* countryside, where limestone was first quarried by the Romans, past the 12th-century walls of the Château d'Antoing, to Tournai, one of Belgium's oldest towns and earliest bishoprics. A boat trip along this pretty river from the quay beside the 13th-century Pont des Trous – a survival, with its flanking towers, of the medieval ramparts destroyed by the English in the 16th century – takes you through this charming town, which the river bisects before winding on to Gent.

Towering over the centre, its five distinctive towers forever catching the eye as you explore the town, is the Cathédrale de Notre-Dame, with a lofty, light Romanesque nave, and a choir of equal length which is the first example of Gothic architecture in Belgium. Inside there are Romanesque murals, 16th-century stained glass, a rare 14th-century Arras tapestry, and masterpieces by Rubens, Jordaens and Pourbus. In the Treasury Museum is a jewelled Byzantine cross-reliquary.

Tournai is an art town. The Musée des Beaux Arts (Fine Arts Museum) displays paintings by Tournai artists, such as Rogier Van der Weyden; the Flemish artists Jan Brueghel and Pieter Brueghel the Younger; and two Impressionists, Edouard Manet and Claude Monet. The cathedral and the Museée d'Histoire et d'Archéologie have examples of Tournai porcelain, and there is a museum of Tournai tapestries. The Beaux Arts was designed by Victor Horta, the Belgian pioneer of Art Nouveau, and there are many Art Nouveau houses to be seen on walks around the town.

Life in Tournai is quiet and slow. The tourist office has details of current films and theatre in the Cultural Centre, there are good restaurants, and the evening hours can be pleasantly whiled away in the bars on the Grand-Place. But night life is confined to a few discos (there's no red-light district: Bishop's orders). So Tournai really is a place for a restful break from noise and stress.

In the course of its history, Tournai has belonged to Flanders, Hainaut, France, England, the Spanish Netherlands, and Austria. Today it makes a good base for visiting some of the many castles in this formerly turbulent region – Antoing nearby, Ath and Attre, and Beloeil near Mons, Hainaut's capital – worth a day trip to see its museums.

Henry VIII's Tower

The Tour Henri VIII in the leafy place Vert was the keep of a citadel built to garrison English troops in the 16th century. Tournai was a French possession from the late 12th century, and Henry VIII seized the town when at war with France. The tower has a small museum of arms and armour as well as some illuminated manuscripts, including a psalter said to have been used by Henry himself. The museum also commemorates the Belgian Resistance during the World Wars. Henry's psalter is one of only 23 illuminated manuscripts that survived the heavy German air bombardment that destroyed the City Archive in May 1940.

Bruges

Once a powerful trading port close to a North Sea estuary, Bruges is almost surrounded by water. Its narrow cobbled streets and peaceful old squares are linked by picturesque waterways spanned by the 50 bridges that give the town its name. Bruges is the capital of West Flanders, and the gallery for the region's most remarkable art collections. It has some of the best-preserved medieval buildings in Europe.

One of Bruges' most famous landmarks, the 13th-century belfry, towers 86m/266 ft above the central market building, the Halle.

Bruges (Brugge in Flemish) was founded more than a millennium ago. It grew within a stronghold built by the first Count of Flanders as a defence against Norse raiders – the encircling canal and the four gates of the old town mark the course of its 9th-century fortifications. In medieval times Bruges became a great centre for the manufacture of cloth and clothes from wool imported from England, and a focus for European trade in rare and costly goods. By the 14th century, the city had become the principal market and banking centre of the Hanseatic League, an association of medieval trading cities. So wealthy did its burghers become, they were famed for their luxurious lifestyle.

What to see

Bruges' finest buildings – the Gruuthuse, a former mansion; the Stadhuis, or Town Hall; St-Salvatore Cathedral (St Saviour's Cathedral), the Basiliek Heilig Bloed (Basilica of the Holy Blood), and the Onze Lieve Vrouwekerk (Church of Our Lady), an early Gothic church with the tallest spire in Belgium – all date from this prosperous era. The Groeninge and Gruuthuse museums, and the Memling Museum in Sint Jans Hospitaal display many great works of fine and decorative art commissioned by medieval Bruges' wealthiest citizens.

The decline of the wool trade and the silting up of the Zwin estuary, its outlet to the sea, weakened Bruges' industrial and trading base. By the middle of the 16th century it was becoming an industrial outpost. Its decline and isolation can be thanked for the town's excellent state of preservation – some buildings are replicas or restored, but there are so many architectural treasures to see that wandering around, 'just looking', is the most favoured tourist activity in this atmospheric spot.

When to go

Summer is high season in Bruges. The threading waterways edged with trees and flowers, and the placid Minnewater – the once-clamorous central dock of the medieval port, rechristened the Lake of Love – are cool and relaxing on hot days. But tourism is now Bruges' main industry. From May or June until September, throngs of chattering visitors crowd the narrow streets from mid-morning to late evening, fill the cafés, bars, restaurants, hotels, and dozens of seasonal tourist shops, and have the museum tour guides, canal boats and horse-drawn carriages working to rush-hour schedules.

Bruges is at its best out of season. The Begijnhof, a charming group of convent buildings founded 800 years ago, is at its most beautiful in early spring, when the central garth is bright with daffodils. Most festivals take place at the time of the spring blossom and early flowers. The major museums and galleries are less crowded between October – when the trees turn the same glorious golden colour as the mellow gabled brick buildings – and March. A crisp wintry look to the canals seems appropriate in Flanders, and when it is chilly there are pleasant cafés to warm up in.

Redolent of the past, Bruges is perfect for short, tranquil breaks from stress and pressure, and an important stop for any lover of art, artefacts, or architecture. Only an hour away from northern Belgium's major tourist towns, it makes a good base for sorties to explore the region. Illuminated buildings reflected in still water make this lovely town a romantic place on fine evenings; good beer bars, and more than 300 restaurants serving Belgian, French, and oriental cooking make drinking and dining in picturesque surroundings an option at the most reasonable prices. But Bruges is not a night spot. Although there are several cinemas with repertoires of films in English, the theatre is mainly Belgian, there is little live music, only one night club, and out of season the town lives up to its epithet *Bruges-la-mort.* Night owls might plan to take in Bruges on a day trip from livelier Ostende or Gent. Or a series of day trips. Those magnificent museums need time.

Bruges Fact File

BRUGES (Flemish **Brugge**) from **Calais** N1/N39/A18 107 km/ 68 miles. To: **Ostende** N9 24 km/16 miles; **Gent** A10 44 km/27 miles; **Ypres** N32/N313 53 km/33 miles; **Brussels** A10 83 km/53 miles; **Tournai** A17/N50 94 km/ 59 miles; **Antwerp** N9/N44/N49 91 km/56 miles.
Tourist information Burg 11 8000-Brugge. Tel: 050 44 86 86. Fax 050 44 86 00. ***Open*** *Apr-Sept* daily 9.30am-6.30pm; *Oct-Mar* Mon-Fri 9.30am-5pm, Sat 9.30am-5.30pm. The tourist office runs guided walking tours *Jul-Aug* daily 3pm.
Parking 't Zand; underground Dweerstraat, Naaldenstraat, Katelijnestraat. Cars are discouraged by heavy fees.

SIGHTSEEING
Basiliek Heilig Bloed (Basilica of the Holy Blood) Burg 13. ***Open*** *Apr-Sept* daily 9.30am-noon, 2-6pm; *Oct-Mar* Mon, Wed-Sun 10am-noon, 2-4pm.
Belfry and Halle, Markt. ***Open*** *Apr-Sept* daily 9.30am-5pm; *Oct-Mar* daily 9.30am-12.30pm, 1.30-5pm. Carillon concerts Mon, Wed, Sat 2-3pm.
Beguinhof Wijngaardplein. ***Open*** *Apr-Sept* Mon-Sat 10am-noon, 1.45-5.30pm, Sun 10.45am-noon, 1.45-6pm. *Oct-Mar* Wed-Thur, Sat-Sun 2.45-4.15pm, Fri 1.45pm-6pm. Old convent and church.
Groeninge Museum Dijver 12. ***Open*** daily *Apr-Sept* 9.30am-5pm; *Oct-Mar* Mon, Wed-Sun 9.30am-12.30pm, 2-5pm. About £2. Paintings of the Bruges school.
Gruuthuse Dijver 17. ***Open*** *Apr-Sept* daily 9.30am-5pm; *Oct-Mar* 9.30am-12.30pm, 2-5pm. Museum of furniture, tapestries and artefacts. About £2.
Kathedraal St Salvator Steenstraat. **Museum *Open*** *Apr-Sept* Mon-Tue, Thu-Sat 10-11.30am, 2-5pm, Sun 3-5pm; *Oct-Mar* Mon-Tue, Thu-Sat 2-5pm.
Memling Museum in **St Jans Hospitaal** Mariastraat 38. ***Open*** daily 9.30am-noon, 2-5pm. A medieval dispensary. The chapel is now a gallery of paintings by the Bruges artist Hans Memling.
Onze Lieve Vrouwekerk (Church of Our Lady) Gruuthusestraat. ***Open*** *Apr-Sept* Mon-Fri 10-11.30am, 2.30-5pm, Sat 2.30-4pm, Sun 2.30-5pm; *Oct-Mar* Mon-Fri 10-11.30am, 2.30-4.30pm, Sat 2.30-4pm, Sun 2.30-4.30pm. Early Gothic church.
Stadhuis Burg 12 (off the A17 near Exit 8 off the E40). ***Open*** *Apr-Sept* daily 9.30am-5pm; *Oct-Mar* Mon, Wed-Sun 9.30am-12.30pm, 2-5pm. Belgium's oldest town hall, dating from 1376.
Straffe Hendrik Brewery Walplein 26. Tel 050 33 26 97. *Mar-Sept* daily 10am-5pm; *Oct-Mar* daily 11am-3pm. **Tours** by appointment. About £1. A 19th-century family brewery.

FOR CHILDREN
Boudewijnpark and **Dolphinarium** A. de Baeckestraat 12. Tel 050 38 38 38. ***Open*** *Mar-Sept* (check with tourist office for opening times). All-in ticket about £7. A children's fun park.
St Janshuysmolen Kruisvest. **Open** *May-Sept* daily 9.30am-noon, 12.45-5pm. About 50p. A 17th-century windmill to explore.

CAMPING
St Michiel Tillegemstraat 55, 8200 St Michiels (3 km/2 miles from Bruges; leave E40 motorway at Brugge-Torhout exit and head for city centre). Tel 050 38 08 19. Fax 050 80 68 24. ***Open*** all year.

EATING AND DRINKING
Brugs Beertje Bar Kemelstraat 5. Tel 050 33 96 16. ***Open*** 4pm-1am. A bar selling over 300 beers.
De Karmeliet Langestraat 19. Tel 050 33 82 59. From about £50.
Duc de Bourgogne Huidenvettersplein 12. Tel 050 33 20 38. Elegant canalside hotel. From £20 to £33.
L'Estaminet Park. Park 5. Tel 050 33 09 16. A jazz café with a young clientele.

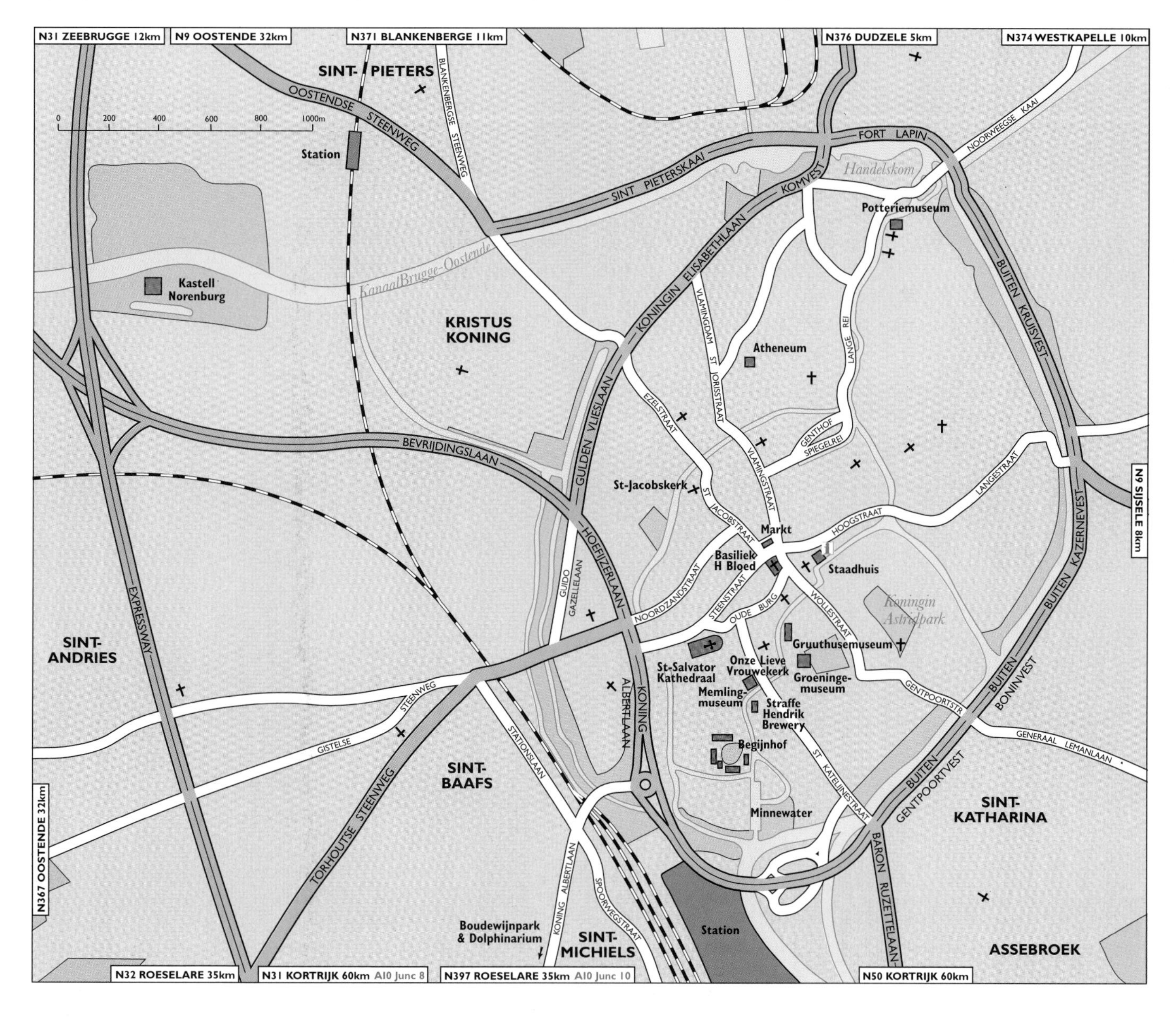

9
Patrick Anciaux
ANTIQUITES

Brussels

A weekend in **Brussels**

The secret of a city break in Brussels is to pick a theme to explore. Art, Art Nouveau architecture, the Battle of Waterloo. Such an interest will take you all around the city. But as twilight falls, be sure to head off to one of the café tables in the Grand'Place to see the floodlighting begin to bathe the magnificent gabled guildhouses in golden light. This magical heart of Brussels' medieval town deserves every word of the praise it gets.

For all its status as capital of Europe, Brussels (Bruxelles in French, Brussel in Flemish) is a mini metropolis, with a population of only 1 million, and an area of about 160 sq km/62 sq miles. So a walking tour, taking in most of the main central sights, is a feasible option for a weekend stay.

Previous pages: Leopold Park (main picture). Insets: The attractions of Brussels include exploring its cultural treasures, shopping for antiques, and being tempted by some of the city's superb *pâtisseries*.

Around town

The Grand'Place is a good place to start. It is the natural centre of the Lower Town, which runs west and south-west of St Michael's Cathedral. It has cheerful restaurants and shops; old churches; peaceful squares – and a tawdry red-light district. The neo-classical Théâtre de la Monnaie is the city's opera house, and the place de la Monnaie in front of it is a music venue for live bands.

Brussels' art galleries and many Art Nouveau buildings, its main museums, parks, and palaces, and the European quarter, are in the Upper Town (see page 103), on high ground east and south-east of the cathedral. The place Royale is its heart, overlooked by the Palais Royal. This part of town, bordered by the rue Royale, is an example of spacious neo-classical town planning, with rows of elegant houses and sumptuous mansions built for the city's aristocrats, and several large parks laid out in formal 19th-century style.

The Leopold Quarter, to the east, was also laid out in the 19th century with parks, wide boulevards, grandiose museums, and the great Cinquantenaire Arch, Brussels' answer to Paris's Arc de Triomphe. But the Parc du Cinquantenaire beneath it is bisected by lanes of roaring traffic, and King Leopold's elegant scheme has been eroded by the encroaching European quarter.

Alternative tour

In 1993, a group of Belgian architects ran alternative tours to show how Brussels is being affected by its political status. Visitors saw how a soulless glass and concrete desert has replaced terraces of lovely 19th-century mansions in the European quarter, and how the boulevards following

the line of the old ramparts have become the confusing *petit ring* (inner ring road) – a network of highways and tunnels. 'Brusselisation' is a term coined by today's town planners to describe the sacrifice of a city to offices and cars.

Contrarily, recession may hasten conservation. All over Belgium steeples are being hidden beneath scaffolding, guild houses regilded and façades refurbished as part of government policy to beat the slump. In Brussels, whole areas are being renovated by government and private capital. The formerly rundown district of St-Géry, centring on Ste Catherine's Church in the Lower Town, is emerging from under wraps, many of its buildings restored. The lively, crowded shops and markets in the places Ste-Catherine and St-Géry ensure the area retains some of its old character.

The rue des Bouchers in the medieval Lower Town: a street of restaurants noted principally for cheerful ambience and massive bowls of *moules*.

Markets and shopping

If you like street markets, you can take part in one of the favourite weekend activities in Brussels. The morning antiques market on the place du Grand Sablon, Brussels' main antiques area, is quite pricey, but there is a cheaper Sunday morning secondhand market on the place de la Reine-Astrid, and a cheerful bric-a-brac market at the Gare du Midi.

Indoor shopping on rainy or cold days is easy – Brussels boasts more covered galleries than any other European city. The huge 19th-century Galeries St-Hubert on the rue des Bouchers in the Lower Town was Europe's first iron and glass shopping arcade. The galleries and streets in the St-Gilles district, south-west of the boulevard Waterloo in the Upper Town, is the most fashionable shopping area for designer and ethnic (African) clothes and jewellery.

Eating, drinking, and nightlife

There are more than 1,800 eating places in this gastronomic capital (pages 103-104), varying from street stalls for fast food and bars offering regional dishes, to the spectacular delights of Belgium's finest gourmet restaurants. Pricewise, eating out in Brussels is not particularly cheap – but happily, portion control is the only culinary concept of which Belgian chefs seem unaware.

Capture Brussels' cheery cosmopolitan atmosphere by investigating the bars. They range from the trendy to the quiet and unassuming, and across American, Irish, tourist, singles, live music, jazz, wine, and cocktail bars. Famous examples include the 1920s La Mort Subite ('Sudden Death') on the rue Montagne-aux-Herbes-Potagères, an aesthetic, atmospheric café that gave its name to a now famous dark beer; the Cercueil in the rue des Harengs, a music bar with a macabre atmosphere – the tables are coffins and the drinks served in skulls. Moeder Lambic at rue de Savoie 68 in the St-Gilles district sustains Brussels' reputation as a beer capital with a list that includes all Belgium's 500 brews plus a further 500 from the rest of the world.

Bars and restaurants open late. In addition, Brussels has all the entertainment potential of an international city, so remember it for city breaks out of season, as well as summer weekends. There are films and even some theatre in English, as well as French and Flemish; opera, ballet, excellent contemporary dance, and classical music. The city is not famous for its clubs and discos, but there are plenty – some free (you pay high prices for drinks), some members only, many with dress codes. Brussels excels in the area of live music from top and rising groups and artists.

All events are listed in *The Bulletin*, a publication available in the tourist offices, and in the Thursday evening editions of *Le Soir*. Bookings may be made through the tourist office.

Left: Majestic buildings overlook Brussels' Grand'Place, making it an impressive setting for all kinds of festivals and celebrations.

Intriguing doorways in the winding streets of the Lower Town may lead into elegant antiques shops or specialist shops selling Brussels' lace.

Lower & Upper Town

The Grand'Place is at its most majestic during the Ommegang Festival in July. The two days of pageantry recall past civic splendours, when the city's ancient marketplace was the setting for tournaments, ceremonies, official pronouncements – and executions. The Ommegang is a celebration, the reenactment of a feast held in 1549 in honour of Charles V, King of Spain and Holy Roman Emperor. The guildhouses, hung with banners, become the backcloth to the festivities. Townspeople in late medieval dress parade before the Imperial Court, seated on a dais. Later they carry a 14th-century statue of the Virgin Mary, said to have miraculous powers, through the surrounding cobbled streets.

St Michael, in the form of a weathervane, watches over the Grand'Place from the 96 m/315 ft steeple adorning the stately Gothic Hôtel de Ville, whose decorative façade stretches along the south-west side. Its 16th-century Council Chamber and the Gallery of portraits of the Spanish kings may be visited. The gilded Maison du Roi, opposite, built as a royal residence for the Duke of Brabant, is the finest of the surrounding houses, now the Musée communal (Municipal Museum). Its collections include fine tapestries – a major industry in Brussels in the 15th and 16th centuries – and '*Marriage Procession*', a masterpiece by the Flemish painter Pieter Brueghel the Elder, who lived in Brussels in the mid-16th century.

The Musée du Costume et de la Dentelle(Costume and Lace Museum), just behind the Hôtel de Ville, is a favourite. It displays exquisite lace produced between the 17th and 19th centuries, when lace-making was a thriving industry in Brussels. Tourism has revived the craft. Several shops around the Grand'Place sell modern hand-made Brussels lace. The museum also displays the wardrobe (complete with two British military uniforms) of the famous Manneken Pis, a bronze fountain in the form of a naked boy perpetually urinating. The statue (on the corner of rue de l'Etuve, south-west of the square) is now much hyped as a symbol of the city's rebellious spirit – it has been stolen and broken many times since it was first cast in the 17th century, but always reappears.

Shopping and eating are the main activities north of the Grand'Place. The rue des Bouchers, best known for its restaurants and the Galeries St-Hubert shopping arcade, is also the home of Toone VII, Belgium's oldest puppet theatre. Marionnettes were a subversive form of theatre in the 16th century, when Brussels was under Spanish rule and live theatre was suppressed. The shows (usually, but not always, in French) are loosely based on folk tales and religious events. The place de la Brouckère, farther north, is surrounded by pavement cafés, and the rue Neuve, beyond, is Brussels' mainstream shopping street.

The river Senne, on whose marshy floodplain ancient Brussels was founded, was crossed by a trade route between Cologne and the Flemish trading cities. Brussels grew around the crossing. The rue du Marché-aux-Herbes north of the Grand'Place marks where the route passed through the centre of the medieval town. The Tour Villers, south-east of the Manneken Pis, and the Tour noire, near the Baroque Ste Catherine's Church north-west of the Grand'Place, were part of the medieval walls.

The network of streets centring on Ste Catherine's in the St-Géry district still gives a flavour of old Brussels. The Senne was covered in the 19th century, but the Quai au Bois-à-Brûler and the Quai aux Briques were the quays of the old river port. The fishmarket is held here and there are good seafood restaurants around. There is a peaceful square in front of the Baroque church of St-Jean-Baptiste-au-Béguinage. The daily market held medieval-style around Ste Catherine's Church and the flower market in the Grand'Place continue the capital's trading tradition.

The July Ommegang festival is a re-enactment of events from the city's medieval history in the splendid Grand'Place.

Upper Town

St Michael's Cathedral, on rising ground east of the central station, no longer dominates the capital as it did from the 13th century, when the choir was built, until the 1960s, when it became increasingly hemmed in by high-rise buildings. The foundations date from an earlier, 11th-century church and the towers from the 15th century. It has some beautiful 16th-century stained glass, the tombs of Duke John II of Brabant and Margaret of York, and paintings from the school of Rubens.

The place Royale is the centre of a complex of monumental neo-classical buildings south of the cathedral. There are tours of the state rooms in the Royal Palace (the Royal residence in Laeken Park out to the north of Brussels is also open to the public in August), and the Musée de la Dynastie in the rue Brederode presents the history of the Belgian royal family. The world-famous Musées Royaux des Beaux-Arts attract huge numbers of visitors to Brussels to see the outstanding collections of masterpieces by Pieter Brueghel the Elder and the other great Flemish primitives, and Rubens, in the Musée d'Art ancien, and by the Surrealists in the Musée d'Art moderne.

Children love gliding by escalator between spheres inside the Atomium, a 110-m/360-ft model of a molecule near the Centenaire Park. One sphere encloses a museum of atomic energy; another a simulated trip through the human body; one is a restaurant. Opposite is the Brupark, a leisure complex with a heated swimming pool, a wave machine and waterslides, and the National Planetarium. Huge museums in and around the Cinquantenaire Park include Autoworld, displaying racing cars and fire engines plus hundreds of other motor vehicles, as well as science and military museums.

The EC quarter (between the Leopold Park and the Cinquantenaire Park) was a huge building site as we went to press. The Berlaymont Building, the former EC HQ, was a forlorn shell being stripped of asbestos. Tours around the main buildings can be arranged for parties, but there is little of visual interest.

Winning the competition for skyline prominence over modern Brussels is Poelart's massive Palais de Justice, south-west of the European quarter. The terrace gives the best view across the Lower Town.

A walk through the Marolles quarter, sprawling southwards down the slope beneath it, restores a feeling of humanity. The 12th-century Notre-Dame de la Chapelle, Brussels' oldest church, is currently under restoration.

In the 17th century the Marolles was the craftsmen's district; now it is mainly the home of poor immigrant communities, with decaying houses and cheap cafés and restaurants. Parts – especially around the place du Jeu de Balle – have been restored, the old buildings converted into art galleries, antiques shops, pricey cafés and restaurants, and chichi residences, but the area retains great character. Its people still speak the Brussels dialect, called Marollien, and the capital's best flea market is held every morning, but most colourfully at weekends, on the place du Jeu de Balle.

The luxurious art of the *chef pâtissier* attains its most tantalising manifestation in the displays of *pâtisseries* such as Wittamer, above.

Cafés and cuisines

It takes willpower to walk down the appropriately named rue au Beurre, off the Grand'Place to the north – you have to pass the Biscuiterie Dandoy's seductively aromatic streetside waffle counter.

The scent of waffles poses a constant threat to sensible dietary intentions, waffle stands being as plentiful in Brussels as *pâtisseries.* From Wittamer on the place du Grand Sablon (the priciest and most famous) downwards, these make short work of guilt, stacked high as they are with absorbing displays of *gâteaux* and *tartes* – masterpieces by *chefs pâtissiers* who must own majority shareholdings in creameries.

Then there are the sensational smells emanating from Godiva on the Grand'Place and two dozen other hand-made chocolate shops; the *confiseries* (crowned by Confiserie Mary, Confectioners By Appointment – strategically located on rue Royale); and the ubiquitous aroma of irreproachable Belgian coffee from cafés packed along streets and shopping arcades, and ringing the squares.

The fact is that delicate whiffs wafting from a multiplicity of caterers to every gastronomic weakness, from *frites* to *feuilletés,* compete for airspace in the streets of central Brussels. In and around the rue des Bouchers, seafood restaurants have squeezed out almost all other trades in their fight for table space. There are schools of thought about their worth: natives are sniffy about the quality of their speciality – *moules* – but foreigners love them. The consensus view is that this has to be Europe's liveliest tourist trap, and that Chez Léon at Nos. 19-22 is outstanding.

French, Flemish, and the ubiquitous Italian pizza and pasta restaurants predominate, but in Brussels a variety of foreign cuisines is represented. Spanish and Portuguese restaurants are numerous, but pricey. Greek restaurants (around the Gare du Midi) and Turkish restaurants (around the St-Josse district) are cheaper, and generally higher quality than those in the UK. Henri J. Beans has gone continental in the S.A.S. Royal Hotel east of the place de la Monnaie, and there's the odd New York-style deli (Au Suisse, 73-75 boulevard Anspach), plus East-European, Moroccan, African, and South American restaurants. The main oriental cuisines are Chinese and Japanese, but there are Thai, Vietnamese, Indonesian and Indian restaurants, and Buddhist vegetarian cafés. Café Strauss (boulevard du Midi) is a German *pâtisserie.*

Brussels backs up its claim to be Europe's gastronomic capital with 25 Michelin-starred restaurants (at the last count). Three have three stars: Bruneau (avenue Broustin 73-75, out near the Laeken Park) is a pair of restaurants run by a husband-and-wife team; first-class nouvelle cuisine in an elegant setting is the speciality of chef Pierre Wynants at Comme Chez Soi (place Rouppe 23), the most central; and light, modern cooking is the hallmark of chef Pierre Romeyer at his eponymous restaurant in a beautiful setting at chaussée de Groenendaal in Hoeillaart (about 11 km/7 miles outside Brussels). L'Ecailler du Palais Royal (rue Bodenbroeck 18) is famous for seafood, and Chef Gert Jan Raven at The Four Seasons in the Royal Windsor Hotel (rue Duquesnoy 5), whose brigade won the *Bocuse de Bronze* award 1991, maintains Brussels' reputation for fine hotel restaurants with light, imaginative, beautifully presented dishes and faultless service.

Belgium's noted restaurant critics have joined forces to produce a useful guide, *Gourmet Restaurants,* giving full details of more than 100 eating establishments, including foreign cuisines from the Antilles to Scandinavia, and restaurants open after midnight. Restaurants are rated for quality and value for money (but there are no reviews). It is available (about 50p) from the tourist offices.

Beers and breweries

Don't ask for a beer in a Belgian bar. You'll be served the standard lager the bar has on tap. In Belgium you ask for the beer list. The list at Moeder Lambic's at rue de Savoie 68 in St Gilles tops out at more than 1,000, but most Brussels' bars have long beer lists. All will include *Lambics,* spontaneously fermented beers from Brabant, from which the Gueuze, Krieks and Framboise are derived. It's worthwhile being adventurous.

Broadly speaking, the bars in the Lower Town are cheaper and more casual than those up the hill, but few are really pricey and most also serve inexpensive food. Many close around 1am or when the last customer leaves. Try any that seems interesting. Or ask for recommendations (in the tourist office, your hotel, a likely-looking person in another bar) – in Brussels, it's the best way to get to know people.

You can watch brewing in action in the Gueuze Brewery Museum in Anderlecht, out to the West of Brussels. Back in the Grand'Place, the Maison des Brasseurs at No.10 is the only guild house still to be owned by a guild. The Guild of Brewers offers a free beer to visitors touring the small brewery museum inside.

Art Nouveau

The swirling, stylised plant forms of Art Nouveau houses are as great an attraction in Brussels, where Art Nouveau architecture emerged at the turn of the century, as the curled and stepped gables of its Renaissance guildhouses.

Many buildings by Victor Horta – including his seminal Maison du Peuple (1896-9) – have been bulldozed away over the last 30 years, but several remain: his house and studio (1898) at 25 rue Américaine, now the Horta Museum; the Tassel House (1892) at rue P.E. Janson 6, and the Van Eetvelde House (1898) avenue Palmerston 2-6 (above). Horta also designed the airy Magasins Waucquez in the rue des Sables in the Lower Town, now a museum of the Belgian comic strip.

Bloemenwerf (1895-6) in the suburb of Uccle is virtually the only remaining example in Brussels of the work of the Dutch architect, Henry Van de Velde, but the Cité Moderne (1922-5), one of Europe's first flat-roofed, concrete housing estates at Berchem-Ste Agathe is the work of Victor Bourgeois, a Belgian who was strongly influenced by his work.

The Brussels tourist office publishes guides and walking tours of Brussels' main Art Nouveau buildings, including some of the many façades – around the avenue Palmerston in the Upper Town; the avenue Louise and the chaussée de Waterloo in the St-Gilles borough south of the *petit ring,* and around the two lakes in the Maelbeek Valley in Ixelles, the borough to the south-west.

A tour should not miss some of the capital's more sober buildings: Antoine Pompe's Clinic for Dr. Van Neck at 53 Rue Wafelaerts (1910), and especially the tasteful, restrained Stoclet House (1904-11) by the Austrian Josef Hoffman, at 179-281 avenue de Tervuren. Finish the tour in the Falstaff, an exuberant Art Nouveau bar near the Stock Exchange (Bourse) on rue Henri Maus, open until 3am.

Below: The Gueuze Brewery Museum explains the history of local brewing. All Brussels' beer bars serve *lambics,* spontaneously fermented beers native to Brabant, from which Gueuze is derived.

Around **Brussels**

Bourgeois Brussels continues as it began: spreading erratically outwards as its wealthier citizens buy plots of land and build houses, with gardens, on the outskirts. So Waterloo, nominally 20 km/12 miles south of Brussels on the N5, is really only just beyond its expanding suburbs. It is a pleasant drive alongside the vast green Soignes forest to Waterloo town, where the Duke of Wellington's HQ – an inn in which he spent the night before the battle – is now the Wellington Museum. It's a good place to start a battlefield tour, because maps and descriptions give a clear picture of the phases of the battle.

To reach the battlefield, continue through and out of Waterloo town until you spot the Butte du Lion (Lion Hill) west of the Waterloo-Gordon crossroads. This artificial mound roughly marks the centre of Wellington's position. From the top you get a lion's eye view of the whole battlefield. The Battle of Waterloo was fought in the afternoon of 18 June, 1815 between an army of about 68,000 British, Belgians, Dutch and Germans under Wellington, and a French army of about 72,000 mustered by Napoléon after his escape from Elba. On the morning of 18 June, Napoléon reviewed his troops at the farm La Belle Alliance (about 1 km/⅔ mile south of the Butte on the N5) – which is preserved essentially as it was in 1815. In the evening, the victorious Wellington met the German General Blucher there.

Napoléon's HQ was the 18th-century Ferme du Caillou, about 2 km/1 mile south along the N5. This is now a museum, with Napoléon's bed and table, plans and maps. Roads east and west follow the lines of battle and are studded with memorials to cavalry charges, decisive stages of battle and particular acts of heroism. Return via the church opposite the Wellington Museum, where some of the 39,000 soldiers who died are buried and commemorated. Touring the battlefield and returning through the lovely Soignes forest makes an interesting and varied day out from the city.

Leuven

Beyond the suburbs, just over 24 km/15 miles east of Brussels and a pleasant day trip away, is the university town of Leuven (Louvain), Brabant's old capital. The ornately traceried and turreted 15th-century town hall survived both world wars undamaged, while bombing destroyed most of the town's old houses and all but a handful of ancient churches. Bombardments exposed the Romanesque crypt of St Peter's Church, but the 15th-century walls survived. The ambulatory is a museum of religious art, with treasures dating from the 12th century. Leuven is famous for its Catholic university, the oldest in Belgium and one of Europe's great medieval academic centres. It was founded in 1425 – Mercator studied geography here in the 16th century – and it is now Belgium's principal seat of Flemish learning.

The Lion of Flanders stands proudly at the top of the Butte du Lion on watch over the battlefield of Waterloo. The Wellington Museum in the town of Waterloo (inset), has a collection of souvenirs of both Wellington and Napoléon.

Brussels Fact File

BRUSSELS (French Bruxelles, Flemish Brussel) from **Calais** A16, N1, N39, A18, A10 197 km/127 miles.
Tourist information Hôtel de Ville, Grand'Place 02 513 89 40. Fax 02 514 45 38. ***Open*** *Apr-Sept* Mon-Sat 9am-6pm, Sun 9am-6pm; *Oct-Nov, Feb-Mar* Mon-Sat 9am-6pm, Sun 10am-2pm. Rue du Marché-aux-Herbes 63. Tel 02 504 03 90. Fax 02 504 02 70. ***Open*** *Jan-May, Oct-Dec* Mon-Sat 9am-6pm, Sun 9am-1pm, 2-6pm; *Jun-Sept* Mon-Sat 9am-7pm, Sun 9am-6pm.
Parking E of Grand'Place and close to rue Marché-aux-Herbes on blvd de l'Impératrice and Keizerinlaan. A tourist office map shows city car parks.

SIGHTSEEING
Walking tours: *The Brussels Guide and Map*, published by the tourist office, suggests walking tours.
Coach tours Brussels City Tour offers a 2½-hour walking tour of the Grand'Place with a coach tour of the Upper Town *2 Nov-25 Mar* daily at 10 and 11am, and at 2 and 3pm. About £14 adult, £7 child.
Hôtel de Ville Grand'Place. ***Open*** *Apr-Sept* Tue-Fri 9.30am-12.15pm, 1.45-5pm; Sat-Sun 10am-noon, 2-4pm; *Oct-Mar* Tue-Fri 9.30am-12.15pm, 1.45-4pm; Sat-Sun 10am-noon, 2-4pm. About £1.50.
Maison des Brasseurs (Brewery Museum) Grand'Place 10. ***Open*** Mon-Fri 10am-noon, 2-5pm, *Apr-Oct* also Sat 10am-noon.
Musée du Costume et de la Dentelle (Museum of Costume and Lace) rue de la Violette 6. ***Open*** *Apr-Sept* Mon-Fri 10am-12.30pm, 1.30-5pm, Sat-Sun 2-4.30pm; *Oct-Mar* Mon-Fri 10am-12.30pm, 1.30-4pm, Sat-Sun 2-4.30pm. About £1.50.
Musée de la Dynastie place des Palais 7 (3rd floor, Bellevue Palace in the Royal Palace). ***Open*** Mon-Thur, Sat-Sun 10am-4pm. History of the Belgian royal family.
Musée Gueuze rue Gheude 56. ***Open*** Mon-Fri 8.30am-4.30pm; *Jan-May 15 Oct-Dec* Sat 10am-6pm; *Jun-14 Oct* Sat 9.30am-1pm. About £1.50.
Musée Horta rue Américaine 25. ***Open*** Tue-Sun 2-5.30pm.
Musée royal des Beaux-Arts Collection in two parts, linked internally: **Musée d'Art ancien** entrance at rue de la Régence 3; **Musée d'Art moderne** entrance at place Royale 1-2. ***Open*** Tue-Sun 10am-noon, 1-5pm. Free.
Musée de la Ville de Bruxelles (Museum of the City of Brussels) Maison du Roi, Grand'Place. ***Open*** *Apr-Sept* Mon-Fri 10am-12.30pm, 1.30-5pm; Sat 10am-1pm; *Oct-Mar* Mon-Fri 10am-12.30pm, 1.30-4pm; Sat 10am-1pm. About £1.50.
WATERLOO:
Butte du Lion route du Lion 242-254. ***Open*** *Apr-Oct* daily 9.30am-6.30pm. About £2.
Musée Wellington chaussée de Bruxelles 147. ***Open*** *Apr-15 Nov* daily 9.30am-6.30pm; *16 Nov-Mar* daily 10.30am-5pm.

FOR CHILDREN
Atomium blvd du Centenaire. ***Open*** daily *Sept-Apr* 10am-6pm; *Jul-Aug* 9.30am-6pm. About £3.
Autoworld parc du Cinquantenaire 11. ***Open*** daily *Apr-Sept* 10am-6pm; *Nov-Mar* 10am-5pm. About £3.
Centre belge de la Bande dessinée (Comic Strip Centre) Waucquez Warehouse, rue des Sables 20. ***Open*** Tue-Sun 10am-6pm. About £3. Tintin and other Belgian heroes, comic strips and animated cartoons are made, plus a comics bookshop.
Brupark blvd du Centenaire 20. ***Open*** *27 Mar-9 Jan* daily 9.30am-6pm (*27 Jun-Aug* Mon-Fri 9.30am-8pm; Sat-Sun 9.30am-9pm).
Musée des Enfants (Children's Museum) rue du Bourgmestre 15. ***Open*** Wed, Sat 2.30-5pm. About £3.50.
Musée de l'Institut royal des Sciences naturelles rue Vautier 29. ***Open*** Tue-Sat 9.30am-4.45pm; Sun 9.30am-6pm. About £3. The dinosaur collection includes 30 skeletons of iguanodons and mosasaurs. Also the evolution of elephants, undersea life, and live spiders in a vivarium.

CAMPING
Warandeberg Camping Wolfhaegenstraat (take the A3 towards Liège, then A1 towards Charleroi, leave at the Wezambeek/Oppen exit, the second exit on the left after underpass). Tel 32 16 47 75 13. ***Open*** *Apr-Sept.*

Statues, fountains and rows of trees lend a serene and formal atmosphere to the 19th-century Parc de Bruxelles in the neo-classical Upper Town. It is the perfect place to stroll while digesting some of the city's famed culinary delights (inset) in which it is all too easy to indulge.

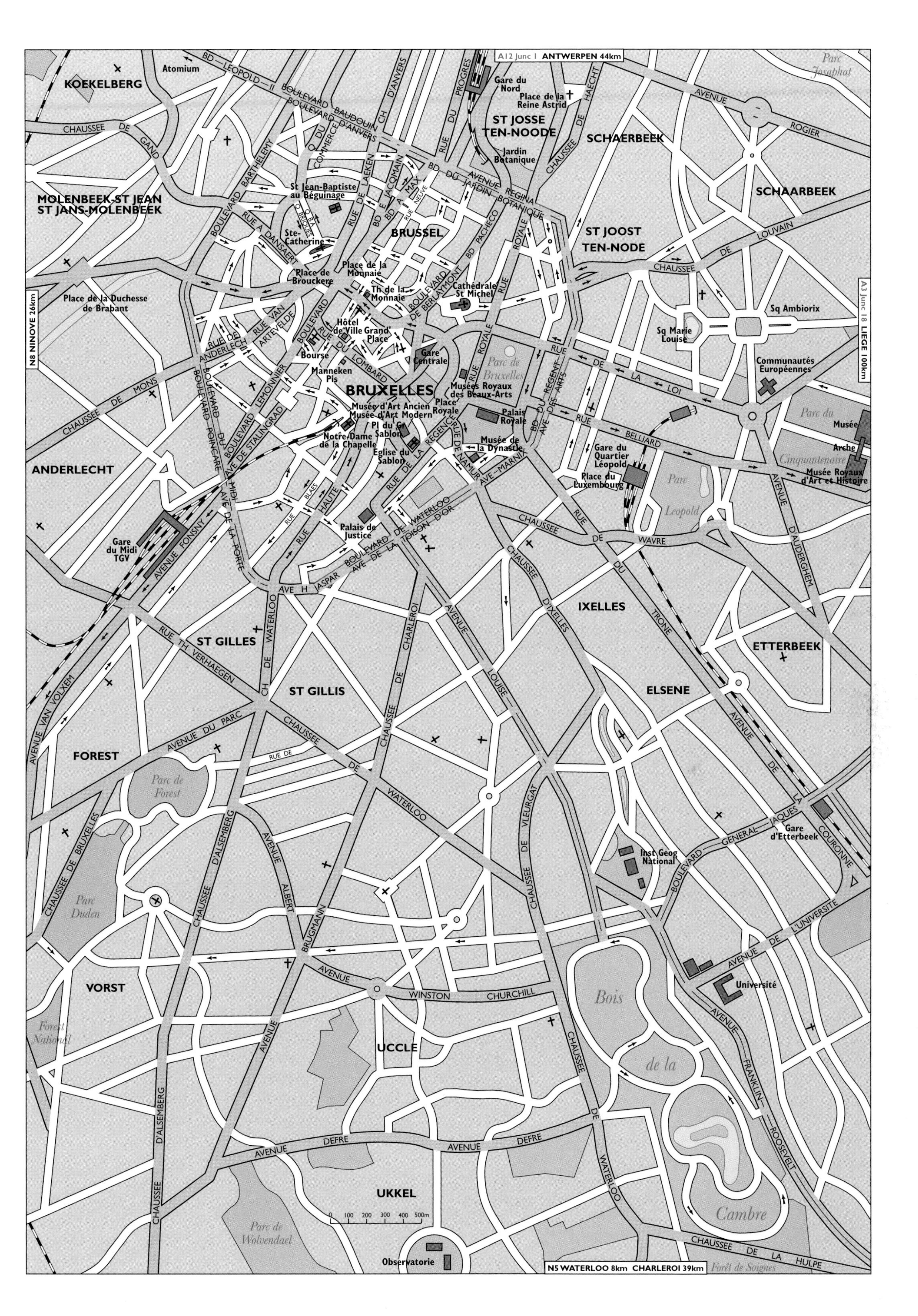

A12 Junc 1 ANTWERPEN 44km
A3 Junc 18 LIEGE 100km
N8 NINOVE 26km
N5 WATERLOO 8km CHARLEROI 39km
KOEKELBERG
Atomium
MOLENBEEK-ST JEAN
ST JANS-MOLENBEEK
ST JOSSE
TEN-NOODE
SCHAERBEEK
SCHAARBEEK
ST JOOST
TEN-NODE
BRUSSEL
BRUXELLES
ANDERLECHT
ST GILLES
ST GILLIS
IXELLES
ELSENE
ETTERBEEK
FOREST
VORST
UCCLE
UKKEL
Gare du Nord
Place de la Reine Astrid
Jardin Botanique
St Jean-Baptiste au Béguinage
Ste-Catherine
Place de Brouckère
Place de la Monnaie
Th de la Monnaie
Place de la Duchesse de Brabant
Cathédrale St Michel
Hôtel de Ville
Grand' Place
Bourse
Manneken Pis
Gare Centrale
Musées Royaux des Beaux-Arts
Parc de Bruxelles
Musée d'Art Ancien
Musée d'Art Modern
Place Royale
Palais Royale
Pl du Gr Sablon
Notre-Dame de la Chapelle
Eglise du Sablon
Musée de la Dynastie
Palais de Justice
Gare du Midi TGV
Sq Ambiorix
Sq Marie Louise
Communautés Européennes
Parc du Cinquantenaire
Musée
Arche
Musée Royaux d'Art et Histoire
Gare du Quartier Léopold
Place du Luxembourg
Parc Leopold
Parc Josaphat
Parc de Forest
Parc Duden
Forest National
Inst Geog National
Gare d'Etterbeek
Université
Bois de la Cambre
Parc de Wolvendael
Observatorie
Forêt de Soignes
0 100 200 300 400 500m
BD LEOPOLD II
BOULEVARD BAUDOUIN
BOULEVARD D'ANVERS
CH D'ANVERS
RUE DU PROGRES
CHAUSSEE DE HAECHT
AVENUE ROGIER
CHAUSSEE DE GAND
BOULEVARD BARTHELEMY
RUE DU COMMERCE
RUE DE LAEKEN
BD E JACQMAIN
BD A MAX
RUE NEUVE
BD DU JARDIN BOTANIQUE
AVENUE REGINA
BD PACHECO
RUE ROYALE
CHAUSSEE DE LOUVAIN
RUE A DANSAERT
BOULEVARD DE BERLAIMONT
BOULEVARD ANSPACH
RUE DU LOMBARD
RUE VAN ARTEVELDE
RUE DE ANDERLECHT
CHAUSSEE DE MONS
BOULEVARD LEMONNIER
BOULEVARD DU MIDI
BOULEVARD POINCARE
AVE DE STALINGRAD
RUE DE LA LOI
BD DU REGENT
AVE DES ARTS
RUE BELLIARD
RUE DE LA REGENCE
RUE DE NAMUR
AVE MARNIX
RUE HAUTE
RUE BLAES
BOULEVARD DE WATERLOO
AVE DE LA TOISON D'OR
AVE DE LA PORTE
AVENUE FONSNY
AVE H JASPAR
CHAUSSEE DE WAVRE
CHAUSSEE D'IXELLES
RUE DU TRONE
AVENUE D'AUDERGHEM
CH DE WATERLOO
CHAUSSEE DE CHARLEROI
AVENUE LOUISE
RUE TH VERHAEGEN
AVENUE VAN VOLXEM
AVENUE DU PARC
CHAUSSEE DE WATERLOO
RUE DE
AVENUE DE LA COURONNE
BOULEVARD GENERAL JAQUES
CHAUSSEE DE BRUXELLES
CHAUSSEE D'ALSEMBERG
AVENUE ALBERT
CHAUSSEE DE VLEURGAT
BRUGMANN
AVENUE DE L'UNIVERSITE
AVENUE WINSTON CHURCHILL
AVENUE FRANKLIN ROOSEVELT
AVENUE DEFRE
CHAUSSEE DE LA HULPE

Bulbfields & the Dutch coast

Alkmaar & Bergen
IJmuiden
National Park de Kennemerduinen
HAARLEM
Zandvoort
Heemstede
Bulb Fields
Vogelenzang
Hillegom
Keukenhof
Noordwijk
Lisse
Sassenheim
Kager plassen
Katwijk
Wassenaarse Slag
Wassenaar
LEIDEN
Scheveningen
DEN HAAG
Kijkduin
Zoetermeer
SOUTH HOLLAND
DELFT
Hoek van Holland
Europoort
Nieuwe Waterweg
Maassluis
Vlaardingen
Schiedam
ROTTERDAM
Euromast
Delfshaven
Oostvoorne
Voorne
Brielle
Rockanje
Haringvlietdam
Hellevoetsluis
Spijkenisse
Goedereede
Goeree
Putten
Oud-Beijerland
Zwijndrecht
Piershil
's-Gravendeel
Hoekse Waard
Haringvliet
Brouwersdam
Grevelingen
Middleharnis
Renesse
Brouwershaven
Overflakkee
Haringvlietbrug
Strijen
Schouwen
Duiveland
Gravelingendam
Volkerakdam
Hollands Diep
Willemstad
Zierikzee
Bruinisse
Krammer
Volkerak
Delta Expo
Oosterscheldedam
Roompot
NOORD-
Etten-Leur
Zeelandbrug
Stavenisse
Steenbergen
Veersegatdam
Nord Beveland
Tholen
Oudenbosch
Oostkapelle
Veere
Veerse Meer
Zandkreekdam
Oosterschelde
Sherpenisse
Walcheren
ZEELAND
ROOSENDAAL
Westkapelle
Goes
BERGEN OP ZOOM
MIDDELBURG
Kapelle
Oesterdam
Vlissingen
Zuid Beveland
Kruiningen
Ovezande
Hoogerheide
(F)
Westerschelde
Breskens
Schelde R.
Kloosterzande
BELGIUM
Oostburg
Ijzendijke
Terneuzen
Sluis
NOORDZEE
Alp
GO
Kinde
Moerdijk
Zund

Touring *the* bulbfields

Holland – the two western provinces of the Netherlands – is the most northerly region that falls within our short-break driving limit. The curve takes in Zeeland, near the Belgian border; South Holland and Den Haag; Amsterdam; and North Holland up as far as Haarlem, in the heart of the bulbfields.

Previous pages: Windmills typify the Dutch countryside, and the area around Leiden has many of the most interesting. This part of the Netherlands is also famed for its horticulture (inset).

Opposite and below: Aalsmeer, between Leiden and Amsterdam, has Europe's largest concentration of glasshouses – and its biggest auction for flowers and pot plants. Its buildings cover 135 hectares/334 acres, and it deals with some 4 billion flowers and 400 million plants every year. From the visitor's gallery, you can watch the spectacle of millions of flowers being auctioned in the early morning.

From the beginning of April up to early May, rectangles and stripes of pink and white, and startling primary blues, reds and yellows, carpet the landscape of the north-west Netherlands from the coast to the eastern horizon. Occasionally and strangely, a ship sails along a canal through the fields of flowers, looking as if it were floating through a fantasy sea of colour.

Bulbs are the main industry. Flowers are the by-product. But they have become the reason for an early start to the tourist season, as thousands of spring visitors flock to enjoy the lovely sight.

The centre of the Dutch bulb-growing industry is between Leiden and Haarlem, where there is a 60-km/37-mile signposted driving route through the bulbfields, with marked points for the best views. Bulbs are grown in other parts of the Netherlands too – there is an even longer bulb route around the Noordoostpolder near the Ijsselmeer Lake.

The flowers bloom for only a short while before they are cut to allow the bulbs to develop. They are heaped into flat-bottomed boats and transported – cargoes of yellow or red, pink or blue – along the canals to the towns. There they are sold off cheaply to tourists, and made into garlands and floats for the local flower festivals. Every town contributes a float to the annual spring pageants.

South Holland's acres of sun-reflecting glasshouses make the Netherlands the European country most easily visible by day from outer space. The plant and flower-growers open their glasshouses to visitors during the first week in April. You can look around, ask questions, and get a preview of new strains and colours to be launched on the market in the future. Frans Roozen, the Netherlands' biggest grower of bulbs and other flowering plants, opens its gardens and greenhouses outside Haarlem throughout April and May, and invites the public to its spring and summer bulb and flower shows.

The three largest Dutch flower auctions are open to everyone – but they only handle wholesale trade. If you want to buy flowers, bulbs or plants to take home, head for the flower markets in Amsterdam, Delft or Utrecht, and ask for a box with a certificate of health, required for British customs clearance. The Dutch have thought of everything.

If you miss the spring flowering in the bulbfields, head for Lisse, midway between Leiden and Haarlem, and the Keukenhof Gardens, the world's largest flower gardens. They were opened on the 28-hectare/70-acre estate of a horticulturally minded 15th-century countess, to try to encourage people to buy bulbs for their gardens. They display some 6 million flowering bulbs, plus shrubs, trees, aquatic plants, and several show gardens. These display the latest varieties in bloom – tulips looking like orchids, and species you've never heard of – and sell them to the public. You can order them and have them sent home.

The Dutch are even more enthusiastic than the English about plants. Driving routes are marked around every district that can claim to have a flowering season. There are blossom routes in the fruit-growing areas, even tours around yellow rapeseed fields in some areas. There are gardens open to the public in almost every major town, and flower pageants and processions the year round.

Leiden

The Netherlands' oldest gardens are in Leiden, a photogenic university town in the heart of the bulbfields. Beside a canal in the south-west corner of the old medieval centre is the Hortus Botanicus, one of Europe's earliest botanical gardens, first planted in 1590. Its lawns and huge tropical houses are beautifully landscaped with rare trees and shrubs. Across the canal bridge is the Clusiustuin, a reconstruction of the first such garden to be arranged systematically. It is named after its founder, the botanist Carolus Clusius, who imported the first tulip into the Netherlands in the 16th century.

Leiden is built with concentric squares of canals surrounding the old town, and grids of canals flowing into the town dock. Visitors can't resist strolling along the canalsides, admiring the pretty gabled houses and discovering medieval gems, like the old Fish Market, the Corn Bridge, where corn was once exchanged, or the 14th-century St Pancraskerk.

John Robinson, leader of the Pilgrim Fathers, is buried in the 13th- to 14th-century St Pieterskerk (now deconsecrated, and the home of a Saturday antiques market). The Pilgrim Fathers fled here from religious persecution in England, and lived here from 1609 to 1620. They started their journey to America from the nearby Vliet River. There are walking tours that take visitors around key sites in the life of the community, and a museum showing a video about the Pilgrim Fathers.

One of the prides of Leiden's museums is the 1st-century Egyptian Temple of Taffeh, in the courtyard of the archaeological museum. The temple was a gift of the Egyptian government after Dutch archaeologists discovered important remains in what is now part of Ethiopia. There is a windmill museum, a clay pipe museum, and a museum of science history in the building where one of the first surgeons, Dr. Boerhaave, worked in

Leiden's Windmill Museum (below), in an 18th-century brick-built flour mill, shows how a miller lived. On the 7th floor is the mechanism that makes the sail turn.

Top: The view from Leiden's prestigious university, founded in 1575. Beautiful old university buildings overlook its calm waterways.

Above: The Rijksmuseum, Leiden.

the Middle Ages. The old cloth hall – the Lakenhal – is an art gallery, with works by Rembrandt and other important 16th- and 17th-century artists.

But Leiden's greatest charm is that indefinable atmosphere unique to old university towns, of peaceful absorption and energetic undergraduate-café-society life.

Haarlem

At the northern centre of the bulbfields is the riverside town of Haarlem, built around its large and splendid Grote Markt. Among the buildings surrounding it are the old meat market, the Vleeshal, and the Stadhuis, the 14th-century town hall, both with decorated stepped gables. The mighty and very high St Bavo's cathedral is famous for its massive 18th-century organ, which Handel and Mozart are said to have played.

Just 7 km/4 miles from the sea to the west, and 15 km/10 miles from Amsterdam to the east, Haarlem's age and present size reflect its strategic importance at the narrow neck of North Holland. Its centre is 1,000 years old, the former seat of the medieval Counts of Holland. It is also a provincial capital and a spreading industrial city. Some visitors love its quaint old centre which does not have the crowds of Amsterdam.

Some find the old town pretty, but the new town soulless, lacking the vibrant character of Amsterdam. Impressions aside, Haarlem counts as essential on any tour of the Netherlands' heartlands. Besides its central square, its chief attraction is the Frans Hals Museum close by. The museum includes galleries of paintings by other artists – Frans Hals' masterful portraits are in the west wing. Ask at the tourist office for the dates of evening openings, when the paintings are sometimes illuminated by candlelight.

Haarlem's other famous museum is the oldest in the Netherlands: the Teyler Museum, founded in the 18th century by a cloth trader to promote arts and sciences. The museum has a collection of drawings by Michelangelo, Raphael and others, and, in the science section, some dinosaur fossils. A third, extraordinary museum, opened only in 1988, is the simple house and shop of a family of watchmakers who sheltered Jewish and other persecuted people from the Nazis in tiny hidden rooms during World War II. All but one of the family of five died in concentration camps, but a daughter, Corrie Ten Boom, was freed at the age of 52, and lived in the house until her death in 1983.

Spring, when the surrounding fields are brilliant with massed daffodils, crocuses, tulips and hyacinths, is the time to visit Haarlem. Dutch tulip-growing began in Haarlem in the 17th century, and the city records bulb exchange booms, when amazing prices were paid for tulip bulbs at one time, hyacinths at another. Today, Haarlem is a world centre for the export of bulbs.

The Frans Hals Museum building (below) is one of the Leiden's several *hofjes* – old almshouses, themselves one of the city's attractions. In this one, the Flemish painter Hals is believed to have passed his final years.

The coast

The Netherlands' coast is a broad swathe of golden sands and grassy dunes. From Den Haag to Haarlem there are beautiful, clean, wide beaches. South of Rotterdam are the islands of Zeeland, with historic ports and harbours of great character – and engineering works so audacious they number among the wonders of the 20th-century world.

Bergen, up in North Holland near the cheese town of Alkmaar, is perhaps the most attractive bathing resort along the North Sea coast. The beach and dunes at Bergen-aan-Zee are extensive and uncrowded. Inland, the little village of Bergen, a traditional retreat of artists, with several art galleries in its pedestrianised streets, is prettily situated in woodland. Among the trees are discreetly sited, luxurious villas.

The coast's extended beaches backed by high protective dunes are great for sunbathing on hot days. But there are no elegant bathing resorts along the Dutch coast, and the North Sea can be murky for swimming. The beaches may be best for invigorating morning or evening walks, especially if you've spent the day in the car, or shuffling around crowded tourist sites.

The Mesdag Panorama in Den Haag is the world's largest circular painting, showing the resort of Scheveningen as it was in 1881. Modern Scheveningen is a western extension of Den Haag, South Holland's busiest, perhaps most fashionable, resort and harbour, with a casino, large breakers for surfing, lifeguards on patrol, children's games and sports, museums, a pier, and a boardwalk with shops and bars, cafés and restaurants. Noordwijk, the next major resort to the north, has a beach miles long and very wide. Sports are the attraction: horses to ride; a swimming pool, sailing, tennis, indoor bowling. Kijkduin and Wassenaarse Slag are quieter beaches for families, with entertainments for children.

The wind never dies down for long on the North Sea coast, even in an August heatwave, and the Dutch deserve prizes for ingenious windbreaks. People sink into hooded wicker chairs, and dig themselves into dunes. *Windschermen* (tarpaulin suntraps), huts and chalets may be hired. Café tables, deckchairs, even boardwalks are glassed in.

Such facilities are normally owned by the beach cafés. The system is to install yourself in a deckchair in one of their suntraps and order the odd coffee, drink or ice cream from time to time. Prices are not extortionate.

Zandvoort, near Haarlem, is the favoured summer escape for Amsterdamers. There's lots going on – jazz on the beach in August; car-racing at Easter; a casino; a dune nature reserve; and bulbfields in the spring. The beach is 15 km/9 miles long. Sea-fishing is the main activity at Ijmuiden, further north.

South of Den Haag, the waves are calmer and the wide beaches safer for children. There are dunes to explore at Oostvoorne and Rockanje, south-west of Rotterdam, and windsurfing on the beaches. With a permit from the tourist office you can walk in the woods between Oostvoorne and Rockanje.

Ports and harbours

There are beaches on the western tip of Zeeland, but its quaint old ports are the main attraction. Veere, just north of the capital, Middelburg, has been a freshwater lake resort and watersports centre since the Veerse Gat Dam cut it off from the sea. It has a Gothic town hall, its original fortifications, and some appealing old houses. In the 15th and 16th centuries it had a monopoly of the

Scottish wool trade, and the old warehouses are now a museum. Zierikzee is a beautiful port on the island of Schouwen-Duiveland, with a medieval gateway and many other buildings dating from the Middle Ages, when it handled the important trade with Belgium.

Just north of the Belgian border is Sluis, Bruges' outer harbour in grander days before the Zwin silted up (see pages 96–7). Though not as unspoilt as Damme, Sluis has preserved some medieval charm. Its town hall and 14th-century belfry, now a museum, and carillon, have been restored after World War II bombing. Sluis is, however, much busier than Damme. Because of its proximity to Belgium, its shops are allowed to open on Sundays and in the evenings.

Den Haag

The antique, small-town charm of this semi-coastal city explodes the preconceptions created in the minds of foreigners by its many titles: administrative capital of the Netherlands; seat of the Dutch government; capital of South Holland; third largest Dutch city.

Den Haag's aristocratic beginnings were as a lodge in the hunting forests of the Counts of Holland. The lodge became a castle under a 13th-century king, then a royal residence – the present Binnenhof. A town grew up around it. By the 16th century, Den Haag had become the seat of the central government. By the early 20th century it was becoming a focus for international organisations, and its suburbs were spreading west to link with the resort of Scheveningen and so reach the sea.

The centre of Den Haag is small and easy to get around and park in. The city's oldest central church is the grand 16th-century hall church, St Jacob's Kerk.

The old town also has several *hofjes* or almshouses, some with chapels and courtyards. Pieter Post, a native architect, designed the Hofje van Nieuwkoop in 1660. *Hofjes* are tourist attractions in many Dutch towns; the tourist office publishes a walking tour of the *hofjes* in Den Haag.

Den Haag is an art town. Preeminent among its museums is the Mauritshuis, a Renaissance mansion by the Dutch architect Jacob van Campen. It displays the national art collection of 15th- to 18th-century paintings by Flemish and Dutch artists: Hans Memling, Rogier van der Weyden, Hans Holbein the Younger, Adriaen Brouwer, Pieter Paul Rubens, Pieter Brueghel the Elder, Anthony van Dyck, Frans Hals, Jan Vermeer. There are more paintings of the period in the Prince William V Gallery. The Gemeentemuseum to the north has an outstanding modern collection, including a unique exhibition of paintings by Piet Mondrian.

People who like Den Haag are specially fond of the small, cosy galleries and museums, the elegant private galleries, and the Dutch furniture and design stores. Artists live and work in the city, just as they did in the 17th century, when Jan van Goyen, Jan Steen, Paulus Potter, Pieter Post and the philosopher Benedictus de Spinoza lived in the old Dunne Bierkade quarter.

Around the old town, Den Haag has over 20 parks. The Clingendael park has a 19th-century Japanese garden, and on the road to Scheveningen is Madurodam, a park with a working scale model of a Dutch town. It was founded by the parents of a soldier who distinguished himself in World War II, but was imprisoned by the Nazis and died in Dachau concentration camp.

Uncrowded, elegant Den Haag is a good base for exploring South Holland. Delft, about 8 km/5 miles away, is a charming town of old houses and narrow streets. It is invaded annually by tourists shopping for pottery souvenirs. The town was the birthplace of the artist Vermeer, and its museums and old buildings are best visited out of season. If you are really interested in Delftware, you can tour the Delft pottery factory.

Main picture: Among the attractions of the Dutch coast are the windswept dunes, where some unspoilt areas are protected as bird sanctuaries. Inset: Kinderdijk is a village between Rotterdam and Dordrecht with 19 windmills, the largest concentration of windmills in the Netherlands. On Saturdays in July the sails of many mills are set to turn. One of these 18th-century mills is open as a museum.

The Houses of Parliament in Den Haag

The charming, very typically Dutch canal town of Gouda is only 25 km/16 miles from Den Haag. It is most famous for its Thursday morning cheese market (held only in summer). Nearby is Oudewater, with attractive gabled houses overlooking the river Hollandse Ijssel. In the 16th-century weigh-house, women accused of witchcraft were weighed, and issued with certificates if they were judged too heavy for broomstick-riding.

At weekends in Delft (below) sellers of bric-a-brac and antiques – and pottery, although most on view is either of modern design or reproduction – help to bring a festive atmosphere to the city's tree-lined canals.

Rotterdam

The 185-m/607-foot Euromast gives a stunning view over an energetic, exciting city. Rotterdam has some medieval buildings to attest to its origins as a 13th-century dam across the river Rotte. But it has no pretensions to old-world charm: this is a city that has thrown in its lot with the 21st century. In the 1920s, Rotterdam was at the forefront of the Netherlands modern architecutre movement, with the Van Nelle Factory and J.P. Oud's modern housing estate.

Salvaged from the German bombing that destroyed the town in 1940 is the 15th-century Grote Kerk, built close to the site of the original Rotte dam. In front of the church is a statue of the Renaissance scholar and humanist, Erasmus, who was born in the city. Between the city centre and the docks is Delfshaven, the old port, which survived the bombing. Before sailing for Plymouth, the Pilgrim Fathers held a service in Delfshaven's Oude Kerk.

The town's history is on display in the Schielandhuis Museum, in a 17th-century town house. The Boymans-Van Beuningen Museum, towards Delfshaven, has impressive collections of paintings, from Flemish religious paintings to the works of the late 20th century. The Surrealists, Dutch masters, Rembrandt, and modern European painters are especially well represented.

There is an impromptu maritime museum in the old harbour, where owners of old and historic boats and ships bring their vessels for repairs and reconstruction. The

Rotterdam-Europoort (main picture below) is the busiest port and the largest artificial harbour in the world. Other features (insets below) of the Netherlands' second largest city include Kijk-Kubus, cube houses by architect Piet Blom, and the Maritime Museum.

Zapata Nordic drilling platform in the Maas River has been turned into an offshore museum.

Sights in this fascinating city range from pewter-making in Delsfhaven to windmills and extraordinary specialist museums, such as the Tax Museum near the Euromast, with a well-informed 'story of smuggling' display. But the most unmissable excursions have to be to the record-breaking Europort, extending into the North Sea, which opened in 1960. It has the world's largest oil terminal, the first terminal for containers, and can handle the biggest tankers: the statistics go on and on; the sight is stupendous. Dockland tours run day and night from the Willemsplein, south of Centraal Station.

In Zeeland's Delta Project, the Netherlands can claim a second wonder of the 20th-century world. In 1953, a combination of high tides and persistent high winds produced a surge tide that pierced the coastal dunes and flooded Zeeland.

Work was quickly begun on the 30-year Delta Project, to build dams across the large estuaries and inlets of the Zeeland coast. To protect the fish nurseries and shellfish beds in the Oosterschelde estuary, however, a storm surge barrier – the pioneering precursor of the Thames Barrier – was built instead of a dam, and the bridge across the Scheldt River estuary is the longest bridge in the world at 5,022 m/5,492 yards. Delta Expo, an exhibition built out on the barrier, has a working model of water control in the area, films, and a guided boat tour along the barrier, with commentaries explaining how it works.

Canalside houses of Old Rotterdam. (below left) are now more tranquil than they would have been when trade was carried by sailing ships and barges. The Euromast (below right) stands higher than any other point in the Netherlands. There is a restaurant half way up.

South Holland Fact File

SOUTH HOLLAND from **Calais** 280km/175 miles.

AALSMEER
Flower Auctions Legmeerdijk 313. ***Open*** Mon-Fri 7.30-11am. About £2.50 adult, child free.

ALKMAAR
Cheese Market Waagplein *15 Apr-15 Sept* Fri 10am-noon.
Cheese Museum Waagplein. ***Open*** *Apr-Oct* Mon-Sat 10am-4pm, Fri 9am-4pm. About £1.

DELFT
De Delftse Pauw Pottery Factory Delftweg 133. ***Open*** *Apr-15 Oct* daily 9am-4pm; *16 Oct-31 Mar* Mon-Fri 9am-4pm, Sat-Sun 11am-1pm.

DELTA EXPO
Burgh-Haamstede Neeltje Jans. Tel 01115 2702. Fax 01115 3164. ***Open*** *Nov-Mar* daily 10am-5pm. About £4.50 adult, £2.50 5-18s.

GOUDA
Tourist information VVV Gouda Markt 27. Tel 1820 13666. Fax 1820 83210. ***Open*** Mon-Fri 9am-5pm, Sat 10am-4pm.
Cheese Market Markt *Jul-Aug* Thur mornings 10am-noon.

HAARLEM
Tourist information VVV Haarlem Stationsplein 1. Tel 023 319059. Fax 023 340537.
Corrie Ten Boom Museum Barteljorisstraat 19. ***Open*** *Apr-Oct* Tue-Sat 10am-4pm, *Nov-Mar* Tue-Sat 11am-3pm.
Frans Roozen Nurseries Vogelenzangseweg 49, Vogelenzang. Tel 02502 47245. ***Open*** (gardens and greenhouses) *26 Mar-31 May* daily 8am-6pm. Summer show *Jul-30 Sept* Mon-Fri 9am-5pm. Phone for details of other shows.

DEN HAAG
Tourist information Koningin Julianaplein 30, Babylon Centre, near Centraal Station. Tel 070 3546200. Fax 070 3472102. ***Open*** *15 Apr-15 Sept* Mon-Sat 9am-9pm, Sun 10am-5pm; *16 Sept-14 Apr* Mon-Sat 9am-6pm.
Boat trips: tours of Den Haag and Delft; reservations RVH Rondvaartbedrijf Spui 256. Tel 070 346 24 73. North Sea fishing trips *Jun-Sept* daily 4pm; reservations Sportviscentrum Trip, Dr. Lelykade 3, Scheveningen. Tel 070 354 11 22.

KINDERDIJK
Windmill Museum ***Open*** *Apr-Sept* Mon-Sun 9.30am-5.30pm.

LEIDEN
Tourist information VVV Leiden Stationsplein 210. Tel 071 146846. Fax 071 125318. ***Open*** Mon-Fri 9am-5.30pm, Sat 9am-4pm.
Hortus Botanicus Rapenburg 73. ***Open*** *Apr-Sept* Mon-Sat 9am-5pm, Sun 10am-5pm. About £1.
Clusius Garden ***Open*** Mon-Fri, Sun 9am-5pm.
De Valk Mill Museum 2e Binnenvestgracht 1. ***Open*** Tue-Sat 10am-5pm, Sun 1-5pm. About £1.50 adult, 75p 6-15s.
Pilgrim Fathers Documents Centre Vliet 45. ***Open*** Mon-Fri 9.30am-4.30pm. Free.

LISSE
Keukenhof Bulb Gardens Stationsweg 166a. ***Open*** *25 Mar-23 May* daily 8am-6pm. About £6 adult, £3 under-13s.

OUDEWATER
Witches' Weigh House Leeuweringerstraat 2. ***Open*** *Apr-Oct* Tue-Sat 10am-5pm, Sun noon-5pm.

ROTTERDAM
Tourist information VVV Rotterdam Coolsingel 67. Tel 010 4136000 Fax 010 4130124. ***Open*** Mon-Thur 9am-5.30pm, Fri 9am-9pm, Sat 9am-5pm; *Apr-Oct* Sun 10am-4pm.
Boat trips tours of the port via Spido Haven Rondvaarten, Willemsplein. Tel 010 4135400. About £5, £2.50 child.
Euromast and Spacetower Parkhaven 20. ***Open*** *Apr-Sept* daily 10am-7pm. *Oct-Mar* daily 10am-5pm; **Spacetower** *Jan-Feb* Sat-Sun 11am-4pm. *Mar-Dec* daily 11am-4pm; About £5, £3.50 under 12s.
Schielandhuis Museum Korte Hoogstraat 31. ***Open*** Tue-Sat 10am-5pm, Sun 1-5pm.

ZEELAND
Tourist information VVV Middelburg Markt 65a. Tel 01180 16851. Fax 01180 40764.

FOR CHILDREN
Madurodam nr. Scheveningse Bosjes, Haringkade 175. ***Open*** *Apr-May* daily 9am-10.30pm; *Jun-Aug* daily 9am-11pm; *Sept-Dec* daily 9am-6pm. About £4.50 adult, £2.25 child. Miniature Dutch town.

CAMPING

DEN HAAG
Campingplatz Ockenburgh Wijndaelerweg 25 (follow signs for Kijkduin/Hoek van Holland) Tel 070 325 23 64. ***Open*** *Mar-Oct.*

NOORDWIJK
Camping Club Soleil (S of Noordwijkerhout, turn W, signposted). Tel 025 237 42 25. ***Open*** *Apr-Oct.*

ROTTERDAM
Camping Kanaalweg Kanaalweg 84 (follow signs from Rotterdam-Centrum exit from A20 Rotterdam-Utrecht or A13 Rotterdam-Den Haag). Tel 010 4159772 (for information).

Amsterdam

Exploring Amsterdam

Conservation-conscious Amsterdam has a heart of traditional beauty, where more than 150 canals section the city into islands made picturesque by multi-storey, decoratively gabled 17th- and 18th-century houses. Other attractions are manifold: wonderful art galleries and historic churches; timeless café society; plenty of entertainment. Yet Amsterdam is one of Europe's smallest capitals, quiet and uncrowded by comparison with London or Paris, and compact enough to get around on foot.

In the Anne Frank House, you can see where the Jewish Frank family hid from the Nazis from 1941 until they were discovered in 1944.

Use the quaint but efficient water taxis, trams, even buses or your feet to get around Amsterdam. But leave your car in the hotel car park, where it will be safe from thieves, regulations, restrictions, and fines. It's easy to orientate yourself. The canals fan out in concentric semicircles from Centraal Station in the north, along the port of Amsterdam on the Ij.

Cutting through the centre of the old town is the Amstel River. With 1,250 bridges, Amsterdam could rightfully be called Bruges. But the Magere Brug over the Amstel is the only one of the 17th-century wooden bascule bridges left (a bridge that can be raised to allow large ships through).

What to see

Dam Square in the north-west marks the site where Amsterdam began: a dam built by fishing people to separate the Amstel from the Ij. The narrow streets around are the town's medieval centre – Schreierstoren, opposite Centraal Station, was part of the old town wall.

In Zeedijk, running south to the medieval weigh-house is the oldest house in the city, believed to date from the 15th century. But this is a sleazy part of town, with the red-light district just to the left. Don't walk round there alone, or displaying obvious signs of wealth.

Previous pages: Amsterdam's canals have a charm of their own, even at night. And in the daytime (insets) the bright and youthful colours of the city, its traditional crafts and its distinctive food, such as this array of Dutch cheese on a stall in the Albert Cuyp market, all contribute to the liveliness for which the city is justly famed.

You will glimpse residues, though, of Amsterdam's golden age of maritime history if you stroll along the busy Prins Hendrikkade along the docks towards the Scheepvaart Museum, the National Maritime Museum.

Right on the edge of the red-light district, at No. 40 Voorburgwal, the house of a wealthy 17th-century Catholic merchant's family has been preserved with its kitchens and furnishings. It dates from a time when Catholic families were only allowed to worship in their own homes. So this house is known as Amstelkring or 'Our Dear Lord in the Attic', because the loft, and those of adjoining houses, were converted into a church.

The oldest and most magnificent canalside houses are arrayed along the ring of three 17th-century canals: Herengracht, Prinsengracht, and Keizersgracht – where No. 672 has been preserved as a museum.

The Anne Frank House is at Prinsengracht 263, just north-west of the Dam. Anne Frank died in Belsen, but her diaries survived to be published. In the Jewish Museum in the old Jewish quarter, near Waterlooplein in the town's geographical centre are photographs and records of Amsterdam workers, who came out on strike against the deportation of the Jews.

Art and music

The tree-lined canals, huge pancakes in cafés, street stalls selling raw herring and chips with mayonnaise, street performers in the square in front of the 19th-century railway station, all say 'this is Amsterdam' to most summer visitors. But Amsterdam is the Netherlands' cultural capital, and its art galleries are reason alone for a visit at any time of year. Many are grouped with the home of the celebrated Amsterdam Concertgebouw Orchestra, on Museumstraat in the south-west of the town.

De Stijl architect Gerrit Rietveld designed the Vincent Van Gogh Museum. It opened in 1973 and quickly became a very popular gallery. It displays the works collected by Van Gogh's brother, representing all the key periods in his life, including a *Sunflowers* canvas, plus a collection of drawings and letters.

The museum is a branch of the Rijksmuseum, justifiably Amsterdam's most famous museum, itself in a neo-classical building by the 19th-century Dutch architect, P. J. H. Cuypers. It has an unparalleled collection of Dutch art, especially 17th-century paintings, and of old masters from the 15th century. And people flock to Amsterdam just to see 20 paintings by Rembrandt, whose house, now a museum, is in the Jewish quarter.

Aficionados of modern art should head for the Stedelijk Museum, with its world-class permanent exhibitions on show in the summer, and a kaleidoscopic succession of temporary exhibitions all year round. Modern architecture fans should find time for H.P. Berlage's innovative Stock Exchange and New South district, and Michel de Klerk's 1913–1921 Eigenhaard housing estate, plus the Maritime Museum in the docks, both characteristic of the Amsterdam School.

In summer, there is drama and sometimes music in the Vondelpark near the Rijksmuseum – and also on the canals, as the players of Amsterdam's Water Theatre demonstrate.

From the top of the Domtoren, the graceful belltower of Utrecht, just half an hour away by train, you can see the towers and spires of old Amsterdam on a clear day. The oldest are the towers of the 14th-century Oude Kerk (marooned in the red-light district), with fine 16th-century stained glass. The tower (with carillon) of Hendrick de Keyser's 17th-century Zuiderkerk, adorns the first Protestant church built after the Reformation. The Mint Tower, once part of the town's defences, and the dome of Jacob van Campen's Palladian Royal Palace in Dam Square, can be spotted near the fleche on the impressively high Nieuwe Kerk. Easily visible is the yellow onion dome on top of Long John, Amsterdam's tallest tower at 85 m/280 feet, belonging to de Keyser's Westerkerk on Prinsengracht, as is his spire on the 16th-century Montelbaanstoren in the docks.

There is an antiques market every day but Sunday on Waterlooplein and a Sunday morning flea market on Niewmarkt in summer. The metal sculpture above was snapped up at an occasional crafts market in Rembrandtsplein.

Where to stroll and browse

The most pleasant central shopping areas are around Dam Square, in the old streets around the Nieuwe Kerk, and around Spuistraat on the opposite side of the square, an area known as Spui. This is a lovely place to browse through shops, try out bars, and wander into the tranquil courtyard of the peaceful Begijnhof – a collection of women's convent houses built around a church and central courtyard.

The best flea market is on Waterlooplein. Art and antique dealers crowd the Spiegel quarter near the Rijksmuseum.

Away from the centre, the western Jordaan district is a favourite place to stroll. It developed in the 17th century as a working-class area of narrow streets and canals, interesting houses, and old *hofjes*, or almshouses built around secluded courtyards. In recent years it has become a haunt of artists and students, and is full of little bars and lots of boutiques. As you wander, you come across small, lively street markets.

Nightlife

It is the sheer variety of events and entertainment that make visiting Amsterdam worthwhile at any time of year. Evening life centres on the capital's many theatres (with frequent performances in English) and cinemas; opera and dance at the Muziektheater in Waterlooplein and

Stadsschouwburg in Leidseplein; and the Royal Concertgebouw Orchestra. The Meervaart in Osdorpplein and the Melkweg in Lijnbaansgracht are famous arts centres, with multimedia events, discos and tea-rooms. Live music bars and nightclubs change all the time, as in any capital, and can be disappointing. The free *Uitkrant* from the tourist offices give a guide. Otherwise, experiment and use your sixth sense.

In the evening, stroll along to the Leidseplein for atmosphere, for the Art Nouveau Hotel American, pavement cafes (above), bars, and any number of things that might be going on in the square.

Eating and Drinking

Restaurants in Amsterdam, Den Haag, Rotterdam, and other large Dutch cities serve ethnic food from all over the world. The 13,677 Spice Islands – now the Republic of Indonesia – were once the Dutch East Indies, and there are Indonesian restaurants everywhere in the Netherlands.

RIJSTAFFEL

On Indonesian restaurant menus in the Netherlands, the *rijstaffel*, literally 'rice table', the name given to Indonesian cooking by Dutch colonizers, is often listed. The *rijstaffel* is a banquet of dishes, from satay and chicken in sambal sauce to *babi madoera* (pork in coconut sauce with kmiri nuts), and a dozen other dishes. **Tampat Senang**, Laam Van Meerdervort 6, tel 070 347 21 02, a restaurant close to the Peace Palace in Den Haag, specialises in *rijstaffel*, but most of the larger restaurants serve them.

VEGETARIAN EATING

There is plenty of vegetarian choice in Indonesian restaurants, and over 40 varieties of pancakes offered by the Dutch pancake houses, such as Amsterdam's **Egg Cream**, Sint Jacobsstraat 19. Tel 020 623 05 75. In this land of market gardens, vegetable dishes like red cabbage with apples, hutspot, and salads, are on all restaurant menus. In June, when the southern asparagus is ready, the restaurants serve little else, and everyone turns vegetarian.

BEERS AND BARS

You'll be served a Heineken if you ask for a beer in Amsterdam – but it no longer comes from the old Heineken brewery in the city, now just a suite of offices. You can find out about organised beer tastings from the Amsterdam tourist office. Notable beer bars are **De Wildeman** at Kolksteeg 3 at Nieuwe Zijds Kolk, off Nieuwendijk, tel 020 638 23 48, and **Brouwhuis Maximiliaan** on Kloveniersburgwal 6-8, tel 020 624 27 78. **De Bierkoning**, at Paleisstraat 125, tel 020 625 23 36, is a specialist beer shop.

The traditional places to drink beer are the *bruin kroeg* or brown bars. Their name is descriptive – their walls are always brown from years of tobacco smoke. They serve good food, as well as beer. **Cul-de-Sac** at Oudezijds Achterburgwal 99, tel 020 625 45 48, and **Chris** (the oldest bar in the capital) at Bloemstraat 42 in the Jordaan, tel 020 624 59 42, are two examples.

GENEVER

De Drie Fleschjes at Gravenstraat 18, tel 020 624 84 43, is one bar that serves no beer, but a range of *genever* (Dutch gin). Gin was first produced in the Middle Ages – for medicinal use, of course – by a Dutch apothecary. *Genever* is made by a different process from the English gin we drink with tonic, and is flavoured with juniper as well as other herbs and spices that give the *genever* on sale in Dutch bars a range of colours and flavours. *Bessen-genever*, for example, is sweet and blackcurranty. Bartenders and owners of shops specialising in the spirit, such as the one below, will gladly explain the composition of other *genevers* in their range. *Genever* is served in small tumblers, to which you lower your head to take the first sip.

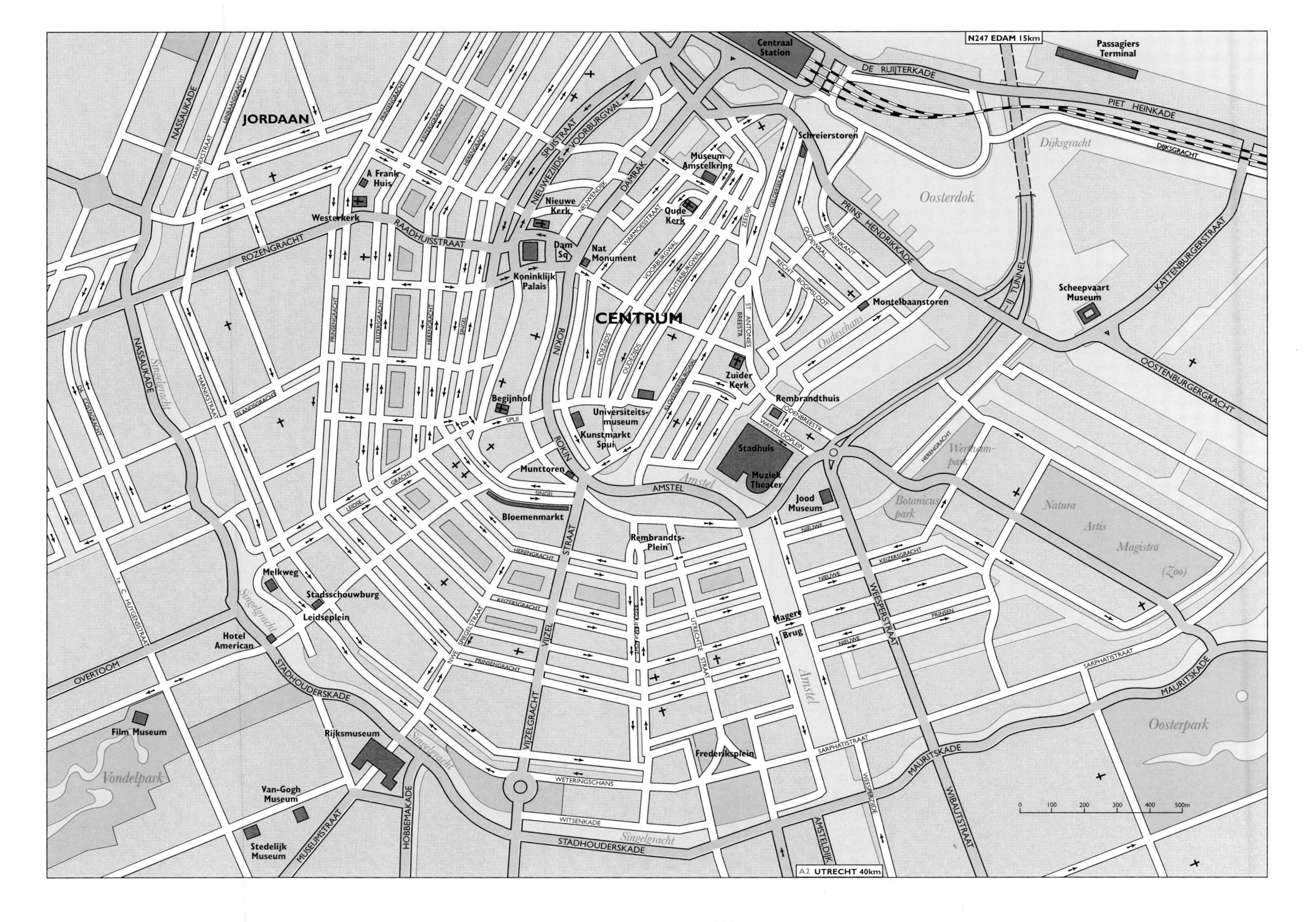

N247 EDAM 15km
Passagiers Terminal
Centraal Station
DE RUIJTERKADE
PIET HEINKADE
DIJKSGRACHT
Dijksgracht
KATTENBURGERSTRAAT
OOSTENBURGERGRACHT
Scheepvaart Museum
IJ TUNNEL
Oosterdok
PRINS HENDRIKKADE
Schreierstoren
Montelbaanstoren
Oudeschans
Rembrandthuis
JODENBREESTR
WATERLOOPLEIN
Stadhuis
Muziek Theater
Zuider Kerk
ST ANTONIES BREESTR
Wertheim-park
HERENGRACHT
Botanicus park
Natura Artis Magistra (Zoo)
MAURITSKADE
Oosterpark
SARPHATISTRAAT
WIBAUTSTRAAT
WEESPERSTRAAT
WEESPERZIJDE
A2 UTRECHT 40km
AMSTELDIJK
Amstel
Magere Brug
Jood Museum
NIEUWE
PRINSEN
KEIZERSGRACHT
Museum Amstelkring
Oude Kerk
ZEEDIJK
GELDERSEKADE
BINNENKANT
OUDEWAAL
RECHT BOOMSLOOT
ACHTERBURGWAL
VOORBURGWAL
KLOVENIERSBURGWAL
OUDEZIJDS
WARMOESSTRAAT
CENTRUM
DAMRAK
Nat Monument
Dam Sq
Nieuwe Kerk
NIEUWENDIJK
Koninklijk Paleis
ROKIN
Universiteits-museum
Kunstmarkt Spui
Begijnhof
SPUI
Munttoren
SINGEL
Bloemenmarkt
AMSTEL
Rembrandts-Plein
UTRECHTSE STRAAT
Frederiksplein
REGULIERSGRACHT
VIJZELSTRAAT
VIJZELGRACHT
WETERINGSCHANS
WITSENKADE
STADHOUDERSKADE
Singelgracht
NWE SPIEGELSTRAAT
PRINSENGRACHT
HOBBEMAKADE
Rijksmuseum
MUSEUMSTRAAT
Van-Gogh Museum
Stedelijk Museum
Film Museum
Vondelpark
OVERTOOM
1e C HUYGENSSTRAAT
Hotel American
Leidseplein
Stadsschouwburg
Melkweg
LEIDSE
NIEUWEZIJDS VOORBURGWAL
SPUISTRAAT
RAADHUISSTRAAT
A Frank Huis
Westerkerk
ROZENGRACHT
JORDAAN
LIJNBAANSGRACHT
MARNIXSTRAAT
NASSAUKADE
DA COSTAGRACHT
0 100 200 300 400 500m

Day trips *from Amsterdam*

Trips from Amsterdam run north to the polders and to the banks of Ijsselmeer, the Netherlands' huge freshwater lake, formed when the Zuider Zee was dammed. Along what was the sea coast of Marken were old fishing villages, whose traditional income was cut off when the dam was built. These tiny villages, with their traditional wooden houses where people always wore traditional dress, have discovered a new source of income in tourism.

While the townspeople of Marken are Calvinist, those of Volendam are Roman Catholic. The town has a 17th-century wooden church. Older people still wear folk dress, and tourists can be photographed dressed up in traditional outfits.

Edam, in the polders, is a traditional Dutch town with some interesting Gothic buildings. It has a large hall church, with the Netherlands' oldest carillon, dating from 1560, and 17th-century stained glass.

These villages are so tourist-oriented these days that you might almost find it more rewarding to drive directly north of Amsterdam to Zaanse Schans, a Dutch village made up of houses and windmills of different styles, with workshops where traditional crafts are demonstrated.

Further north, but still an easy drive, are the old port towns of West Friesland, Hoorn and Enkhuizen, with picturesque old harbours overlooked by 17th-century gabled houses.

Amsterdam Fact File

AMSTERDAM from **Calais** 338km/210 miles.
Tourist information: VVV Amsterdam, Stationsplein 10 (opposite Centraal Station). Tel 06 34034066. Fax 020 625 28 69. Call for times and various locations. Museum card about £16 adult, £6 under-18s. *What's on in Amsterdam* free.

SIGHTSEEING
Boat trips Canal Bus every 20 min between Centraal Station, Leidseplein, Leidsestraat/Keizersgracht, Prinsengracht and Rijksmuseum. Day ticket about £6 adult, £5.50 child. **Museum Boat Canal Cruises** (booking at tourist office). Tel 020 622 21 81. Day ticket about £8 adult, £6 under-13s; day ticket plus museum entrance about £14 adult, £13 under-13s. Get on and off at any of 7 stops along the route. Check with tourist office for details of many canal cruises.
Amstelkring (Ons Lieve Heer op Solder/Our Dear Lord in the Attic) Oz Voorburgwal 40. ***Open*** Mon-Sat 10am-5pm, Sun 1-5pm. About £2 adult, £1.50 under-19s.
Amsterdam Diamond Centre Rokin 1-5. Tel 020 624 57 87. One of Amsterdam's many diamond houses open daily for guided tours.
A. Frank Huis (Anne Frank's House) Prinsengracht 263. ***Open*** *Oct-Apr* Mon-Sat 9am-5pm, Sun 10am-5pm; *May-Sept* Mon-Sat 9am-7pm, Sun 10am-7pm. About £3 adult, £1.50 10-17s.
Koninklijk Palais (Royal Palace) Dam Square. ***Open*** *Easter, Jun-Aug* daily 12.30-5pm. *Sept-May* Tue-Thur 1-4pm. Guided tours Wed 2pm.
Nederlands Scheepvaart Museum (National Maritime Museum) Kattenburgerplein 1. ***Open*** Tue-Sat 10am-5pm, Sun noon-5pm, *15 Jun-15 Sept* Mon 10am-5pm. About £4 adult, £3 7-18s. Museum of Dutch seafaring history.
Rembrandthuis (Rembrandt's House) Jodenbreestraat 4-6. ***Open*** Mon-Sat 10am-5pm, Sun 1-5pm. About £2 adult, £1.50 10-15s.
Rijksmuseum Stadhouderskade 42. ***Open*** Tue-Sat 10am-5pm, Sun 1-5pm. About £10 adult, £5 OAP, child.
Stedelijk Museum P. Potterstraat 13. ***Open*** daily 11am-5pm. About £3 adult, £1.50 7–16s.
Vincent Van Gogh Museum P. Potterstraat 7. ***Open*** daily 10am-5pm. About £4 adult, £2 under-17s.
Westerkerk Prinsengracht 281. Tel 020 624 77 66. ***Open*** *Apr-Sept* daily. Check for opening times.

CAMPING
Camping Vliegengbos Meeuwenlaan 138 (N from Amsterdam centre through Yijs tunnel, then follow signs). Tel 020 636 88 55. ***Open*** *Apr-Sept.*

EATING AND DRINKING
J.G. Beune Haarlemmerdijk 156. A famous tea-room, part of a chocolate shop.
Café américain Leidseplein 28. ***Open*** daily 10.30am-1am.
Egg Cream St Jacobstraat 19. Recognised as one of the best pancake/vegetarian cafés. From about £5.
Haesje Claes Spuistraat 273. Tel 020 624 99 98. Good Dutch food. From about £16.
Restaurant D'Vijff Vlieghen Spuistraat 294. Tel 020 624 83 69. Modern Dutch cuisine in a 17th-century house. From £30.
Selecta Vijzelstraat 26. Tel 020 624 88 94. One of the better – but pricier – Indonesian restaurants. From about £16.

Trips out of Town

Enkhuizen
Zuider Zee Museum Wierdijk 18. **Indoor Museum *Open*** all year 10am-5pm. **Outdoor Museum *Open*** *Apr-Oct* daily 10am-5pm.
Marken
Marken Museum Kerkbuurt 44-47. ***Open*** *Apr-Oct* Mon-Sat 10am-5pm, Sun 1-5pm. **Marken Express** boat trip on the Gouwzee to Volendam. Rederij Veerman & Co, Schoklandstraat 111 Volendam. Tel 02993 63331. ***Open*** *Apr-Sept* daily every 30 min between 10am and 6pm, *Sept-Oct* daily between 10am and 5pm.
Volendam
Museum Zeestraat 37. ***Open*** *Apr-Oct* daily 10am-5pm.
Zaanse Schans
Zaandam on the A8 N of Amsterdam. ***Open*** *Apr-Oct* daily 8am-6pm (most museums and workshops). **Open-air museum** of windmills and traditional houses on River Zaan.

The winged cap, which identifies Dutch national costume for most foreigners, is worn only on Sundays. Strong feelings for tradition prompt men and women in Volendam (far left) and Marken (left) to continue to wear Dutch dress.

Hotel
Guide

On the following pages is a selection of a few hotels for the areas covered by this guide. Most are listed in the RAC *French Hotel and Holiday Guide* and *European Hotel Guide*, updated annually.

Use the tourist offices if you particularly need a hotel (or a camping or caravanning site) in a local area for which no hotel is listed here. All have lists of local hotels, detailing facilities and prices, and all run booking services, some for a small fee. The French tourist offices also stock booklets listing northern France's many splendid château hotels, and the Relais du Silence (ideal for those escaping from city life and pressurised jobs), which guarantee a quiet and peaceful stay.

The listings below give roughly converted prices for a double room in mid-season. Bear in mind that prices are likely to be higher during high season, and lower off-season – and that hotels may alter their prices at the beginning of a new season. The French government has introduced a hotel residency tax which can vary throughout the country according to the hotel category. Many hotels also close for a period, usually in January, but sometimes in July or at other times of year. Always book in advance to be sure of a room.

The Opal Coast

BERGUES
Mercure 2 Bordure du Lac. Armbouts-Cappel. Tel 28 60 70 60. Fax 28 61 06 39. A modern lakeside hotel, just off the motorway. From about £35.

BOULOGNE
de Lorraine** 7-9 place de Lorraine. Tel 21 31 34 78. Fax 21 32 91 42. A hotel on a quiet town centre square. From £20 to £33.
Métropole*** 51 rue Thiers. Tel 21 31 54 30. Fax 21 30 45 72. A good central hotel with a garden. From £52.

CALAIS
du Golf** Digue Gaston-Berthe (on road marked 'La Plage' from town centre). Tel 21 96 88 99. Fax 21 34 75 48. A modern hotel just outside town overlooking the sea. From £35 to 40.
Georges V 36 rue Royale. Tel 21 97 68 00. Fax 21 97 34 73. From £27 to £57.
Métropol' 43 quai du Rhin. Tel 21 97 54 00. Fax 21 96 69 70. From £48.
Meurice*** 5 rue Edmond-Roche. Tel 21 34 57 03. Fax 21 34 14 71. An old-established hotel in a quiet area near Richelieu Park. From about £35.

HARDELOT
du Parc 111 av François Ier. Tel 21 33 22 11. Fax 21 83 29 71. From about £64.

LE TOUQUET
Manoir*** (opposite golf course) Le Touquet-Paris-Plage. Tel 21 05 20 22. Fax 21 05 31 26. A hotel in Le Touquet Forest, with swimming, golf, and tennis. From £97.
Red Fox corner of rue St-Jean and rue de Metz. Tel 21 05 27 58. Fax 21 05 27 56. English-style hotel. From £40 to £64.

LILLE
de la Paix** 46bis rue de Paris. Tel 20 54 63 93. Fax 20 63 98 97. From £43 (weekends) and £47 (week).
Sofitel av de la Marne, Marcq en Barœul suburb (exit 12 off E17 Lille-Gent motorway). Tel 20 72 17 30. Fax 20 89 92 34. A comfortable and well run hotel conveniently located off the motorway. From £56 to £85.

RECQUES-SUR-HEM
Château de Cocove*** av de Cocove (off D218 and N43). Tel 21 82 68 29. Fax 21 82 72 59. A restored 18th-century château in a beautiful park, with a notable restaurant and riding stables. The proprietors also run a wine shop. From £55 to £87.

ST-OMER
Hostellerie St-Hubert**** 1 rue du Moulin, Hallines. Tel 21 39 77 77. Fax 21 93 00 86. A pretty château hotel near St-Omer. From £75 to £100.
Château Tilques, Tilques (off N43 6km/4 miles from St-Omer). Tel 21 93 28 99. Fax 21 38 34 23. A château hotel in parkland. From £62 to £74.
St-Louis 25 rue d'Arras. Tel 21 38 35 51. Fax 21 38 57 26. From about £32 to £37.

WISSANT
Normandy* 2 place de Verdun (on N40 between Boulogne and Calais). Tel 21 35 90 11. Fax 21 82 19 08. A hotel in an 18th-century building overlooking the sea. From £50 to £82.

Canche, Authie & Somme
The Fields of War

ABBEVILLE
de France 19 place du Pilori. Tel 22 24 00 42. Fax 22 24 26 15. A tasteful and supremely comfortable modern town centre hotel. From about £43.

AMIENS
"Best Western" Grand Hôtel de l'Univers 2 rue de Noyon. Tel 22 91 52 51. Fax 22 92 81 66. From £32 to £85.
Ibis 4 rue du Maréchal-de-Lattre-de-Tassigny. Tel 22 92 57 33. Fax 22 91 67 50. One of a chain of good hotels and motels, this one is close to the cathedral. From about £36.
Le Prieuré 17 rue Porion. Tel 22 92 27 67. A pleasant hotel near the cathedral. From about £47.

ARRAS
Le Manoir** 35 route nationale, Gavrelle (take N50 Arras/Douai, then exit 16). Tel 21 58 68 58. Fax 21 55 37 87. Just outside Arras. Airy in summer and cosy in winter. From about £34.
Trois Luppars 47 Grand'Place. Tel 21 07 41 41. Fax 21 24 24 80. Comfortable, inexpensive hotel in 15th-century building (the oldest in Arras). From £35.

BETHUNE
du Vieux Beffroi** 48 Grand'Place. Tel 21 68 15 00. Fax 21 56 66 32. A useful base for battlefield tours. From £32.

CAMBRAI
Château de la Motte-Fénelon square du Château. Tel 27 83 61 38. Fax 27 83 71 61. A château hotel with a notable restaurant. From £125.
France 37 rue de Lille. Tel 27 81 38 80. Fax 27 78 13 88. Central, close to the church of St-Géry. From £17 to £27.

CANCHE VALLEY
Le Val de Canche* 2 Grande-Rue, Beaurainville (off N39 between Montreuil and Hesdin). Tel 21 90 32 22. A family hotel run by English owners. From £17 to £28.

MONTREUIL-SUR-MER
Château de Montreuil**** 4 chaussée des Capucins. Tel 21 81 53 04. Fax 21 81 36 43. A country house hotel with a celebrated restaurant. From £188 to £238.
Les Hauts de Montreuil 21-23 rue Pierre-Ledent. Tel 21 81 95 92. Fax 21 86 28 83. From £40 to £52.
Shakespeare**
7 rue de Change. Tel 21 86 16 04. A family hotel run by English owners. From about £28 to £35.

PERONNE
St-Claude** 42 place Louis-Daudre. Tel 22 84 46 00. Fax 22 84 47 57. Central hotel with a basement disco. From about £35.

RANCOURT
Le Prieuré, Rancourt (on N17 Péronne–Bapaume). Tel 22 85 04 43. Fax 22 85 06 69. A hotel much used by parties exploring the nearby World War I battlefields and memorials. From £27 to £37.

Rouen & the Caux

CAEN
Climat de France** avenue Montgomery, quartier du Mémorial. Tel 31 44 36 36. Fax 31 95 62 62. A useful inexpensive hotel just outside the city. From about £34 to £43.
Holiday Inn 4 place Foch. Tel 31 27 57 57. Fax 31 27 57 58. From £57 to £72.
Le Dauphin 29 rue Gémare. Tel 31 86 22 26. Fax 31 86 35 14. A simple hotel with a notable restaurant, in a former priory. From £44 to £64.
Moderne 116 blvd Maréchal-Leclerc. Tel 31 86 04 23. Fax 31 85 37 93. From £55 to £79.

CAUDEBEC-EN-CAUX
Normotel La Marine** 18 quai Guilbaud. Tel 35 96 20 11. Fax 35 56 54 40. A riverside hotel with a good restaurant. From £32 to £52.

DEAUVILLE
Clos St-Gatien***. St-Gatien-des-Bois. Tel 31 65 16 08. Fax 31 65 10 27. From £35.
De l'Amirauté*** Touques. Tel 31 81 82 83. Fax 31 81 82 93. A fitness-orientated hotel with golf, exercise facilities, squash, sauna and jacuzzi. From £87 to £98.
Hélios** 10 rue Fossorier. Tel 31 88 28 26. Fax 31 88 53 87. A hotel close to the beach, with swimming pool. From about £47 to £57.
Normandy**** 38 rue Jean-Mermoz. Tel 31 98 66 22. Fax 31 98 66 23. A hotel for a holiday of sheer luxury in a picturesque half-timbered building, surrounded by gardens. It has a notable restaurant, a swimming pool and private access to the casino. From £188.

Dieppe
La Présidence*** 2 blvd Verdun. Tel 35 84 31 31. Fax 35 84 86 70. Sea-front hotel at the foot of an old château. From £40 to £53.
Duclair
de la Poste parc de Brotonne. Tel 35 37 50 04. Fax 35 37 39 19. Seine Valley hotel with a good restaurant. From about £30.
Forges-les-Eaux
Auberge du Beau Lieu Le Fossé (on D915). Tel 35 90 50 36. Fax 35 90 35 98. A small hotel in the Pays de Bray, with a good restaurant. From about £42.
Honfleur
Castel Albertine*** 19 cours Albert-Manuel. Tel 31 98 85 56. Fax 31 98 83 18. A small hotel in an 18th-century building near the old port. From £44 to £75.
Le Havre
d'Angleterre** 1 rue Louis-Philippe. Tel 35 42 48 42. Fax 35 22 70 69. A small hotel near the beach. From about £35.
Ouistreham
Normandie** 71 av Michel-Cabieu. Tel 31 97 19 57. Fax 31 97 20 07. A modern hotel on the Normandy coast, close to Caen and handy for the sites of the Normandy landings. From £38.
Pont-Audemer
Belle Isle-sur-Risle**** 112 route de Rouen. Tel 32 56 96 22. Fax 32 42 88 96 A hotel on a river island in the Seine, with indoor and outdoor swimming pools, and tennis. From £100.
Rouen
Astrid 121 rue Jeanne-d'Arc. Tel 35 71 75 88. Fax 35 88 53 25. A central hotel, opposite the station. From about £45.
de Dieppe*** place Bernard-Tissot. Tel 35 71 96 00. Fax 35 89 65 21. A pleasant hotel near the station, run by the Gueret family since 1880. From about £58 to £73 (week), £44 (weekends).
de la Cathédrale 12 rue St-Romain. Tel 35 71 57 95. Fax 35 70 15 54. A pleasant, inexpensive hotel beside the cathedral. From £36 to £43.
de Québec** 18-24 rue de Québec. Tel 35 70 09 38. Fax 35 15 80 15. An inexpensive hotel, close to the old town. From £20 to £40.
Trouville
Beach*** 1 quai Albert Ier. Tel 31 98 12 00. Fax 31 87 30 29. A seaside hotel in the heart of Trouville. From about £55.

Senlis & the Forests of South Picardy

Beauvais
du Palais** 9 rue St-Nicolas. Tel 44 45 12 58. Fax 44 45 66 23. A useful base for visiting the cathedral. From £15 to £32.
Chantilly
Château de la Tour chemin de la Chaussée, Gouvieux. Tel 44 57 07 39. Fax 44 57 31 97. From £79 to £112.
Hostellerie du Lys 63 Septième Avenue, rond-point de la Reine (from Chantilly take the N16 towards Lamorlaye). Tel 44 21 26 19. Fax 44 21 28 19. A hotel in a beautiful wooded setting. From about £62.
Compiegne
A la Bonne Idée*** 3 rue des Meniers. St-Jean-aux-Bois (6km/4 miles from Compiègne). Tel 44 42 84 09. Fax 44 42 80 45. A hotel in the heart of Compiègne Forest, with a restaurant specialising in regional cooking. From about £54.
Elincourt-Ste-Marguerite
Château de Bellinglise**** route de Lassigny (exit 11 at Ressons-sur-Matz on A1 from Paris, drive E through Margny on D15 to Elincourt): Tel 44 76 04 76. Fax 44 76 54 75. A 16th-century manor in its park with a gourmet restaurant. From £77 to £85.
Senlis
Château de Raray 4 rue Nicolas-de-Lancy, Raray (signposted off the D932A and A1 motorway from Senlis exit 8). Tel 44 54 70 61. Fax 44 54 74 97. A historic château, location of Jean Cocteau's film *Beauty and the Beast*. Excellent cuisine and a golfing club in the park. From about £162.

Paris & the Ile de France

Hotel reservations the tourist offices make on-the-spot hotel reservations for a small fee (about £2-£5)
A l'Hôtel 2 av du Professeur André-Lemière, 20e. Tel 1 43 63 16 16. Fax 1 43 63 31 32. From about £55.
Abaca Messidor*** 330 rue de Vaugirard, 15e. Tel 1 48 28 03 74. Fax 1 48 28 75 17. A Montparnasse hotel overlooking a garden square. A building of character, with rooms individually decorated. From about £113.
Bailli de Suffren*** 149 av de Suffren, 15e. Tel 1 47 34 58 61. Fax 1 45 67 75 82. A left-bank hotel with each room individually decorated, furnished with antiques. From about £83.
Britannique*** 20 av Victoria, 1e. Tel 1 42 33 74 59. Fax 1 42 33 82 65. An understated hotel in a quiet central location. From about £90 to £104.
Ermitage 24 rue Lamarck, 18e. Tel 1 42 64 79 22. Fax 1 42 64 10 33. A very pleasant hotel behind the Sacré-Cœur. From about £55.
L'Horset-Opéra 18 rue d'Antin, 2e. 1 44 71 87 00. Fax 1 42 66 55 54. From £163.
Lecourbe** 28 rue Lecourbe, 15e. Tel 1 47 34 49 06. Fax 1 47 34 64 65. An elegant central hotel with a courtyard garden, not far from the Champs-Elysées. From about £57.
Méridien-Montparnasse 19 rue du Commandant-Mouchotte, 14e. Tel 44 36 44 36. Fax 44 36 49 00. From £116 (two nights), £156 to £206 (one night).
Nouvel** 9 rue d'Austerlitz, 12e. Tel 1 43 42 15 79. Fax 1 43 42 31 11. A modern hotel near the Bastille. From £44.
Le Parc Victor-Hugo**** 55 av Raymond-Poincaré, 16e. Tel 1 44 05 66 66. Fax 1 44 05 66 00. In the centre of Paris, near the Champs-Elysées. A luxurious, spacious hotel. From about £275.
Le Pergolèse**** 3 rue Pergolèse, 16e. Tel 1 40 67 96 77. Fax 45 00 12 11. A luxurious hotel near La Défense, decorated and furnished in contemporary style by designer René Dumas. From about £106 to £188.
Queen Mary*** 9 rue de Greffulhe, 8e. Tel 1 42 66 40 50. Fax 1 42 66 94 92. A comfortable, refined hotel in the centre. From about £85 to £112.
Rome*** 18 rue de Constantinople, 8e. Tel 1 45 22 14 52. Fax 44 70 05 38. A comfortable, central hotel near the Opéra. From £90.
Utrillo** 7 rue Aristide-Bruant, 18e. Tel 1 42 58 13 44. Fax 1 42 23 93 88. A pleasant hotel in the heart of Montmartre. From £47.
Fontainebleau
De l'Aigle Noir**** 27 place Napoléon-Bonaparte. Tel 1 64 22 32 65. Fax 1 64 22 17 33. Opposite the château, a château-hotel, former residence of the Dukes of Retz offers total luxury. From about £119.
Manoir de St-Herem** parc Jean-François-Millet, Barbizon (take Fontainebleau exit from the A6, then RN7). Tel 1 60 66 42 42. Fax 1 60 69 20 98. A manor house hotel in parkland, situated behind Millet's house in Barbizon town centre. Gourmet cuisine. From about £44.
Versailles
Residence du Berry*** 14 rue d'Anjou. Tel 1 39 49 07 07. Fax 1 39 50 59 40. A hotel in the town centre, 5 minutes' walk from the palace. From about £57.

Laon & the Aisne

Chateau-Thierry
Ile de France*** route de Soissons (RN37, A4). Tel 23 69 10 12. Tel 23 83 49 70. A modern hotel in extensive grounds, near Château-Thierry, EuroDisney. From £42 to £50 (Adjoining rooms for family of 4 £62).
Laon
Mercure, Hôtel du Golf de l'Ailette Parc nautique de l'Ailette, Chamouille. Tel 23 24 84 85. Fax 23 24 81 20. From £57.
St-Vincent** av Charles-de-Gaulle. Tel 23 23 42 43. Fax 23 79 22 55. A hotel in the lower town, overlooking a park, with a seafood restaurant. From £37.
Liesse
Château de Barive Sainte-Preuve. Tel 23 22 15 15. Fax 23 22 08 39. A beautifully restored, château hotel with a Baroque garden, surrounded by woodland, about 10 km/6 miles from Laon. Good restaurant with cuisine based on farm produce and local game. Sports facilities include an indoor swimming pool. From £48 to £98.
St-Quentin
de la Paix et Albert Ier 3 place du 8-Octobre. Tel 23 62 77 62. Fax 23 62 66 03. From about £38.
Grand Hotel 6 rue Dachery. Tel 23 62 69 77. Fax 23 62 53 52. From £69 to £75.
Vervins
La Tour du Roy*** 45 rue du Général-Leclerc. Tel 23 98 00 11. Fax 23 98 00 72. A friendly hotel built on the town's ramparts, with an excellent restaurant serving regional cuisine. From about £50 to £75.
Villers-Cotterets
Le Régent*** 26 rue du Général-Mangin. Tel 23 96 01 46. Fax 23 96 37 57. Hotel in an 18th-century post-house in the town centre. From £33 to £45.

Reims & Champagne Country

Colombey-les-Deux-Eglises
Les Dhuits*** (on the N19). Tel 25 01 50 10. Fax 25 01 56 22. A modern hotel on the Champagne Route. From £35.
Epernay
Château d'Etoges*** Etoges (25 km/16 miles S of Epernay on D33). Tel 26 59 30 08. Fax 26 59 35 57. Hotel in an authentic 17th-century moated castle. From £60 to £119.
Reims
Château de la Muire 40 av Paul-Vaillant-Couturier. Tinqueux. Tel 26 04 15 56. Fax 28 04 15 69. A comfortable hotel with a notable restaurant in extensive grounds on an avenue on the outskirts of the city. From £60 to £138.
Univers** 41 blvd Foch. Tel 26 88 68 08. Fax 26 40 95 61. A reasonably priced central hotel in a 1930s building. From £36.

Rocroi
du Commerce** place Aristide-Briand, Rocroi. Tel 24 54 11 15. Hotel situated in the main square of the town. From about £30.

Bruges & Northern Belgium

Antwerp
Hotel reservations tourist offices can book rooms for a deposit of about £4, deducted from hotel bill.
Ibis** Meistraat 39. Tel 0323 231 8830. Fax 0323 234 2921. Modern hotel near the main port. From about £80.
Crowne Plaza**** Gerard Legrellelaan 10. Tel 0323 237 2900. Fax 0323 216 0296. A Holiday Inn usefully near the E3/E10 junction and the town centre. From £180.
de Rosier Rosier 23. Tel 0323 225 0140. Fax 0323 231 4111. An elegant 17th-century hotel, centrally located, with sports facilities. From about £160.
Eden Lange Herentalsestraat 25. Tel 0323 233 0608. Fax 0323 233 1228. One of the cheaper central hotels. From about £60.
Tourist Pelikaanstraat 22. Tel 0323 232 5870. Fax 0323 231 6707. Basic and inexpensive. From about £40.
Bruges
Hotel reservations the tourist office provides a free booking service. A seasonal service in the Bruges railway station is open *Apr-Sept* Mon-Sat 2.45-9pm; *Oct-mid Nov* Mon-Sat 1.45-8pm.
Adornes*** St Annarei 26. Tel 050 34 13 36. Fax 050 34 20 85 Situated along canal. From about £60.
Holiday Inn Crowne Plaza Burg 10. Tel 050 34 58 34. Fax 050 34 56 15. From about £132.
Jacobs*** Baliestraat 1, off the Langerei. Tel 050 33 98 31. Fax 050 33 56 94. B&B in a 100-year old gabled house on a quiet street. From about £45.
Navarra*** St Jacobstraat 41. Tel 050 34 05 61. Fax 050 33 67 90. From about £93.
Portinari**** 't Zand 15. Tel 050 34 10 34. Fax 050 34 41 80. Modern B&B in the town centre. From about £85.
Sositel**** Boeveriestraat 2. Tel 050 34 09 71. Fax 050 34 40 53. Modern hotel in a 17th-century monastery building. Indoor swimming pool, garden. From about £105.
Wilgenhof*** Polderstraat 151, St Kruis. Tel 050 36 27 44. Fax 050 36 28 21. Cosy, country hotel overlooking a canal, 2 km/1 mile north of Bruges. From about £75.
De Haan
Auberge Des Rois**** Zeedijk 8420, De Haan aan Zee. Tel 059 23 30 18. Modern beach hotel, 10 km/4 miles from Ostende. From about £100.
De Panne
Host. Le Fox**** Walckiersstraat 2. Tel 058 41 28 55. Fax 058 41 58 79. From about £60.
Gent
Hotel reservations the tourist office runs a free booking service.
Cours St Georges St Jorishof, Botermarkt 2. Tel 092 24 24 24. Fax 092 24 26 40. Modern hotel in beautiful gabled house built in 1228, in city-centre. From about £65
Express* Ottergemsesteenweg 703 (off Corneel Heymanslaan). Tel 092 21 80 41. Fax 092 20 40 84. Basic hotel beside E17, useful during high season and festivals when central hotels are full. From about £60.
Knokke-Heist
Memlinc Palace**** Albert Plein 23, Knokke-Zout. Tel 050 60 11 34. Fax 050 61 57 43. Facing the sea. From about £80.
Ostende
Hotel reservations the tourist offices can help you find a hotel.
New Astoria Van Iseghemlaan 38A. Tel 059 70 99 61. Fax 059 70 50 68. A central hotel close to the beach in a 19th-century building. Book during October beer festival. From about £35.
Die Prince 41 Albert 1 Promenade. Tel 059 70 91 85. Fax 059 80 78 51. Family hotel facing the beach. From about £50.
Bero**** Hofstraat 1A. Tel 059 70 23 35. Fax 059 70 25 91. Pleasant city-centre hotel with fitness centre. From about £60.
Tournai
The tourist office has a list of hotels.
De la Cathédrale place St-Pierre 11 (between the cathedral and the river). Tel 069 21 50 77. Fax 069 21 50 78. Pleasant hotel in a small central square. From about £60.
Le Manoir de St-Aubert rue Crupes 14, Mont-St-Aubert. Tel 069 21 21 63. Fax 069 84 27 05. A comfortable hotel and restaurant in a pleasant park. From about £55.
Tour St-Georges place de Nedonchel 2. Tel 069 22 53 00. An inexpensive central hotel. From about £30.
Ypres
Hotel reservations the tourist office provides a free booking service.
Hostellerie Kemmelberg**** Berg 4, Kemmel-Heuvelland (14 km/8 miles NE of Ypres off the N331). Tel 057 44 41 45. Fax 057 44 40 89. A beautiful hilltop hotel on the site of a World War I battlefield and close to the French border, offering haute cuisine, tennis, hillside walks and golf. From £75.

Brussels

Hotel reservations the tourist offices can make reservations, for a percentage of the price as a deposit, deducted on payment of the hotel bill. Flats can also be rented through the tourist office from about £200 per week. If possible, book ahead for the summer months.
Amigo rue de l'Amigo 1-3. Tel 02 547 47 47. Fax 513 52 77. A luxury hotel with excellent service in a quiet street just north of the Grand' Place. From about £160.
Arcadie place Ste-Catherine. Tel 02 513 76 20. Fax 02 514 22 14. From about £70.
Bosquet rue Bosquet 70. Tel 02 538 19 14 Fax 02 534 27 11. From about £25.
Rembrandt rue de la Concorde 42. Tel 02 512 71 39. Fax 02 511 71 36. From about £50.
Waterloo
Grand Hotel chaussée de Tervuren 198. Tel 02 352 18 15. Fax 02 352 18 88. From about £130.
Le Joli-Bois rue Ste-Anne 59. Tel 02 353 18 18. Fax 02 353 05 16. From about £55.

Bulbfields & the Dutch Coast

The tourist offices will make reservations for about £3.50.
Delft
Juliana*** Maerten Trompstraat 33. Tel 015 567 612. Fax 015 565 707. Close to the Delft Factory. From about £145.
Den Haag
Europa Scheveningen**** Zwolsestraat 2. Tel 070 351 26 51. Fax 070 350 6473. Luxurious, seaside hotel with indoor swimming pool. From about £90.
Parkhotel den Haag**** Molenstraat 53. Tel 070 362 4371. Fax 070 361 4525. In the old centre near the Royal Palace gardens. From about £80.
Petit*** Groot Hertoginnelaan 42. Tel 070 346 5500. Fax 070 346 3257. A small, inexpensive hotel. From about £65.
Rotterdam
Atlanta**** Aert van Nesstraat 4, Cool Singel. Tel 010 411 0420. Fax 010 413 5320. From about £95.
Van Walsum*** Mathenesserlaan 199, Oldenzaal. Tel 010 436 3275. Fax 010 436 4410. A fair priced hotel on a quiet street. From about £50.
Sluis
Sanders de Paauw*** Kade 42. Tel 011 781 224. Fax 011 782 102. On the Belgian border, near both Bruges and the North Sea beaches. From about £45.

Amsterdam

The tourist offices will make reservations for about £3.50.
Ambassade*** Herengracht 341. Tel 020 626 2333. Fax 020 624 5321. A canalside hotel occupying eight 17th-century merchant houses. From about £95.
Asterisk** Den Texstraat 16. Tel 020 626 2396. Fax 020 638 2790. Family- run hotel. From about £50.
Canal House*** Keizersgracht 148. Tel 020 622 5182. Fax 020 624 1317. A comfortable, friendly hotel in a beautifully restored 17th-century building. From about £85.
Estherea**** Singel 303. Tel 020 624 5146. Fax 020 623 9001. A canal house very close to Dam Square. From about £110.
King* Leidsekade 85. Tel 020 624 9603. Fax 020 620 7277. A 17th-century canal house overlooking the Grand Canal. From about £35.

Hotel chains

In addition to the selection of hotels listed above, several international chains operate in the countries covered by this book and reservations can be made from the UK.
Campanile
Tel 00 33 1 64 62 46 46.
Fax 00 33 1 64 62 46 61.
Hilton
Tel 0171 734 6000.
Fax 01923 218 548.
Holiday Inn
Tel 0800 897 121.
Fax 013 12 06 06 54 54.
Ibis, Novotel and **Sofitel** hotels are part of the same group.
Tel 0171 724 1000.
Fax 0181 748 9116.
Méridien
Tel 0171 439 1244.
Fax 0171 439 1230.
Trust House Forte
Tel 01345 404040.
Fax 01296 813 91.

Index

In this index of places, **bold** type signifies principal entries. Asterisks (*) refer to hotels in or near the town.